W9-CLR-155

always up to date

The law changes, but Nolo is on top of it! We offer several
ways to make sure you and your Nolo products are up to date:

1 **Nolo's Legal Updater**
We'll send you an email whenever a new edition of this book is
published! Sign up at **www.nolo.com/legalupdater**.

2 **Updates @ Nolo.com**
Check **www.nolo.com/update** to find recent changes
in the law that affect the current edition of your book.

3 **Nolo Customer Service**
To make sure that this edition of the book is the most
recent one, call us at **800-728-3555** and ask one of
our friendly customer service representatives.
Or find out at **www.nolo.com**.

please note

We believe accurate, plain-English legal information should help you solve many of your own legal problems. But this text is not a substitute for personalized advice from a knowledgeable lawyer. If you want the help of a trained professional—and we'll always point out situations in which we think that's a good idea—consult an attorney licensed to practice in your state.

1st edition

SOCIETY FOR HUMAN
RESOURCE MANAGEMENT

The Essential Guide to
Workplace
Investigations

by Lisa Guerin

FIRST EDITION	SEPTEMBER 2007
Editor	LISA GUERIN
Cover & Book Design	SUSAN PUTNEY
Proofreading	SUSAN CARLSON GREENE
Index	THÉRÈSE SHERE
CD-ROM Preparation	ELLEN BITTER
Printing	CONSOLIDATED PRINTERS, INC.

Guerin, Lisa, 1964
  The essential guide to workplace investigations / by Lisa Guerin.
     p. cm.
  ISBN-13: 978-1-4133-0691-0 (pbk.)
  ISBN-10: 1-4133-0691-8 (pbk.)
  1. Employee crimes--Handbooks, manuals, etc. 2. Labor discipline--Handbooks,
manuals, etc. 3. Violence in the workplace--Investigation--Handbooks, manuals,
etc. 4. Discrimination in employment--Investigation--Handbooks, manuals, etc.
5. Sexual harassment--Investigation--Handbooks, manuals, etc. 6.
Investigations--Handbooks, manuals, etc. I. Title.
HF5549.5.E43G836 2007
658.3'14--dc22   2007013047

Copyright © 2007 by Nolo
ALL RIGHTS RESERVED. PRINTED IN THE USA.

No part of this publication may be reproduced, stored in a retrieval system, or transmitted in any form or by any means, electronic, mechanical, photocopying, recording, or otherwise without prior written permission. Reproduction prohibitions do not apply to the forms contained in this product when reproduced for personal use.

Quantity sales: For information on bulk purchases or corporate premium sales, please contact the Special Sales Department. For academic sales or textbook adoptions, ask for Academic Sales. Call 800-955-4775 or write to Nolo, 950 Parker Street, Berkeley, CA 94710.

Acknowledgments

Many thanks to:

Amy DelPo, for her encouragement and suggestions.

Rich Stim, for his excellent editing and his sharp eye for the noir detail.

Laura Lawson, **Dan Cafaro**, and **Allen Smith**, of the Society for Human Resource Management, for their insightful comments on the manuscript and their assistance in making this project a reality.

Jathan Janove, of Bullard Smith Jernstedt Wilson, for his helpful advice on the manuscript on behalf of SHRM.

Kelly Perri and **Sigrid Metson**, for their tireless marketing efforts and their help in shaping the tone and structure of the book.

Ella Hirst and **Stan Jacobson**, for their research assistance.

Susan Putney, for her wonderful cover and book design.

Susan Carlson Greene, for the meticulous proofreading.

Dedication

For my parents, whose five children gave them plenty to investigate.
In loving memory.

Table of Contents

Investigation Basics

Workplace Investigations: An Overview

Chances are good that you picked up this book because you've become aware of a potentially serious problem at your company and you're not quite sure how to handle it. Maybe you've heard a complaint or report of misconduct that sounds something like this:

"Every time I go into John's office, he's looking at porn on the Internet—it's really starting to offend me and some of the other women in the office."

"We've finished our internal audit, and the numbers just don't add up. I think we may have a thief on our payroll."

"I've been passed over for promotion three times, and each time the job has gone to a younger person who doesn't have my experience or training. I feel like I'm being discriminated against."

"Mark has been really angry lately—he keeps talking about his gun collection, and yesterday he told me that 'management is about to get what's coming to them.' I'm afraid of what he might do."

Now you're facing some tough decisions: Whom should you believe? What really happened and why? How serious is this problem? What should you do about it? And, can you handle this without creating legal problems for the company?

A complete, impartial, and timely investigation will help you answer these questions and figure out what to do. In fact, a proper investigation is one of the most important tools for maintaining a safe and productive workplace—and keeping your company out of legal trouble.

This book gives you the tools and information you need to conduct a successful investigation. Part I (Chapters 1 through 4) describes in detail the ten steps to a successful investigation of any kind of workplace problem. Part II (Chapters 5 through 8) takes a closer look at four common workplace problems—discrimination, harassment, theft, and violence—and explains how to handle the special investigation challenges posed by each.

This chapter will help you get started. It introduces the benefits and basic components of a proper workplace investigation, including the actions you will have to take—and decisions you will have to make—along the way. (Each of these steps is covered in detail in Chapters 2 through 4.) It also covers some common investigation mistakes that can lead to legal trouble—and tips that will help you avoid them.

Investigations Require Judgment Calls

Although most investigations will require you to at least consider each of these ten steps, every situation is a little bit different. Workplace problems rarely land on your desk in a tidy package with an obvious solution. Instead, you'll often be faced with conflicting stories, documents that are open to different interpretations, and no clear answers about what happened and what you should do about it. You'll have to decide which problems merit a closer look, whom to interview, and what documents to review—and when your investigation is complete, you'll have to decide what you think really happened.

All of these decisions are judgment calls, and no book can tell you how to handle every possible scenario you might face. However, if you follow the guidelines in the chapters that follow, keep an open mind, and use your best judgment, you should be able to handle most of the issues that come up.

The Benefits of an Effective Investigation

Although you might not be happy to learn that you have a workplace problem, investigating and resolving it in the right way can strengthen and protect your company. Among its many benefits, a proper investigation will help you:

- **Figure out what happened.** The immediate aim of any investigation is to get to the bottom of a problem. You won't know how to handle a situation until you know what really happened. And, acting before you have all the facts could lead you to discipline the wrong employee or allow a workplace problem to continue.

- **Deal with employee problems early.** An investigation will help you figure out who's behind a workplace problem, so you can take action before things get any worse. If you are dealing with a problem employee, he or she can be disciplined. If you discover that employees are breaking the rules because they don't know what's expected from them, you can implement training programs, work harder to publicize and distribute company policies, and make sure managers are enforcing the rules.

- **Enforce company policies.** If a company doesn't enforce its own policies, the company's employees quickly realize that they don't have to follow the rules. Showing employees that there are consequences for misconduct will help deter future trouble and keep employees on the right track.

- **Encourage reporting.** Investigating and dealing with problems quickly will encourage employees to come forward with their issues and concerns. This means that you'll hear about workplace trouble right away, before it has a chance to grow into a more serious problem.

- **Avoid or counter bad publicity.** A company that ignores complaints and problems gives the impression that it doesn't care about its workers or the law. And if your company's failure to deal with a problem becomes public knowledge—through a lawsuit, for example—it could really hurt the company's reputation.

- **Protect your company from lawsuits.** A solid investigation will help your company avoid or defend against legal challenges in the future. If someone who is injured by workplace misconduct—an employee who is sexually harassed, for example—sues your company, you can show that you took action right away, which will protect your company from liability in many cases. If an employee who was disciplined or fired as a result of your investigation files a lawsuit, you will be able to show that you acted reasonably and in good faith, which will undermine the employee's claims.

By the same token, however, a slipshod investigation can *lead* to employee lawsuits, by giving employees the ammunition they need to demonstrate that your company was careless, discriminated, spread false information, or treated employees poorly, among other things. And failing to investigate at all is even worse—if an employee can show that company management knew about a problem and didn't do anything about it, the company will be legally responsible for any harm that employee suffered.

So how do you conduct the right kind of investigation? By being fair and thorough and making good-faith efforts to get to the truth. Even if you come to the wrong conclusion, your company should be able to show that it was legally entitled to take action (for example, to discipline or fire an employee) based on the results of your investigation, as long as you investigated properly and your decisions were reasonable based on the information available to you.

EXAMPLE: Ralph was accused of sexually harassing two female coworkers. The company immediately performed a complete investigation, interviewing the women, Ralph, and a number of witnesses—including five Ralph suggested. Based on these interviews, the company concluded that Ralph had in fact harassed his coworkers and fired him.

Ralph later sued the company, claiming that he had a consensual affair with both women, no harassment had occurred, and the women were angry with him for two-timing them. (Ralph did not tell any of this to the company's investigator.) The jury found in Ralph's favor. However, an appeals court decided that it didn't matter what really happened. As long as the company conducted a fair and thorough investigation and reached a good-faith conclusion based on the information available to it at the time, it was not liable for firing Ralph based on the investigation's results.

> **Your Role in the Investigation**
>
> This book addresses every aspect of workplace investigations, from start to finish. Depending on your role at your company, you may be responsible for all, most, some, or just a few of the actions and decisions described in this book. For example, you may be called upon to decide whether an investigation is necessary, but your company may then use an outside investigator to handle the legwork. Or, you may be responsible for performing the investigation, but not for deciding what discipline or other action to take based on your findings.
>
> No matter what aspects of the investigation fall within your job description, you'll find the information you need in this book. We've covered all of the duties associated with an investigation, to make sure that all of our readers are fully equipped to handle every part of the investigation for which they are responsible.

Ten Steps to a Successful Investigation

The best way to tackle an investigation—like any other project—is to divide it up into manageable tasks. Fortunately, most workplace investigations follow a similar pattern, although the details can vary considerably. Once you become aware of a problem or complaint, you'll have to follow these ten steps:

1. **Decide whether to investigate.** Although there are some situations that don't warrant an investigation, you should generally err on the side of investigating. Sometimes, you won't know how serious a problem really is until you start asking questions. Chapter 2 explains how to decide whether to investigate, including how to scale the size of your investigation to the problem.

2. **Take immediate action, if necessary.** You might have to act right away, before you begin to investigate, to protect employees or the company itself. For example, an employee accused of serious sexual harassment or stealing company trade secrets should be suspended,

with pay, until the investigation is complete. For information on taking interim measures—including tips that will help you avoid legal claims based on your pre-investigation actions—see Chapter 2.

3. **Choose an investigator.** If you won't handle the investigation yourself, you'll need to pick someone else to do it. The right investigator is experienced, impartial and perceived as impartial by the employees involved, and capable of acting—and if necessary, testifying—professionally about the investigation. Chapter 2 explains these requirements, including when it makes sense to bring in an outside investigator.

4. **Plan the investigation.** Start by organizing your thoughts and information: What do you know? What do you need to find out to decide what happened? Who might have relevant information? What's the best way to get it? A little careful thought up front can help you avoid wasting time or overlooking important facts as you investigate. Chapter 2 explains how to prepare to investigate, including tips on letting others in the company know your plans.

5. **Interview.** The heart of any investigation is gathering information —and the most basic way to do that is by asking people questions. Typically, you'll have to interview the employee accused of wrongdoing, the employee who complained or was the victim, and any witnesses to the incident(s). You'll learn the most by asking open-ended questions that encourage disclosure without giving too much away. Chapter 3 explains how to conduct successful interviews, including whom to interview, what to ask, and how to get the facts you need.

6. **Gather documents and other evidence.** Documents play a role in many investigations—and decide the outcome in more than a few. You might have to review personnel files, email messages, personal notes, performance reviews, and other documents to figure out what really happened. You might also have to gather physical evidence, such as a weapon, photographs, or clothing. You'll find information on gathering evidence, including a document checklist, in Chapter 3.

7. **Evaluate the evidence.** The most challenging part of the investigation—especially if witnesses disagree or contradict each other—is figuring out what actually happened. There are some proven methods of figuring out where the truth lies, methods all of us use in our everyday lives. Chapter 4 explains how to sift through the evidence and come to a conclusion—and what to do if, despite your efforts, you can't get to the bottom of things.

8. **Take action.** If you conclude that an employee committed serious misconduct, you'll have to act quickly to avoid legal liability for that employee's behavior and to protect other employees from harm. Chapter 4 explains how to decide which actions to take after the investigation, including how to communicate with the employees involved.

9. **Document the investigation.** Once your investigation is complete, you should write an investigation report that explains what you did and why. This will not only give the company some protection from lawsuits relating to the investigation, but also provide a written record in case of future misconduct by the same employee. Investigation reports are covered in Chapter 4.

10. **Follow up.** Your last step is to make sure the problem that led to the investigation has been solved. You'll need to follow through with the complaining employee and the accused employee, and you might have to take other steps—such as training employees or developing new workplace policies—to deal with systemic workplace problems. Chapter 4 explains how to follow up after the investigation.

CD-ROM

Forms, checklists, and more. You'll find all of the forms, checklists, and other tools described in the book in Appendix B and on the CD-ROM inside the back cover. The CD-ROM also includes audio tracks of investigative interviews.

What a Good Investigation Looks Like

Here's how one California employer won a lawsuit by conducting a timely, thorough, and fair investigation:

Lucky Stores (a supermarket chain) received two complaints from female employees that John Silva had sexually harassed them. After conducting a month-long investigation, Lucky concluded that Silva had committed sexual harassment and fired him. Silva filed a lawsuit against Lucky, claiming that he didn't harass the women and, therefore, should not have been fired.

The court found in Lucky's favor because it had good reason to believe, based on its investigation, that Silva committed the harassment. The court detailed the qualities that made Lucky's investigation so reliable:

- Lucky chose Jeff Szczesny, a human resources representative who had been trained on how to conduct an investigation, to investigate the complaint. Szczesny was not involved in the underlying incident.
- Szczesny began investigating immediately.
- Szczesny interviewed 15 Lucky employees and documented the interviews. He asked open-ended questions and tried to elicit facts, not opinions. He encouraged the witnesses to contact him if they wanted to talk to him again.
- Szczesny told Silva of the charges against him and gave him a chance to tell his side of the story.
- Szczesny met again with important witnesses, including Silva, to give them a chance to hear new information and to clarify or correct their own statements.
- Szczesny memorialized the investigation in a written report, detailing the conclusions he reached and why.

Common Investigation Mistakes— and How to Avoid Them

There are a number of legal traps waiting for companies that conduct an improper investigation or fail to investigate at all. Generally, these traps come in the form of lawsuits brought either by an employee who was a victim of inappropriate behavior in the workplace or by an employee who was disciplined or fired after being accused of misconduct. In either situation, a company that performed an incomplete, biased, or late investigation—or that never investigated at all—begins the lawsuit in a fairly deep hole. Not only has the company ignored its workers' legal rights, but it has also shown a lack of concern for its workers' well-being—something that many jurors (most of whom are or were employees themselves, not employers) find offensive.

In addition to these legal issues, companies that don't investigate problems or that conduct half-hearted investigations will face practical problems. These employers are sending precisely the wrong signals to employees, managers, and customers: that they don't want to hear about workplace problems, they don't really care what's going on in their company, and they won't enforce their own workplace rules.

Finally, failing to investigate or doing a poor job will exact an emotional cost as well. Wrongly accusing an employee of serious misconduct not only invites a lawsuit, but also ruins that employee's reputation and relationships with coworkers. As if the legal and practical traps described above aren't bad enough, imagine how bad you'll feel if you make the wrong call—and your mistake brings unhappiness, anxiety, and possibly even career ruin to a blameless employee.

Fortunately, it isn't too hard to avoid these mistakes. By following the strategies outlined in this book—and using your common sense—you can keep your investigation on the right side of the law. Here are some common investigation errors, along with tips that will help you avoid them.

Failing to Investigate

If company management is aware of serious misconduct or dangerous activity in the workplace and doesn't do anything about it, the company could have significant legal exposure. Generally, any harm that comes to a company's employees—and sometimes, to people who aren't on the payroll, such as customers, clients, or bystanders—after the company has notice of a problem will be the company's legal responsibility. This means, for example, that an employee who suffers sexual harassment after a manager learned about the problem will be able to sue the company for damages.

Your company might also face a lawsuit if it fires an employee for workplace wrongdoing without first conducting an investigation. If that employee has an employment contract—whether written, oral, or implied—limiting the company's right to fire, that employee might sue for breach of contract if you don't investigate before terminating his or her employment. The lawsuit would claim that (1) the employee didn't commit the misconduct for which he or she was fired; (2) your company didn't bother to investigate to figure out what really happened; and, therefore, (3) your company didn't have good cause to fire the employee.

Usually, this won't be an issue because most employees don't have employment contracts. Instead, they are "at-will" employees, which means that they can quit at any time, and you can fire them at any time, for any reason that is not illegal (illegal reasons for firing include discrimination and retaliation). However, some employees have employment contracts that limit the employer's right to fire at will. For example, the contract might state that the employee can be fired only for "good cause"—a common provision—or for specified reasons (such as "gross misconduct" or "financial malfeasance"). If you fire the employee for reasons other than those stated in the contract, the employee can sue your company for breaching the contract.

Failing to Fire Dangerous Employees Can Lead to Lawsuits

Someone who is injured by one of your company's employees might have a legal claim against your company if it was careless in supervising or retaining that employee— that is, if company management knew or should have known that the employee was unfit for the job, yet did nothing about it. These are called "negligent retention" or "negligent supervision" claims. Although these lawsuits have not yet appeared in every state, the clear legal trend is to allow employers to be sued for hiring or keeping on a dangerous employee.

Failing to investigate can give rise to this type of lawsuit. If you failed to perform an investigation that would have revealed that a particular employee posed a danger to others, your company could be on the hook for damages if the employee harms someone.

EXAMPLE: John works at a machine plant. His coworkers notice that John has not been himself lately—his appearance is somewhat disheveled, he seems distracted, and he loses his temper easily. He complains that company management is trying to force him to retire, but that he "won't go quietly." Coworkers bring this to the attention of the human resources department but are told, "That's just John. He complains a lot, but he does high-quality work." A month later, John sabotages a major piece of equipment, which malfunctions and injures several employees and a few students visiting from a local vocational school. The company might face a lawsuit for negligent retention.

Negligent retention and supervision claims can always be brought by outsiders— those who don't work for your company. Your employees, on the other hand, may not be able to sue you for negligence. The workers' compensation insurance system, which guarantees compensation to employees who are injured in the workplace, prohibits employees from suing their employers for injuries that are covered by workers' comp. For more on this issue, see Chapter 8.

An employee might also have a contract that hasn't been reduced to writing. For example, some employees have spoken agreements with the employer (known as oral contracts). Whatever the employer and employee agreed to orally will govern the employer's right to fire. In other cases, an employee might have an implied contract: a contract that was never explicitly reduced to words, whether written or spoken, but arose from the conduct and statements of the employer and employee. For example, if an employer tells a worker "as long as you do a good job, we'll keep you on," that could be interpreted as an implied contract restricting the employer's right to fire the employee unless the employee performs poorly.

To avoid the legal problems that can result from failing to investigate, take workplace problems seriously. Never ignore complaints of wrongdoing. Even if a situation seems simple or straightforward, always do some initial research before deciding that an investigation isn't warranted. And make sure you know all the facts before taking disciplinary action against an employee.

Delay

Even if you eventually decide to investigate and do a good job, your company can get into legal trouble if you wait too long to get started. If an employee suffers harm—from harassment or workplace violence, for example—after you learned about the problem but before you took action, your company will usually be legally responsible to that employee. The longer you postpone the investigation, the more serious this legal liability could be.

> **EXAMPLE:** Kristen worked as a checker at a grocery store. She complained that a coworker harassed her by calling her names, propositioning her, commenting on her appearance, and touching her. Kristen complained to the store's assistant manager several times; each time, the manager confronted the coworker, who denied the allegations. After Kristen's fourth complaint—two months after her first complaint—the accused harasser was transferred to a different shift, where he had no further contact with Kristen.

Kristen filed a lawsuit against the grocery store for sexual harassment. The employer tried to have her case thrown out, arguing that it stopped the harassment by transferring the alleged harasser. However, the court found that the store's two-month delay before taking action was too long, even if it eventually did the right thing by moving the alleged harasser to another shift. The court allowed Kristen's lawsuit to go forward.

Postponing the investigation could also lead the complaining employee to claim that he or she was retaliated against—disciplined or otherwise treated badly for making the complaint. (For more on this issue, see "Retaliation," below.) If the employee is threatened by the wrongdoer, given the cold shoulder by other employees, or even disciplined by a supervisor for coming forward, that could well constitute illegal retaliation for which your company would be legally liable.

Of course, there's a simple solution: Don't delay your investigation. Once you learn of a serious problem or complaint, get moving right away. If you absolutely have to wait a bit before getting started (because the victim is on vacation, for example), document the reasons for the delay. (Chapter 3 explains how to do this.)

Inconsistency

Some companies get into trouble by acting inconsistently—that is, by handling similar situations differently. In the employment arena, inconsistent treatment can lead to claims of discrimination. An employee who feels that he or she was treated differently because of a protected characteristic—an inherent quality, such as race or gender, that cannot legally form the basis for an employment decision—might bring a discrimination lawsuit.

Federal laws prohibit employers from making workplace decisions based on an employee's or applicant's race, color, national origin, sex, religion, age (if the employee is at least 40 years old), or disability. These laws don't apply to smaller employers; only employers with at least 15 employees—or 20 employees, for age discrimination—are required to follow them. In addition, almost every state has adopted an antidiscrimination law. Although some of these laws mirror the federal rules, some prohibit additional kinds of discrimination (based on sexual orientation or marital status, for example) and some apply to smaller employers. (For more on discrimination laws and protected characteristics, see Chapter 5. You'll find information on your state's antidiscrimination laws in Appendix D.)

If you aren't even-handed in your investigations, you could risk a discrimination claim. For example, if you decide not to investigate a complaint against a white man for sexual harassment but you do investigate a harassment complaint against an African-American man, you and your company might be accused of race discrimination. Similarly, if you don't investigate a claim of discrimination brought by a Muslim employee, that employee might argue that your decision was based on hostility to his or her religion.

EXAMPLE: Kwik & Klean, a janitorial company, investigates an incident of sexual harassment. The company concludes that Tom, a white employee on one of the night crews, has been telling X-rated jokes and stories, which have made some of his female coworkers uncomfortable. Tom is given a written warning and is required to attend sexual harassment training.

Several months later, a worker on a different crew complains that Eduardo, a Latino employee, has been making lewd sexual comments to coworkers. The company investigates and concludes that the complaint is valid. The company is concerned that it has had two incidents of harassment in the past few months and decides that it has to take steps to demonstrate its commitment to rooting out the problem, so it decides to fire Eduardo.

Eduardo sues, claiming that he was treated more harshly than Tom because of his race. Even if the company's decision wasn't based on the race of either employee, it will have trouble defending its inconsistency in court. Because the employees committed similar offenses, the best course of action is to impose similar discipline. The company can take other steps—like requiring sexual harassment training for the entire workforce—to show employees that harassment won't be tolerated.

Avoid discrimination claims by treating similar problems similarly. If you decide to investigate one claim but not another, make sure you have a valid, business-related reason for doing so. If you punish one employee more harshly than another, be prepared to justify the difference. And always check your motives: Most of us don't want to admit to any prejudice, but we all have preconceptions that can affect our decisions. Inconsistency is sometimes justified, but it can also be a sign of unconscious bias at work.

Retaliation

Your company may not take any negative action against an employee for coming forward with a complaint or participating in an investigation. As the U.S. Supreme Court recently held (in the context of discrimination and harassment complaints), any action that could deter a reasonable worker from coming forward with a complaint might constitute retaliation. (*Burlington Northern & Santa Fe Railway Co. v. White,* 126 S. Ct. 2405 (2006).) An employee need not show that he or she was fired or demoted to bring a retaliation claim: Lesser forms of mistreatment might also qualify as retaliation, if they could discourage employees from bringing complaints.

Most conscientious employers realize that punishing an employee for bringing a workplace problem to their attention is a bad idea, for legal and practical reasons. However, even savvy employers sometimes retaliate against an employee without intending do. This comes up most often when employees have to be separated for some reason. For example, if one employee is harassing another, your first instinct might be to move one of the workers to another position, so they won't have to work together. However, if you move the worker who complained, that worker might feel that he or she is being punished for complaining—especially if the new position, workspace, or shift is less prestigious or desirable.

To protect against retaliation claims, warn everyone involved in an investigation that retaliation won't be tolerated. Ask the complaining employee—and perhaps his or her manager—to bring any instances of retaliation to your attention immediately. And if you must separate workers, either move the worker accused of misconduct or make very sure that the worker who complained is in favor of the change you propose.

 CAUTION
Retaliation lawsuits can outlive the original complaint.
Courts have held that an employee can sue an employer who punishes the employee for making a complaint even if the conduct the employee complains about doesn't violate the law. For example, an employee files a lawsuit, claiming that she was fired for complaining about sexual harassment by a coworker. The court decides that the coworker's conduct, while inappropriate, did not meet the legal standards for sexual harassment. However, the court might still allow the woman to sue for retaliation: Even though she wasn't sexually harassed, it is illegal for the employer to fire her for complaining about it in good faith.

Failing to Be Thorough

Performing an incomplete or sloppy investigation—by failing to interview key witnesses, neglecting to review important documents, or ignoring issues that come up during the investigation, for example—can have many of the same negative consequences as failing to investigate at all.

The employee who complained or suffered mistreatment will feel that his or her concerns weren't taken seriously and might sue for retaliation or for harm that continued during and after the investigation. An employee accused of misconduct might believe that your company wasn't interested in his or her side of the story or in finding out what really happened, which could lead to a lawsuit for wrongful termination or discrimination.

And worse, your company won't be able to rely on the results of your investigation in court: If an employee can show that you did an incompetent job, perhaps by hiring an expert witness to testify that you didn't investigate properly, your company will be in an even worse position than if you never investigated in the first place. As great political scandals have shown, the "cover-up" can be more damaging that the underlying problem ever was. If your investigation appears to be inadequate, a jury might well wonder whether you were trying to hide deeper problems or protect someone important at your company, perhaps by making a scapegoat of the employee who was fired.

This is an easy mistake to avoid. Following the simple strategies and steps in this book will ensure that your investigation is thorough and proper—and will stand up in court.

Compromising Confidentiality

Loose lips do more than sink ships—they can also torpedo a workplace investigation. From a practical standpoint, talking too much during the investigation—telling a witness what another witness said, revealing your personal opinion to one of the employees involved, or publicizing the complaint in the workplace, for example—can lead others to doubt your objectivity. They might believe you have already made up your mind and therefore aren't going to investigate fairly. Employees involved in the investigation might change their statements, either subconsciously or intentionally, based on what you say. And you can bet that if you're talking about the investigation, the entire workplace is talking, too, which will lead to a lot of gossip and lost productivity.

As a legal matter, an employee who believes you have maligned his or her reputation by spreading false information can sue for defamation. These claims are sometimes made by the target of the investigation, who argues that the employer falsely accused him or her of wrongdoing, resulting in unfair discipline and a damaged reputation—and perhaps even preventing him or her from getting another job.

EXAMPLE: Tricia was fired from the Reader's Hideaway, a bookstore, after her register drawer was short on several occasions. Tricia claims that she didn't steal any money from the store, and that another employee—David, the owner's son—used her register on each day that it was short. David denies taking the money, and the company never talks to other employees about what they've seen or looks into Tricia's claims further. When Tricia applies for other jobs and Reader's Hideaway is called for a reference, the owner says that Tricia was fired for stealing from the company. Tricia sues for defamation.

Defamation Defenses

Although employers can be held liable for harming an employee's reputation, the law recognizes that employers sometimes have to talk about former employees and the reasons why they are no longer employed. Here are a few legal defenses that will protect an employer who reveals limited information in good faith:

- **Truth.** Someone who is telling the truth can't be sued for defamation. In other words, if you tell someone that an employee was fired for pulling a gun on you, the employee can't make a claim for defamation if that's exactly what happened.

- **Good-faith reference to a prospective employer.** Most states will not allow a former employee to sue an employer for defamation if the employer makes statements that it reasonably believes to be true to a prospective employer seeking a reference. Typically, these statements are "conditionally privileged": This means that the employer won't be liable as long as it acts in good faith (rather than with malice).

- **Good-faith statement to a government agency.** An employer generally cannot be sued for responding in good faith to an official request for information about why an employee was fired. For example, you can tell the unemployment or workers' compensation office your reasons for terminating an employee without worrying about defamation claims. Similarly, statements made by an employer during official proceedings (such as a lawsuit or arbitration hearing) cannot give rise to a defamation claim.

The best way to avoid a defamation claim is to speak only to people who have a legitimate need to know why the employee was fired, and to make only statements that you know to be true. Conducting a proper investigation will help you figure out where the truth lies—and, therefore, what you can safely say about the situation.

A defamation claim can also be brought by an employee who makes a workplace complaint, if you conclude that the complaint is false and make this belief public. In this situation, the employee's claim is that he or she was falsely labeled a liar. Even a witness who participated in a workplace investigation could accuse the employer of lying about what he or she said, if the employer's statements damaged the employee's reputation.

Defamation claims start when investigators or employers talk too much, or say things that they don't know to be true. The best way to avoid this mistake is to reveal information on a need-to-know basis only. Don't talk about the investigation, the evidence, or your conclusions with anyone except those who need to be in on the decisions. If you must make a damaging statement about an employee or former employee, stick to the facts and keep it short.

Losing Objectivity

You've probably developed some personal opinions about most of the people you work with. It's human nature to like some people more than others. But you have to put these opinions aside and look objectively at the evidence when you conduct a workplace investigation. If you let your personal feelings and opinions hold sway, you might be accused of discrimination—and the results of your investigation could be called into question.

It can also be tough to stay objective if you have to investigate—and recommend discipline against—people who outrank you on the corporate ladder. But, if you let the offending employee's position in the company dictate the outcome of the investigation, you aren't doing your job properly.

The best antidote for this problem is to remember your role. When you investigate, you are acting on behalf of the company. If you feel unable to put your personal feelings aside, get some help. Ask someone else within the workplace (or hire an outside investigator) to conduct the investigation or get some advice from a lawyer.

> **CAUTION**
> **You might not like what you discover.** You must follow the evidence wherever it leads, even if that means uncovering serious problems at your company or finding that a popular or high-ranking employee committed wrongdoing. You won't do your company any favors by turning a blind eye to these types of problems: Remember, your job is to figure out what's going on, so the company can take effective action to remedy the situation. Although your findings might make you unpopular or unhappy in the short term, you'll be doing the right thing in the long run.

Strong-Arm Interview Tactics

Some investigators are so intent on getting straight answers from the workers they interview that they restrain workers against their will. For example, an investigator might lock the door to the interview room, physically prevent the employee from leaving, or tell the employee something like "nobody's leaving this room until I find out what really happened." Using physical means to restrain an employee, or taking actions that lead the employee to believe that he or she is not free to go, can lead to a legal claim of false imprisonment.

You can avoid false imprisonment lawsuits by avoiding coercive tactics. If an employee indicates that he or she wants to leave the room or stop an interview, let him or her go. Your company is free to take disciplinary action against an employee who refuses to answer legitimate questions or participate in a workplace investigation. However, you can't use physical means or threats to prevent the employee from leaving.

Invading Employee Privacy

Don't become so zealous in your search for the truth that you invade employees' privacy rights. This can be a tough call; after all, conducting an investigation involves a certain amount of poking around, usually into things that someone doesn't want you to know about. However, if you cross the line from legitimate workplace concerns into private employee property or behavior, you could be inviting a lawsuit for invasion of privacy.

If an employee files a lawsuit for invasion of privacy, a judge will look at why both sides acted as they did: why the employee expected privacy and why the employer searched, monitored, or otherwise got into an area the employee felt was private. Then, the judge decides whose side of the argument seems most reasonable, in what is aptly called a "balancing test."

Searches

When investigating certain types of wrongdoing, you may need to search an employee's work area. For example, if an employee is accused of theft, you may want to look in the employee's desk or locker for the stolen items. You will be on safest legal ground if your company has a policy that reserves the right to search employee workspaces—this type of policy shows that employees should not have expected the contents of their desks or lockers to be private.

The more intrusive the search, the more compelling your reasons for searching must be. For example, if you want to search something an employee brings on company property, such as a lunch pail or backpack, you must have a fairly strong reason to search. And you probably should not undertake this kind of search unless your company has clearly warned employees, in a written policy, that these items are subject to search. If you want to conduct a really intrusive search—for example, turning out a worker's pockets or searching an employee physically—you are asking for trouble. If your investigation reaches a point where this type of search seems necessary, talk to a lawyer. (For more on workplace searches, see Chapter 7.)

Electronic Monitoring

As long as your company has a written policy letting workers know that it might monitor their email or use of the Internet, the company generally has the right to read employee email sent on company equipment or monitor which websites employees visit using the company's computer network. During an investigation, email messages often provide crucial proof of misconduct, such as harassment, discrimination, or threats.

> **EXAMPLE:** Isaac complains that someone is sending him racist cartoons and jokes anonymously, using the office email system. The company has a written policy permitting email monitoring. The investigator reads the email messages and asks for the tech department's help in figuring out where they originated. The employee who sent the offensive messages would have a hard time arguing that the company shouldn't have read the messages or traced them back to their sender.

Monitoring phone calls is another story. An employer is legally allowed to monitor employee conversations with customers or clients for quality control (although some state laws require the employer to inform the parties to the call—either by announcement or by signal—that someone is listening in). However, different rules apply to personal calls. Once the person monitoring realizes that a particular call is personal, the monitoring must stop immediately.

Avoiding Privacy Lawsuits

The best way to avoid violating employee's privacy rights is to ask—or search for—only what you need to know. Exercise restraint: Don't search or monitor employees without a good reason. The further you stray from the complaint or alleged misconduct, the more likely you are to invade someone's privacy.

You can minimize legal exposure by making sure your company adopts written policies warning employees that it reserves the right to search desks, lockers, and email. If your company has a written policy warning that it might search, employees will have a tough time arguing that they reasonably expected those areas to be private.

Using Polygraphs Improperly

You might believe that the easiest way to get to the bottom of a workplace problem is to require everyone involved to take a lie detector test. In many situations, however, polygraph tests will only lead to trouble. A federal law, the Employee Polygraph Protection Act (29 U.S.C. §§ 2001–2009) strictly limits the circumstances in which an employer can require workers to take a lie detector or polygraph test, and it's not easy to meet the law's requirements.

An employer has to fit within one of the law's narrow exceptions to have the legal right to test. (One of the exceptions applies to theft investigations; see Chapter 7 for more information.) And even then, the employer has to meet a long list of technical requirements before it can use the results of the test to make a disciplinary decision about an employee. For example, the employee must receive a variety of written notices, must receive the test questions in advance, cannot be asked certain types of questions, and must receive a copy of the test results, among other things. In addition, the employer may only use a polygraph examiner who meets certain qualifications and reports the results of the test in a particular form.

It can be pretty tough to conduct a legal polygraph test under this law. Even if your company can meet the legal requirements, you'll have to decide how much weight to give the test results. Experts disagree about how easy (or difficult) it is to "beat" the test. Because of these legal and practical problems, most employers should probably just skip the polygraph testing altogether. If you are still inclined to test, make sure the situation falls within one of the law's exceptions—and hire a polygraph examiner who is properly certified and understands the law.

Getting Started

Although your company can reap a lot of benefits from conducting an effective investigation, that doesn't necessarily mean you'll enjoy every minute of it. Investigating can be unpleasant work. If you're looking into a sexual harassment complaint, for example, you might see or hear some pretty graphic things. If you're investigating a violence complaint, you might have to make difficult judgment calls to ensure the safety of employees and customers. And if you're investigating a complaint that involves employees whom you like or work closely with, your investigation may affect those relationships. All the while, you will probably feel some pressure to resolve the situation quickly, without creating legal liability.

In short, you're likely to experience some anxiety when investigating and dealing with workplace problems. The best way to alleviate this anxiety is through careful planning: taking some time before you begin your fact-finding to assess the situation and decide how to handle it.

Preparation can also help you avoid making mistakes that could come back to haunt you and your company. Sometimes, the worst investigation blunders are made before the investigation starts: A company ignores a complaint, chooses an insensitive or biased investigator, or fails to take immediate steps to prevent further harm to its employees. It's often apparent only in hindsight, after a lawsuit is filed, that these problems could have been avoided by paying careful attention to pre-investigation details.

This chapter provides the information you'll need to get ready to conduct a successful investigation. It explains how a problem requiring investigation might come to your attention, how to decide whether to investigate, what actions you might want to take before beginning the investigation, and how to plan and prepare for the investigation. It also covers how to choose someone to investigate a problem (if you won't do it yourself), including the pros and cons of hiring an outside investigator.

Discovering Workplace Problems

The situation that triggers an investigation might come to your attention in any number of ways, but your company's obligation to investigate doesn't depend on how you find out about the problem. Some employers mistakenly believe that they have a duty to investigate only formal complaints. This is wrong, however. No matter how your company learns of a serious workplace problem, it generally has a legal duty to take appropriate action—and to investigate the situation before taking action, if necessary. As a practical matter, if your company ignores misconduct, morale will drop, productivity will suffer, and employees will quickly learn that they don't have to follow workplace rules.

> (!) **CAUTION**
>
> **Once a manager knows, "the company" knows.** Generally, a company is assumed to be aware of a complaint or problem once a manager, officer, or other person responsible for taking action (such as a human resources professional) knows about it. This is true even if the manager or other responsible person doesn't reveal the problem to anyone else. This is one reason why your company should have strictly enforced policies that require managers to bring problems immediately to the appropriate person, such as a human resources representative or the company president, as the sample policy in Appendix A does.

Some investigations do begin with a formal complaint. But you can't count on employees to bring every workplace problem to your attention. Employees sometimes choose not to complain because they don't want to be seen as troublemakers, they fear retaliation, or they simply hope the problem will go away on its own.

In some situations, employees may not even know about the misconduct because they're not being victimized by it. For example, if an employee is stealing from customers, it's possible that no other worker is even aware of the problem. And in some situations, no one wants to come forward because they are all implicated in the misconduct. For example, if employees are selling drugs in the workplace, you probably shouldn't expect their coworkers—who are also their customers—to let you in on the details.

Here are some of the many ways you might find out about a workplace problem requiring an investigation.

Formal Complaints

One advantage of starting an investigation with a formal complaint—in which an employee directly reports a problem to the appropriate person (typically, someone in the human resources department)—is that you can document the source and nature of the problem. A complaint gives your investigation a natural starting point; you can begin by getting the details directly from the complaining employee.

You should have a form for reporting complaints, with blanks to fill in the complaining employee's name, the date of the complaint, the details of the complaint, and so on. (You'll find a sample complaint form in Appendix B and on the CD-ROM.) Although some companies require the complaining employee to complete a complaint form, this could create problems. Some employees will feel intimidated by having to commit their complaint to writing and will balk at this requirement. And you'll be at the mercy of the complaining employee's writing skills (and ability to pinpoint the problem). It's a better idea to have the person who takes the complaint—often a human resources representative or designated manager—fill in the complaint form.

An employer can encourage formal complaints by instituting well-publicized complaint and open-door policies that encourage employees to come forward with their concerns. These policies can:

- give you an opportunity to deal with workplace problems immediately
- tell employees that the company cares about their concerns
- let managers know what their responsibilities are if they learn of a problem

- support other workplace policies (for example, an antiharassment policy or workplace violence policy) by demonstrating that employees will be held to these rules, and

- give your company some legal protection against harassment and discrimination lawsuits (see "Decide Whether to Investigate," below, for more information).

You'll find more information, including sample policies you can use in your workplace, in Appendix A and on the CD-ROM.

What If the Employee Doesn't Want to File a Complaint?

Most experienced managers and human resources professionals have faced this troubling situation: An employee comes to their office, shuts the door, and confides that another employee is causing trouble—perhaps by telling dirty jokes, threatening coworkers, or breaking workplace rules. The confiding employee may want advice, a shoulder to cry on, or simply a safe place to let off some steam about a bad situation. What the employee does not want is to make a formal complaint.

While you might be tempted to act as a friend and respect the employee's request to keep things quiet, that is rarely in the best interests of the company or the complaining employee. Once a manager knows of illegal workplace conduct, the company has notice of the problem—and has an obligation to deal with it, even if the employee doesn't want to file a complaint. And the complaining employee's situation isn't going to improve unless and until the company takes action.

This can be a tough situation for managers, particularly those who are friends with the employees who work for them. Prepare managers by letting them know that they must bring all complaints to the attention of the appropriate people, even if the complaining employee does not want to come forward. Managers can tell reluctant complainers, "I know this is hard and you want to keep it quiet. But I have an obligation to report this, so the company can do something about it. That's the only way we can improve this situation."

Anonymous Complaints

Sometimes, complaints are made anonymously, through an unsigned note in a suggestion box, a letter or memo to a manager, or an unidentified phone message, for example.

An employee might complain anonymously for many reasons. An employee who is being harassed might fear retaliation from the wrongdoer or want to avoid being seen as a complainer. An employee who is threatened with violence or who witnesses illegal activities—such as theft or drug crimes—might fear for his or her physical safety or simply not want to talk to the police.

An anonymous complaint might also come from someone who isn't involved in the situation. For example, a coworker might complain anonymously on behalf of a friend who is too fearful to come forward. A customer, vendor, or client may want to report misconduct but not want to get involved. An anonymous complaint might even be made by someone outside the work environment—for example, a concerned friend, spouse, or partner.

TIP

Publicly traded companies must have a procedure for making anonymous complaints. The Sarbanes-Oxley Act of 2002, a comprehensive federal law that seeks to protect shareholders from fraud, requires public companies to provide a way for employees to submit confidential, anonymous complaints about questionable accounting or auditing practices. This law also requires companies to adopt procedures for receiving, handling, and retaining such complaints. For more information, see Chapter 7.

Reports by Managers and Supervisors

Managers and supervisors are the company's eyes and ears in the workplace. Because they are on the front lines, they are most likely to witness developing problems. In some cases, managers or supervisors might hear rumors or gossip about improper activities; sometimes, they hear complaints directly from unhappy workers.

Your company should train all managers to report any employee complaints, incidents of workplace wrongdoing, or even rumors of troublesome behavior. Requiring managers to report problems will allow your company to remedy the situation early. As a legal matter, once your managers are aware of a problem, the company is generally legally responsible for taking action to deal with the situation. If managers fail to report serious issues, your company may be on the hook for any harm that results—even if no one else ever learns of the problem.

Indirect Complaints

Sometimes, an employee who is unwilling to bring a complaint will let a manager or human resources representative know about a problem indirectly. For example, an employee who receives a poor performance evaluation might explain that he or she has been unable to concentrate at work because of harassment. Or an employee who is interviewed as a witness in an investigation might raise a completely separate problem. Even though these workers are not making formal complaints, they are revealing a possible workplace problem that should be looked into.

Information From Departing Workers

Sometimes, a company learns of workplace troubles from an employee on the way out the door. For example, say that a worker quits, claiming that she has found another job. However, at her exit interview, the worker says that one reason for her departure is that her boss, whom she once dated, won't stop pressuring her to get back together with him. Once she's gone, do you need to look into this further?

The answer is a resounding "yes." The complaining employee's departure doesn't get rid of the potentially serious problem in your company—and it doesn't mean that same departing employee can't sue for sexual harassment. The accused boss may be harassing others. And even if he's not, you have to take action against those who commit sexual harassment to demonstrate your company's commitment to rooting out the problem, both to the departing employee and to other workers. If your investigation reveals that the departing employee was harassed, you should also take steps to make things right for her, such as giving her a chance to return to her old job.

Workplace Observation

Sometimes, a workplace problem is obvious but the source of the problem is not. For example, you might see graffiti on an office wall, pornographic images in the lunch room, threats spray painted in the parking lot, or money missing from petty cash. In these situations, you'll need to investigate to find out who's to blame.

Third-Party Reports

Sometimes, problems are brought to light by an outsider—such as a customer, a client or vendor, an administrative agency, a lawyer, or even the police. Regardless of how a problem becomes apparent, your company's obligations are the same: It must investigate and take action to deal with the situation, if necessary.

However, you might need to adjust your investigation procedures somewhat if outsiders are involved. For example, you might have an obligation to share what you discover with the police, if they are investigating an alleged crime in your company. These issues are covered in more detail in the chapters that follow—for now, simply remember that your obligation to investigate doesn't disappear just because you heard about a problem from an outside source, even if that third party or agency is investigating the situation on its own. Only your company can discipline its own employees and take any other internal steps necessary (such as providing harassment training, developing procedures for dealing with workplace violence, or changing its internal financial controls) to make sure the problem is resolved.

CD-ROM

Listen to a sample complaint. The CD-ROM accompanying this book includes audio files of investigative interviews, including an intake session with an employee who's making a complaint.

If you learn of a problem only after an employee has retained a lawyer, filed a charge with an administrative agency (for example, a sexual harassment charge with the Equal Employment Opportunity Commission), or even filed a lawsuit, you should consult with an attorney right away. In this situation, you are starting the investigation in an adversarial position, and you know that someone will be looking closely to catch any errors or omissions. By talking to a lawyer, you can figure out the best way to protect your company as you try to uncover the truth.

CAUTION

Don't let anyone destroy documents once you know a lawsuit might be in the offing. As you probably know, your company must keep a variety of personnel records for certain periods of time prescribed by law. Once the time period for retention is over, your company is usually free to dispose of the documents—unless the company knows that those documents might be relevant to a pending or possible legal action. After your company knows that there's a dispute, it must retain these documents—in what's often called a "litigation hold"—until the matter is resolved. A lawyer can help you figure out which documents to keep, and give you advice on how to protect documents from disclosure, if legally possible.

Decide Whether to Investigate

Not every workplace problem demands an investigation. To decide whether (and how extensively) you should investigate, you'll need to consider several factors, including:

- whether there is a dispute over what happened
- how serious the alleged misconduct is, and
- how similar complaints have been handled in the past.

Scale the Investigation to the Size of the Problem

Sometimes, a problem bears some further looking into but doesn't warrant a full inquisition. While you don't want to ignore a complaint or incident, you should also exercise your common sense about how deep to dig. For example, you should spend more time and resources on a report that one employee has threatened another with a gun than on a report that one employee parked in the other's space in the company lot, unless the facts take you in a different direction.

Although you should generally follow the ten investigation steps in any situation that requires a closer look, that shouldn't take much time in a fairly simple dispute. If the situation turns out to be more complicated, you can slow down and take a more detailed approach.

EXAMPLE: You are looking into the case of the errant parker, above. You decide that no immediate actions are necessary, that you will handle the investigation yourself, and that you will start by talking to Marie, the complaining employee. Marie tells you that she doesn't know who's been parking in her spot or why. You go to the parking lot, see that the offending car belongs to Jack, and ask him what's going on. He replies that he was recently assigned a parking space and thought the space was his. He says he will happily move his car to wherever he's supposed to park. The person in charge of facility issues tells you that Jack was assigned Space 35, and Marie has Space 53. You tell both employees, Jack moves his car, and it's over and done with.

Are you going to interview witnesses who may have seen Jack actually parking his car, ask Jack if he has a learning disability that might cause him to transpose numbers, or review Jack's and Marie's personnel files for signs of previous problems? Of course not. Going into any more detail would be a waste of time—you've gotten to the bottom of the problem and solved it.

Now change the facts a little. What if Marie, during your first interview, said, "I know that's Jack's car in my space. Ever since I told him I wouldn't go out with him, he's been trying to intimidate me. I found a really nasty note on my chair yesterday, and I'm pretty sure he wrote it. One of our coworkers told me that he called me a bitch and said he was going to teach me a lesson." This is an entirely different situation. Now, you will have other interviews to consider, you have a document to look at, you will want to spend some time planning how you will question Jack, and you will probably want to review his personnel file.

Are the Facts in Dispute?

The first thing to consider is whether there is a disagreement about what really happened. For example, if one employee accuses another of making violent threats and the other employee denies making them, you'll need to investigate to figure out who's telling the truth. On the other hand, if everyone agrees on the basic facts, you can move on to figuring out how to deal with the problem.

Sometimes, employees agree on what was said or done but disagree about what it meant. For example, what seemed like an innocent request for a date to one employee might have seemed like harassment to another. These situations call for a closer look. Otherwise, you won't know if the incident was just a one-time miscommunication or part of a larger pattern of harassment. However, be prepared to adjust the scope of the investigation to fit the facts. If, after completing your interviews of the people involved, you conclude that you're dealing with a simple misunderstanding, that warrants a quicker investigation than if you conclude that the incident is just one example of ongoing misconduct.

How Serious Is the Problem?

Sometimes, employees disagree over what happened, but the underlying problem is not serious. Who left the coffeepot on? Who was supposed to show up early to do inventory? In these situations, the simple fact that there's a dispute doesn't mean you have to investigate—just talk to the employees involved and resolve the situation.

Of course, if you discover that the seemingly minor issue is part of a more serious underlying problem, you may need to go to a full-scale investigation. Using one of the examples above, let's say that Jared didn't come in early to do inventory because he didn't know that it was his turn. In this case, you might make sure that Jared's manager institutes a reminder system to let employees know when they are assigned to do the inventory, and leave it at that. If, however, Jared knew he was supposed to show up but didn't because he's afraid to work alone with Patrick, who has made racist comments about him, that's a much more serious issue that calls for a comprehensive investigation.

Some companies make the mistake of investigating only allegations of potentially illegal behavior, such as harassment or theft. But there are many other types of incidents and issues that might warrant an investigation, such as violation of company policies, ethical concerns, misuse of company property, inappropriate dealings with clients or vendors, and much more. Although these issues might not involve potentially illegal behavior, they certainly merit a closer look and, possibly, disciplinary action. If you don't investigate allegations like these, you're missing an opportunity to root out workplace problems.

How Have Similar Problems Been Handled?

When you are deciding whether an investigation is warranted, think about how your company has handled similar incidents or complaints in the past. If it has generally investigated similar problems, you should consider doing so now. If legal trouble later develops, you will be able to show that your company was fair and consistent with its employees and treated their complaints with equal concern.

Take Immediate Action, If Necessary

In certain situations, you will need to take some precautionary steps right away, even before the investigation begins. If, for example, an employee complains that her supervisor has fondled her repeatedly, an employee threatens to bring a gun to work, or an employee appears to be stealing company trade secrets to give to a competitor, you don't have the luxury of waiting until your investigation is complete. If the safety of employees or your company is at risk, you'll have to take some action immediately to prevent further harm.

The actions you take will depend on the situation. In cases of misconduct between two employees (sexual harassment, insubordination, or fighting, for example), you might choose to separate the employees until the investigation is finished. By assigning one or both to different shifts, managers, or job responsibilities temporarily, you can alleviate the immediate problem and investigate more thoroughly.

> **CAUTION**
>
> **Beware of retaliation.** It is illegal to punish or otherwise take any negative action against an employee who comes forward with a good-faith complaint of harassment, discrimination, illegal conduct, or health and safety violations. The most obvious forms of retaliation are termination, discipline, demotion, pay cuts, or threats of any of these actions. More subtle forms of retaliation may include changing the shift hours or work area of the accuser, or changing the accuser's job responsibilities or reporting relationships. Although it often makes sense to change the work environment so that the accuser doesn't have to report to or work with the accused, those changes cannot come at the accuser's expense. If one employee must move to a less desirable position temporarily, your best bet is to move the accused employee.

If one employee is accused or suspected of extreme misconduct (such as threatening or harming another employee, sexual assault, or large-scale theft), you'll probably want to suspend that employee, with pay, while you investigate the situation. When you suspend the employee, explain the complaint or behavior at issue and ask to hear the accused employee's side of the story. Assure the employee that you will investigate the incident and reach a decision as quickly as possible.

Avoid Unpaid Suspensions

No matter how egregious the misconduct an employee is accused of committing, it's always a bad idea to suspend employees without pay pending an investigation. From both a practical and legal standpoint, paid suspensions are less risky and less inconvenient for employers—less risky because a paid employee is not as likely to sue as one who isn't being paid, and less inconvenient because you don't have to interrupt your regular payroll system.

In some cases, you cannot suspend salaried employees (those who are not entitled to earn overtime pay) without pay. Even if the employee is entitled to earn overtime pay, however, you can still get in trouble for imposing an unpaid suspension. A suspension without pay signals that you believe the employee is probably guilty—which can cause bad feelings and potential legal problems. If your investigation shows that the employee didn't commit misconduct or that the misconduct was less serious than it appeared, you will probably have to provide retroactive pay anyway (along with an apology). It's easier to simply let the employee take a few days off with pay while you figure out what happened.

Choose the Investigator

This book assumes that you will generally be doing the investigating yourself. In some cases, however, it might make sense to choose someone else, whether from inside or outside the company. If you are unavailable, have a personal relationship with either the accused or the complaining employee, or, in a worst case scenario, are the accused or complaining employee yourself, you'll need to choose another investigator.

⇨ **SKIP AHEAD**

If you'll handle the investigation, skip ahead to "Plan the Investigation," below.

The person you choose to investigate a problem will depend on various factors, including the size of your company, the identity of the complaining employee and accused employee (if any), and the nature and severity of the problem. Regardless of how these factors play out, however, the investigator must meet a few essential job requirements: experience, impartiality, and professionalism.

Should You Use a Team?

Some companies use a team of two or more investigators to look into workplace problems. The benefit of using a team is that you'll have an extra set of eyes, ears, and hands during the investigation. This means, for example, that one investigator can ask questions while the other takes notes, one investigator can gather evidence while the other sets up interviews, the investigators can collaborate when making decisions and recommendations about discipline, and both investigators will be available to testify about the investigation if the employer ends up in court.

However, there are also drawbacks to using a team. For one thing, two employees will be pulled away from their usual job responsibilities until the investigation is over, which can be a significant hardship for smaller employers. Some employees may feel intimidated by having to face two questioners, which might make it more difficult to establish rapport. And there's also the "too many cooks spoil the broth" problem—unless the investigators carefully choreograph who will be responsible for what, there's a danger of duplicated effort and crossed signals.

It's probably best to use a team only for more serious complaints—those that involve many employees, substantial misconduct, and/or a high possibility of legal trouble. Your company will reap the greatest benefits (of corroboration and efficiency) in these situations, and they warrant spending the additional time and money a second investigator will require.

Experience

The investigator should have some experience in investigating complaints, or at least some education and training on the subject. An experienced investigator will know what to look for, how to find it, and how to evaluate what he or she finds—and, therefore, will probably do a better job than someone who hasn't tackled a project like this before.

Experience will also come into play if a complaining party files a lawsuit claiming that the investigation was faulty. If your investigator is inexperienced, a jury is more likely to second-guess his or her decisions, question the quality of the investigation, and, ultimately, disregard the findings altogether.

TIP

Train investigators ahead of time. Don't wait until you're facing a problem that you can't handle to start training other investigators. You need to be ready to start investigating serious problems as soon as you learn about them. This means that any other inside investigators you might use should be trained and ready to go before trouble starts.

Some situations call for an investigator with special expertise in certain issues. For example, if the investigation will involve figuring out technical matters (like whether an employee sabotaged a computer program or violated safety rules in a production line) or require advanced knowledge of a particular field (to determine whether an accountant was "cooking the books," for example), you should try to choose an investigator—or make someone available to assist the investigator—who has enough background to understand the details.

Impartiality

The person who investigates must be perceived within the workplace—and particularly by the employees involved in the problem—as fair and objective. Someone who supervises, or is supervised by, either the complaining employee or the accused employee should not perform the investigation. Similarly, you shouldn't choose an investigator who has known difficulties with any of the main players, has expressed an opinion on the matter to be investigated, or has any involvement in the underlying problem. Here are some examples of situations when the investigator's impartiality could be challenged:

- **The manager of a department is chosen to investigate an employee's claim of religious discrimination.** Although the manager has no involvement in the underlying incident, he is a member of the same church as the complaining employee.

- **The HR director decides to investigate alleged improper billing practices by the recruiters who work for her.** If she were to find that the recruiters were not following the company's rules, she could be disciplined for failing to train and supervise them correctly.

- **An HR representative is tapped to look into allegations that an employee is stealing company property.** The representative and the employee carpool to work together.

In each of these situations, the circumstances suggest that it might be difficult for the investigator to be impartial. Even if the investigator were able to conduct a fair investigation, other employees and those outside the company might not trust the results.

Who's the Boss?

When choosing an investigator, you should consider where the accused employee ranks on the corporate ladder—and pick an investigator whose rank is higher, if possible. That way, you can avoid the appearance that the accused employee has any power over the investigator. If this isn't possible, take steps to insulate the investigation from the accused employee (by requiring the employee to take paid leave and refrain from talking to other employees during the investigation, for example). If employees—or a jury, if it comes to that—believe that the accused employee can intimidate the investigator or dictate his or her findings, they won't put much stock in the outcome of the investigation.

Once you have come up with a potential investigator, ask the employees involved if they believe that person can be fair and impartial. If they do not, choose someone else. Of course, in a small business, you might not have a wide range of potential investigators to choose from. In that case, just make sure that whoever does the job doesn't have an axe to grind with any of the employees involved in the problem.

> **TIP**
>
> **Document approval of the investigator.** If the employees involved in the problem agree to the investigator (whether it's you or someone else), make a note of it in your file, including the date and time of the conversation. This might be valuable evidence later, if an employee files a lawsuit and argues that the investigator was biased. Some employers also ask employees to sign a statement verifying that they have no concerns about the investigator's qualifications or impartiality. Although this could also be helpful evidence, it's probably overkill. Your signed statement is evidence of each employee's approval. And an employee who is asked to sign a statement like this may become suspicious that you are more concerned with avoiding a lawsuit than with solving the underlying problem.

Sometimes, the sensitivities of a complaining employee might also influence your choice of investigators. For example, some women might feel more comfortable discussing a sexual harassment complaint with a female investigator. Some larger companies try to make an investigator of each gender available for just this reason.

Professionalism

Professionalism is a quality that's sometimes hard to define, but we all know it when we see it. A professional behaves in a businesslike, dependable way, doesn't inject personal feelings or biases into workplace interactions, and remembers that he or she is always representing the company.

A professional demeanor is an essential quality for an investigator for several reasons. First, a good investigator has to keep his or her emotions in check. During an investigation, the investigator may hear or see things—such as X-rated or racist material, threats, or serious misconduct—that are disturbing. The investigator may also bear the brunt of employees' emotions, including anger at being the subject of an investigation, sadness and fear over making a complaint, and so on. In the face of these emotions, a good investigator must remain calm and try to get to the bottom of things.

Second, the investigator must be discreet and preserve the integrity of the investigation. At some point during an investigation, the investigator will begin to develop some ideas about what really happened—who's lying and who's telling the truth, who committed misconduct and why. Despite these hunches (no matter how well founded they may be), the investigator can't reveal his or her feelings. If the employees involved in the problem believe the investigator has already reached a decision before examining all of the evidence and hearing everyone's statements, they might come to distrust the investigation and any decisions that are based on it. This can lead to lawsuits challenging the fairness of the investigation. On the other hand, an investigator who conveys that he or she has not reached any decisions and will listen carefully and objectively to everyone's statements builds trust in the investigation and its outcome.

Third, the investigator may have to give testimony about the investigation in the future, to an administrative agency, an employee's lawyer, or even a judge or jury. If this worst-case scenario comes to pass, you'll want the investigator to convey confidence, poise, and objectivity. A professional demeanor will help the investigator convince outsiders that the company did the right thing. On the other hand, a jury might have doubts if the investigator is overly nervous, can't answer questions directly, or fails to make eye contact—even if he or she did a bang-up job on the investigation.

Hiring an Outside Investigator

In some situations, it makes sense to ask for professional help to investigate a workplace problem. Many law firms and private consultants will investigate workplace issues for a fee. You might consider bringing in outside help if:

- more than one employee complains about the same serious problem (for example, several women complain that a particular manager is harassing them)
- the accused is a high-ranking official in the business (such as the president or CEO)
- the complaining employee has publicized the complaint in the workplace or in the media
- the complaining employee has hired a lawyer, filed a lawsuit, or filed charges with a government agency, such as the Equal Employment Opportunity Commission, the Occupational Safety and Health Administration, the Wage and Hour Division, or a similar state agency
- the accusations are extreme (allegations of rape, assault, threats, or significant theft, for example), or
- for any reason, no one is available to investigate the complaint fairly and objectively.

CAUTION

Some states require outside investigators to be licensed. If your state has this type of requirement, make sure that any outside investigator has a current license. Don't just take the investigator's word for it—ask to see and copy the license itself. If your investigator is not properly licensed, you may not be able to rely on the results of the investigation in court.

You can get referrals for professional investigators through management newsletters, trade associations, other business contacts, and even listings in the yellow pages. The American Arbitration Association (AAA), a national provider of dispute resolution services, offers fact-finding services—trained, experienced investigators who are prequalified by the AAA to conduct independent investigations. You can find out more about this service at the AAA's website, www.adr.org. For complaints of discrimination and harassment, your state's fair employment practices agency may be able to provide referrals. These agencies are listed in Appendix D.

⊘ **CAUTION**

Your company is responsible for actions you take based on an outside investigator's findings. Hiring an outside investigator doesn't insulate your company from liability for the investigation or the decisions it makes based on that investigation (for example, to discipline or fire an employee accused of wrongdoing). Your company is ultimately responsible to its employees, even if it hires a professional to do some of the investigative work. You must work closely with an outside investigator to make sure that he or she receives all relevant information, conducts a thorough and fair investigation, and documents the findings. And although a professional investigator can certainly give advice about what action to take when the investigation is over, you or another company decision maker should always have the final say in disciplinary matters.

Reporting Requirements for Outside Investigators

Until a few years ago, hiring an outside investigator had a very significant downside (other than the expense): Employers who hired outsiders had to comply with some legal technicalities that had the potential to derail the investigation. Under a law called the Fair Credit Reporting Act, employers who hired an outside investigator had to tell the accused employee that an investigation would be conducted, get the employee's written consent ahead of time, and give a copy of the investigation report to the employee—and wait for a "reasonable period"—before taking any adverse action based on its contents.

These rules were extremely controversial, and were relaxed in 2003. (Although the rules still apply to certain types of investigations, such as credit checks and background checks, they do not apply to workplace investigations of suspected misconduct, violation of the employer's policies, or violation of the law.) Now, employers who hire an outside investigator are no longer required to warn the accused employee or get the employee's consent. If the employer decides to take action against the employee based on the investigation report, the employer has to give the employee only a summary of the nature and substance of the report (which need not identify the employees interviewed). You'll find a form you can use to give this required notice in Appendix B and on the CD-ROM.

Hiring a Lawyer to Investigate

There are many good reasons to hire a lawyer to investigate. An experienced employment lawyer will know exactly what to look for and how to keep your company out of trouble. You can expect the lawyer to know the latest legal developments about investigations and workplace claims, including privacy issues. This specialized knowledge could be a real benefit, especially if your problem is factually or legally complicated.

Another advantage of using a lawyer to investigate is that many (though by no means all) lawyers are experienced in the courtroom. If the investigation is later called into question, the lawyer/investigator should have the presentation skills to come across as a strong witness on your company's behalf.

The fact that the lawyer might have to testify about the investigation illustrates the main drawback to this approach: The lawyer might have to answer questions about the advice he or she provided, what you and other company representatives said during the investigation, and other conversations. Usually, when you seek a lawyer's advice about a legal problem, your communications are privileged—which means that no one can force your company (or the lawyer) to reveal them. (See "Attorney-Client Privilege," below.) If the lawyer testifies as a witness for your company, however, you will probably lose the protection of this privilege. This means that the lawyer can be asked questions about what company representatives said and did throughout the investigation and about what the lawyer said to you.

Attorney-Client Privilege

Whenever you talk privately to a lawyer about legal matters, that conversation is protected by the attorney-client privilege—which means that no one can force you or the lawyer to reveal what either of you said. The purpose of the privilege is to encourage full disclosure, which allows the lawyer to give a candid assessment of your problem and sound advice about what to do next.

However, you can lose this privilege if you don't honor it. For example, if you tell another person what you said to your lawyer, your conversation with the lawyer is no longer privileged—you waived the privilege by revealing the statement. Similarly, if your company puts its lawyer on the stand to testify about what a great investigation he or she performed, the lawyer will have to reveal some conversations he or she had with company representatives. Once again, you've waived the privilege by allowing these statements to be revealed.

TIP

Even if you decide not to use a lawyer to investigate, you can still seek the advice of a lawyer about your investigation. By doing this, you get the best of both worlds: Your company will benefit from the lawyer's expertise, and your conversations will generally be protected by the attorney-client privilege. Of course, your company will also have to pay for the lawyer's time. If you choose to go this route, ask the lawyer—before the investigation begins—how you can make sure that your conversations will stay confidential.

Plan the Investigation

Before you start to interview people and sift through documents and other evidence, you should come up with a careful investigation plan. During your planning, you will review the evidence available to you, then start thinking about what additional evidence might exist that will help you figure out what happened. You should also take a few steps to prepare your company for the investigation, including setting aside some time for the process and telling others what you'll be doing.

Review What You Know

At the outset, you will have some information available—an employee complaint, a report by a manager, or a suspicious situation (an employee who frequently seems to be out of it or money missing from a cash register, for example). Start your planning by figuring out what you already know. What misconduct is suspected or alleged? Your answer to this question will help you figure out what information you will need to decide whether the allegation or suspicion is correct.

> **TIP**
>
> **A timeline can help you sort through complicated facts.** If there are more than one or two allegations, you might want to make a basic timeline to help you keep things straight. For example, if an employee alleges that she was harassed on five or six occasions over a period of months, plotting those incidents on a calendar or timeline may help you see patterns and figure out who might have witnessed the incidents. It will also remind you to ask, gather evidence, and draw conclusions about every incident.

Look over any available documents or other evidence related to the misconduct. Review the complaint or report (if applicable), gather and read through any paperwork relevant to the problem (such as personnel files, attendance records, correspondence, or performance reviews), and collect and review any other physical evidence (a weapon, illegal drugs, graphic images, or work materials, for example). Place these documents and items in a locked file cabinet or other safe place.

You should also determine whether any company policies and guidelines might apply to the situation: For example, a sexual harassment policy, workplace violence policy, or noncompete agreement might be relevant.

Planning for Serious Problems

In some cases, you might have to plan ahead to deal with a major problem. For example, if you suspect an employee of criminal activity (such as embezzlement, rape, or violence), you will have to decide whether to bring in the police. If you are facing issues that could lead to serious legal trouble (like allegations of widespread, egregious harassment or potential workplace violence), this is a good time to get some legal advice. If your workplace problem has been, or might become, publicized in the media, you will need a public relations strategy to handle the situation. If you are facing one of these difficult issues, get some expert advice about how to proceed.

Figure Out What You Need to Know

Once you have gotten a sense of the information and evidence already at hand, you can start thinking about what you need to know or find out in order to make a decision about what happened. Whom will you need to interview? What additional evidence might exist? Are there any witnesses or others who might have helpful information?

Then, begin planning the interviews, including:

• **Whom to question.** Make a list of potential interview subjects. In some cases, only the complaining employee and the accused employee should be interviewed—if the complaint is about an incident that no one else witnessed, heard, or was told about later, for example. In other situations, there may be many potential witnesses. If the incident occurred during a staff meeting or company social event, there may be dozens of witnesses. In these cases, you should plan to ask both the complaining and the accused employee which workers were most likely to have seen or heard the disputed event.

- **What order to follow.** The complaining employee should be interviewed first, followed generally by the accused employee and the witnesses. This order can be changed to accommodate employees' schedules, in the interests of moving as quickly as possible.

- **What questions to ask.** You need not script every interview question in advance. However, after reviewing Chapter 3, you should take some notes on topics you want to cover in each interview. As you interview each witness, you can review and add to these notes.

Follow the Evidence Wherever It Leads

It's important to plan the investigation ahead of time, but it may be even more important to depart from your plan if new or unexpected information comes up. For example, imagine that an employee complained that her boss had sexually harassed her by repeatedly asking her out on dates. You've planned your investigation to speak to the complaining employee, her boss, and a few witnesses who may have heard or seen the proposals. However, when interviewing the first witness, you learn that the boss has also asked her out on dates. You also learn that the men in this work group routinely tell X-rated jokes, ask their female coworkers about their sex lives, and visit pornographic websites during work hours.

Should you stick to your original plan and just try to get to the bottom of the unwanted date requests? Not if you want to solve what is obviously a significant problem in this work group—and protect your company from sexual harassment claims. Once you know this additional information, you should revisit your investigation plan. Because the problem is much larger than you thought, you will have to do a more extensive investigation to find out what's going on and who's responsible.

Prepare Your Company for the Investigation

Before you actually start asking questions and reviewing evidence, you should do a few things to make sure your investigation runs smoothly.

Free Up Your Time

First of all, do what you need to do to give yourself enough time to investigate properly. You'll need to start right away and, depending on how complicated the problem is, you may need to spend a week or more interviewing, reviewing documents, sorting out the facts, drafting your report, following up with everyone, and so on. This means you might have to shift some of your work around, talk to your manager about freeing up some time, or postpone a project or two. The investigation should be a top priority.

Inform the Employees' Manager

You should also prepare the manager(s) of the employees involved. You'll need to spend some time with the accused employee, complaining employee, and witnesses—and their manager will need to know where everyone is disappearing to. If you've decided to suspend the accused employee with pay while you investigate, that employee's manager should know about the decision.

In some cases, the manager will already know about the problem. For example, if the employee initially raised the issue with the manager, who escalated the issue to you, the manager will have a good idea of what's going on. Similarly, if the manager noticed a problem and reported it in the first place, he or she will know about it. In these situations, you can confirm to the manager that you will be investigating and explain how you will proceed.

If the manager isn't already in the loop, how much you tell him or her will depend on your company's practices and on whether the manager is involved in the problem, among other things. Because the manager is the company representative who works most closely with the employees, it's a great benefit if you can tell the manager some basic information about the problem. That way, the manager can keep an eye on the situation, ensure that no one retaliates against the complaining employee, watch out for gossip and breaches of confidentiality, and make sure that there are no further problems once the investigation is over.

If, however, the manager is accused of wrongdoing, you won't be able to count on his or her help. In this situation, it often makes sense to suspend the manager with pay during the investigation, so employees will feel more free to express themselves and won't be subject to possible retaliation and intimidation.

Perhaps the trickiest situation arises when the perpetrator is unknown and, therefore, *may* be the manager. This could occur in a theft investigation, but might also happen if anonymous notes threatening violence or racist or sexist graffiti start appearing in the workplace, for example. In these cases, informing the manager of your investigation ahead of time might give him or her the opportunity to destroy evidence, put pressure on witnesses, and otherwise hamper your efforts. Your best course of action will depend on the facts: If it's possible to conduct interviews without the manager finding out (for example, by interviewing employees who work at remote locations), that might make sense. If not, you might start by interviewing the manager. This is one scenario when a consultation with a lawyer will help you figure out the best way to proceed.

Prepare Experts and Decision Makers

If you'll be working with anyone else on the investigation, you should get that person involved. For example, if you'll be working with the company's in-house or outside counsel, you should inform the lawyer about the investigation. If you'll be investigating and then handing your findings over to someone else in the company who will make disciplinary decisions, that person should be told that the investigation is about to begin. And, if you plan to seek outside help (from a forensic accountant, handwriting analyst, or workplace violence consultant, for example), now is the time to line up your experts. ●

Gather Information

Once you've decided that an investigation is in order, it's time to get to work. This chapter will explain how to gather the information you need to figure out what happened.

Your first priority: Get started right away. This chapter explains why delay can derail your investigative efforts and offers some advice for dealing with unavoidable postponements. It also covers interviews—often your best source of information about workplace problems. Here, you'll find information on how to open and close an interview, sample questions for complaining employees, accused employees, and witnesses, and tips for successful interviewing.

In addition to interviewing, you may also have to do some workplace sleuthing. In some situations, paying a visit to the "scene of the crime"— the place where alleged misconduct occurred—will help you sort out the truth. And in almost every investigation, you'll have to examine documents and other materials, such as inventories, performance evaluations, photographs, or attendance records, to figure out what happened.

Get Started Right Away

Workplace experts agree that delay is one of the most common—and potentially most costly—investigation mistakes. Once you become aware of a serious workplace problem that requires an investigation, don't put off the inevitable. Ideally, you should begin investigating within a day or two of finding out about the problem, and complete the investigation within a week or two, depending on how complicated the allegations are. Of course, there will be times when outside circumstances and conflicting schedules lead to unavoidable delays. However, if you postpone the investigation unnecessarily, you will send the message that the company doesn't take the complaint seriously. And if the misconduct continues in the meantime, a court might find your company responsible for failing to investigate and take care of the problem right away.

> **TIP**
>
> **Document unavoidable delays.** If you can't start your investigation right away, document the reason for delay in the investigation report. (Investigation reports are covered in Chapter 4.) For example, if the accused employee is out tending to a family emergency or the complaining employee is on vacation, make a note of these facts, the date you learned them, and the date the employee will return to work. These notes will help you prove, if necessary, that the company didn't cause the delay.

Conducting Interviews

In most investigations, interviews are the main tool investigators use to find out what happened. More often than not, investigators have to rely almost entirely on statements from the main players and witnesses, who may contradict each other. If the main participants flatly deny each other's claims, you'll have to sort out who is telling the truth.

How can you decide whose story is more credible in these "he said, she said" situations? The first step is to conduct interviews designed to elicit as much information as possible. The more information you can draw out of each witness, the easier it will be to figure out what happened and why. The general interviewing tips that follow will help you elicit the most useful responses, even from the reluctant or contentious witness. This section also includes specific ideas and questions for interviewing the person who complained (if there is one), the person accused, and witnesses.

Tips on Conducting Effective Interviews

Here are some guidelines that will help you conduct complete and informative interviews.

Keep an Open Mind

Some investigators don't want to believe that serious misconduct or harassment could happen in their company, and so tend to make light of possible wrongdoing. Others jump to the opposite conclusion, assuming that an employee would not complain without good cause.

As an investigator, your job is to avoid making assumptions. No matter how serious the problem or how straightforward the situation appears to be, don't reach any conclusions until you have gathered and evaluated all the facts. If you start your investigation believing you already know what happened, you will miss some important details. But if you keep an open mind until your investigation is complete, you will conduct more thorough interviews—and receive more candid answers to your questions.

DON'T ASK:

Why did you pressure Maria to falsify her time card?

ASK:

Did you and Maria discuss her time card last week? What did each of you say?

DON'T ASK:

How could you steal from this company?

ASK:

When are your cash register shifts? Do you count the money in your drawer at the start of your shift? Do you count out your drawer at the end of your shift and write that total down for the manager? Your cash register has been short by quite a bit of money several times in the last month. Can you explain why that happened?

Ask Open-Ended Questions

Your goal when conducting an interview is to get as much information as possible. The best way to accomplish this is to ask open-ended questions. If you ask questions that suggest the answer you want to hear or questions that call only for a yes or no answer, you will be doing all the talking. Instead, ask the witness what he or she heard, said, or did, and why.

DON'T ASK:

Did you arrive at three o'clock?

ASK:

What time did you arrive?

DON'T ASK:

Did you hear John tell Ping that she would not be paid for her overtime work unless she agreed to have lunch with him?

ASK:

Did you hear John and Ping talking last week? Tell me what you heard.

Start With the Easy Questions

The employees you interview are likely to be nervous and uncomfortable. Employees suspected of wrongdoing will probably also be defensive, frightened about what may happen, and perhaps willing to lie to save their jobs. If you begin your interview by asking directly about the alleged misconduct, you will aggravate an already tense situation—and probably limit the flow of information. Someone who feels accused or put on the spot is more likely to clam up. Also, if you cut to the chase too soon, you'll miss your chance to find out important details before the employee knows why you're asking questions (and, therefore, has an opportunity to tailor the answers accordingly).

The better course of action is to start with basic background questions about the employee's job, coworkers, daily schedule, and so on. You'll have to get to the tough questions eventually, but starting with a few softballs will put the employee at ease and give you the opportunity to ask about seemingly unimportant details that could prove very significant to your investigation. It will also help you get a sense of the employee's demeanor and body language when he or she is comfortable and telling the truth. Then, when you get to the tougher questions, you can see whether the witness reacts differently (for example, the witness stops making eye contact, starts fidgeting, or becomes much less certain of the facts). This will help you judge credibility.

DON'T START WITH:

You were seen leaving the workplace very late last Friday, with a bulky package under your coat. On Monday morning, the IT department found that several new modems and some other computer equipment were missing. Did you take these things?

START WITH:

Tell me about your usual schedule. What time do you arrive in the morning? What time do you leave at night? Are you often one of the last ones here? Is your schedule fairly regular, or does it vary? What was your schedule like last week? Do you drive to work or take public transportation? Where do you park? Do you usually come in through the main front entrance or use one of the back doors? Which exit do you use when you leave at night?

DON'T START WITH:

Phyllis says that you refused to promote her to be a floor manager, and that you have never promoted an African-American employee to any management position. Did you refuse to promote her because of her race?

START WITH:

How long have you worked here? What are your job responsibilities in your current position? Do they include promoting people? To what positions? About how many people have you promoted since you began working here? Tell me what you take into consideration when you're deciding whether to promote someone. Do interested employees have to fill out an application? Do you interview the applicants? Do you look at any documents—work samples, performance evaluations, personnel files? Is there anything else you consider? How do you decide whom to promote?

> **TIP**
>
> **Dig a little deeper if an employee's reaction seems odd.** If an employee seems much more upset (or much less so) than you would expect, ask more questions. Although all of us react differently to unpleasant experiences, a response that strikes you as emotionally inappropriate could indicate that there's more to the situation than meets the eye.

Keep Your Opinions to Yourself

As your investigation progresses, you will inevitably start to develop some opinions about what really happened. You should not share these opinions with witnesses, however. If you suggest, through your statements or the tone of your questions, that you have already reached a decision, witnesses will be less likely to speak freely with you. Some witnesses might be afraid of contradicting your version of events; others might feel there is no point in explaining what really happened if you have already made up your mind. In the worst-case scenario, a witness might believe you are conducting an unfair or biased investigation and challenge the outcome in court. Avoid these problems by keeping your conclusions to yourself until the investigation is complete.

DON'T ASK:

I have already heard from several people that Sameh was absent from last week's mandatory meeting. Is that what you remember?

ASK:

Who attended last week's mandatory meeting? Was anyone absent?

DON'T ASK:

Can you confirm that Darrell punched Jeff on the loading dock?

ASK:

Where did you work yesterday? Did you see anything unusual? Tell me what happened. (If the witness claims not to have seen anything unusual, you might ask, "Did you see an incident between Darrell and Jeff?")

Focus on the Facts

On the television series *Dragnet*, Joe Friday had a simple interviewing technique: He asked his subjects to tell him "just the facts." If only it were that easy in real life. Many people have a difficult time distinguishing objective fact from subjective opinion when describing what they have seen and heard. Some witnesses might describe another person's motivations or thoughts, relate rumors as if they were known facts, or exaggerate. Your job is to separate the wheat from the chaff—

that is, to isolate fact from opinion—then find out the basis for the witness's story. By helping your witnesses focus on the facts, you can prevent speculation and rumor from affecting your decisions.

IF YOU HEAR:

Lawrence has been out to get Graciela since the day he started working here. But I'm not surprised; he doesn't like reporting to a woman.

YOU MIGHT ASK:

What have you seen or heard that leads you to believe Lawrence is out to get Graciela? Have you heard him say anything about her? Have you heard Lawrence say anything about reporting to a woman or make any disparaging comments about women in general?

IF YOU HEAR:

Everyone knew that Evelyn was going to lose her temper and get violent. It was just a matter of time.

YOU MIGHT ASK:

What do you mean by get violent? Have you seen or heard Evelyn do anything that seemed violent or angry? Why did you believe Evelyn was going to lose her temper? What did she say or do to make you think she was on edge? When you say everyone knew, do you mean that you discussed this with others? Whom did you talk to about it, and what did they say?

Find Out About Other Witnesses or Evidence

Always look for leads. Ask every person you interview whether they know of other witnesses or physical evidence relating to the incident. If the witness is the accused or complaining employee, ask whether anyone else saw or heard the incidents in question. Ask whether they told anyone about the incident when it happened. Find out if they took any notes about the problem or if any workplace documents—emails, memoranda, or evaluations, for example—relate to the incident.

IF YOU HEAR:

Robert and I had a loud argument by the elevators. He told me I wouldn't get my raise unless I agreed to withdraw my complaint that he had harassed me. Afterwards, I was so upset that I ran back to my office in tears.

YOU MIGHT ASK:

Was anyone else near the elevator when the argument took place? Did anyone hear what Robert said to you? Did you see anyone on your way back to your office? Did you talk to anyone about what happened?

IF YOU HEAR:

Julie sent me an email apologizing for giving me a bad review. She said her manager made her change my performance appraisal after I filed a workers' compensation claim.

YOU MIGHT ASK:

Did you save Julie's email to you? Did she copy anyone on the message? Did you see the performance appraisal before it was changed? Do you have a copy?

Ask About Contradictions

Sometimes, one witness contradicts what another has said. The accused and complaining employees are perhaps most likely to contradict each other, but even uninvolved witnesses might give conflicting stories. The best way to deal with these inconsistencies is to ask about them directly. Once you get down to specifics, you may find that everyone agrees on what happened, but not on whether it was appropriate.

If the witnesses continue to contradict each other even after you have pointed out the conflicts in their stories—if the accused flatly denies the complaining employee's statements, for example—ask each witness why the other might disagree.

IF YOU HEAR:

I never sexually harassed anyone. I treat the women who work for me with respect.

YOU MIGHT ASK:

A complaint was made that you touched Tanya's waist and hips several times while she was distributing paperwork to clients, and that you made jokes about her spending the night at her boyfriend's house. Did this happen? Have you ever touched Tanya? Did you say anything that someone might have interpreted in this way? Can you think of any reason why someone might have reported this if it weren't true?

IF YOU HEAR:

Darnell told us at last week's morning meeting that anyone who complained about safety problems in the warehouse would get in trouble. He basically threatened to fire anyone who reported an accident.

YOU MIGHT ASK:

Other people in your work group described that conversation differently. They said that Darnell told all of you that he had reported two safety violations to his manager. They said he encouraged you to bring any safety concerns to him, and he would bring them to the company's attention. Did this happen? Did you have a separate conversation with Darnell? Why do you think others remember the conversation differently?

Broad Confidentiality Requirements Might Violate the National Labor Relations Act

Under the federal National Labor Relations Act (NLRA), employees have the right to engage in concerted activities to improve their working conditions. This right applies to all employees, whether their employer is unionized or not. Workplace confidentiality rules that prohibit employees from talking to each other about the terms and conditions of their employment (such as how much they are paid) have been struck down because they restrict this right.

More recently, confidentiality rules imposed in conjunction with investigations have been challenged as violations of the NLRA. Employees have claimed that these rules prevent them from exercising their right to discuss working conditions, including sexual harassment. Cases have gone both ways on this issue, depending on the employer's justification for requiring confidentiality, how broad the requirements are, and how long they last. In one case, for example, a company that fired an employee for criticizing its handling of a sexual harassment complaint two years after the investigation was found to have violated the NLRA: Although the company might have had legitimate reasons to require confidentiality during the investigation, those reasons weren't as compelling two years later.

Because the rules in this area are still evolving, it's a good idea to talk to a lawyer before you discipline an employee for violating the confidentiality of an investigation.

Keep It Confidential

Complaints can polarize a workplace. Workers will likely side with either the complaining employee or the accused employee, and the rumor mill will start working overtime. Worse, if too many details about the complaint get out, you may be accused of damaging the reputation of the alleged victim or alleged wrongdoer.

You can minimize these problems by insisting on confidentiality and practicing it in your investigation. Tell each witness only those facts necessary to conduct a thorough interview. For example, accused employees deserve to hear the allegations against them, but peripheral witnesses don't need to know every detail. Caution witnesses that the investigation is confidential and should not be discussed with coworkers or friends. Warn everyone you interview that revealing anything about the investigation is against company policy—and can result in discipline. And set a good example by being discreet. Don't discuss the investigation in the lunchroom, keep your investigation materials in a locked cabinet when you aren't working on them, and avoid gossip.

Hold your interviews in a private space—one where you won't be seen or overheard by others in the workplace, and where others won't be able to see who comes to be interviewed. For example, a conference room with interior windows, a table in the company break room, or a centrally located office would be a bad choice. In some particularly volatile situations (for example, if violence is a possibility or employees have been threatened for coming forward), employees may be hesitant to talk to you in the workplace. In these scenarios, consider meeting an employee offsite, after work hours.

DON'T ASK:

Sylvia says that Roger asked her out several times and tried to bring her back to his room after the holiday party. She also says that Roger made a lot of X-rated jokes in front of clients, and that you might have heard some of these jokes during the meeting with Pets-Nation. Did you hear any of these jokes?

ASK:

Did you attend the pitch meeting with Pets-Nation? Who else was there? Do you remember anyone telling jokes during this meeting? Tell me what was said.

DON'T ASK:

Fernando has complained that Martin gave him a bad performance evaluation, and he thinks it's because Martin dislikes Latinos. Fernando believes that he has made more successful cold calls than anyone else on his shift. He thought you might be able to confirm this, since you compile the monthly productivity reports. Is this true?

ASK:

Do you compile monthly productivity reports? Do these reports contain the cold call success rate for each salesperson? Do you recall who had the highest success rate last month for the afternoon shift? May I see a copy of these reports for the last year?

Don't Retaliate

It is against the law to punish someone for making a complaint of harassment, discrimination, illegal conduct, or unsafe working conditions. And it is against your company's best interests to punish any employee who comes forward with a good-faith complaint, regardless of the subject matter. You want to encourage employees to bring problems to your attention, so they can be resolved before they start draining productivity or stirring up legal trouble. Employees will come forward only if they feel protected from retaliation—and witnesses will tell you the truth only if they know you will not kill the messenger who bears bad news. Assure every person you interview that you want to hear their side of the story and that they will not be retaliated against for coming forward.

IF YOU HEAR:

I'm having some problems working with Maurice, but I don't want to cause trouble.

YOU MIGHT ASK:

I'm glad you brought this issue to my attention. We would really be in trouble if you kept this information to yourself, and your team's work suffered as a result. No one in the company will take any action against you for coming forward. Now, what has been happening with Maurice?

IF YOU HEAR:

I've seen some pretty heated conversations between Maria and Simone, but it's really none of my business. I don't want Simone to think that I'm not a team player.

YOU MIGHT ASK:

I need to find out what's been going on between Maria and Simone, and anything you can tell me about those conversations will help me get to the bottom of this. If there are problems in your work group, everyone's work suffers and everyone feels uncomfortable. No one will be allowed to retaliate against you for speaking to me. Both Maria and Simone have been told that these issues would be investigated, and they both understand that they cannot retaliate against anyone involved in the investigation. What have your heard Maria and Simone say to each other?

Ask Interviewees to Contact You With New or Additional Information

People sometimes freeze up when they're put on the spot. It's very likely that a witness might remember some significant detail—or learn new information—after the interview is over. To make sure you stay in the loop, close every interview by thanking the witness and asking him or her to contact you if anything else comes to mind.

Some witnesses might intentionally hold back important information during the interview, while trying to decide whether to come clean. If you offer every witness an opportunity to continue the conversation, you are more likely to get the full story. And should the investigation be challenged in court, you will be able to show that you made every effort to gather all the facts.

DON'T SAY:

Have you told me everything you remember about these incidents? Because you won't be able to change your statement once I start talking to other witnesses.

SAY:

Please remember that my door is always open, if you remember anything later or there is something you need to add to your statement. Also, if you learn of any new information that relates to the complaint, please bring it to my attention right away.

Document Your Interviews

Take notes during every interview. Include the date, time, and place of each interview, the name of the witness, and whether anyone else was present. Don't just record the witness's conclusions; include all the important facts that the witness relates or denies, using the witness's own words whenever possible. These notes will help you remember what each witness said later, when you are making your decision. They will also help you defend your investigation in court, if it is challenged as biased or incomplete. (You'll find sample notes from interviews in Appendix C.)

Before the interview is over, go back through your notes with the witness to make sure you got it right. It's a good idea to have the witness sign either your notes (if they are legible) or a written statement of what was said during the interview. If you decide to use a written statement, write the first draft yourself. That way, you can make sure to include all of the important facts the witness told you. Give the draft to the witness and encourage changes, additions, or deletions. (Of course, if the witness makes a change that contradicts an earlier statement to you, you should ask about it.)

These statements are great evidence of what a witness told you at the time. A witness who later claims to have said something different will have to explain why he or she signed the statement. Some witnesses are intimidated at the thought of writing up an official statement.

Start your notes from each interview on a clean piece of paper. That way, you won't have to worry about the witness seeing your notes from other interviews.

DON'T WRITE:

I spoke to Joan today. She said that Richard has been acting strange lately but she hasn't really seen any fights between him and Sam. She thinks Richard might act out violently some time soon.

WRITE:

I interviewed Joan Suzuki today, June 14, 200X, regarding Sam Levine's complaint (see complaint form in file). We met in my office at 3 p.m. I asked Joan whether she had seen any incidents between Richard Hart and Sam in the last two weeks. Joan said that she thought Richard has been acting very strange lately. When I asked her to explain, she said that Richard seemed "distracted and angry," and that he had been complaining to others in the work group about his ex-wife's petition for an increase in child support. Richard told her that Sam had denied his request for a raise, and that Sam was responsible for all of his problems. Joan also said that Richard had made several jokes during shift meetings about 'going postal,' and that he told Sam, 'You will be the first to go.' This is the only incident she has seen between Sam and Richard. Joan said that she was frightened by Richard's change in behavior.

Joan confirmed that Jose, Jocelyn, and LeShawn were at the meetings where Richard made these jokes. I thanked her for her information and encouraged her to come forward with any additional information immediately. I asked her to treat the investigation confidentially. I assured her that Richard has been suspended pending the outcome of the investigation, and that the company would act swiftly to deal with the situation as soon as the investigation was complete.

CD-ROM

Listen to interview dos and don'ts. The CD-ROM includes audio tracks of investigative interviews. You'll hear the right way—and the wrong way—to take a complaint, interview the complaining employee, and interview the accused employee.

Speak Into the Microphone

You might think it would be easier to dispense with all the notes and statements and just tape your interview sessions, on video or audio. Taping does offer accuracy, but it tends to make things complicated. For one thing, you'll need to know how to operate the equipment (or have someone at the interview who does, which could raise confidentiality concerns). And you'll have to contend with employee anxiety—most employees will be less comfortable (and more nervous) having their interviews taped. This means that you'll have to work harder to build rapport and trust. Finally, when it comes time to use the tape to remember what was said (for example, when you write your report or have to defend your investigation in court), you'll have to fast forward and rewind your way through the conversation until you find the exact statement you need.

For these reasons, most investigators prefer to simply take notes. But this doesn't mean that you should prohibit the employee from taping the interview, at the employee's request. If you refuse to allow an employee to tape, you open the door to later claims that your notes are incomplete or false—and you will start to look a bit shady. ("The investigator didn't write down everything I said—I asked if I could tape the interview, but she wouldn't let me.") If an employee asks to record an interview session, give the OK—but only on the condition that you receive a copy of the tape right away.

Whatever you do, don't tape employees' statements without their knowledge and written consent. In some states, it is illegal to record a conversation unless both parties consent. Secret taping can lead to an invasion of privacy lawsuit—or even criminal prosecution.

Interviewing the Complaining Employee

If the investigation is triggered by a complaint, then you should start by interviewing the complaining employee. Your goals are to put the employee at ease, explain the process, and find out, in as much detail as possible, exactly what happened.

> **TIP**
>
> **Handle a distressed employee with care.** If the complaining employee is really upset, you may have to alter your usual interviewing procedures to avoid exacerbating the problem. For example, if the employee wants to take some time off work, you might have to postpone your interview for a few days. Or, you might allow the employee to bring a friend or family member to the interview for moral support. If you do make an accommodation like this, document it in the investigation file, especially if it requires you to delay the investigation.

Where to Start When No One Complains

In some situations, wrongdoing is clearly taking place, yet no employee has complained. Perhaps the real victim is the company, not any particular employee (as is often the case when employees steal). Or maybe someone has made an anonymous complaint. Who should you interview first when no employee has come forward?

One possibility is to start with someone who has general or background knowledge of the problem. For example, if racist graffiti suddenly started appearing on the walls of a particular work area, you could start by interviewing the manager in charge of those employees to find out who usually works there, what schedules they work, whether there seem to be any racial tensions among the workers, and so on. If money is missing from the cash register, you might start by asking the bookkeeper when and how the problem became apparent and who has access to the cash. Of course, if you don't know who's responsible for the misconduct, the person you interview for background information may turn out to be the perpetrator —and you should keep this in mind when you ask your questions.

Another option is to start by interviewing the suspected wrongdoer, if there is one. For example, if a worker is suspected of coming to work drunk or on drugs, you could start by interviewing that person directly.

Getting Started

Begin the interview by letting the employee know how the process will work and what to expect. Here are some points you should make at the start of the interview:

- Explain that you will be investigating the employee's complaint by interviewing witnesses and gathering evidence.
- State that you expect the employee to give you complete and accurate information and to answer all of your questions truthfully.
- Explain that, if the investigation reveals misconduct, the company will take appropriate steps to deal with the situation.
- Assure the employee that you will maintain confidentiality to the extent possible, but that it will be necessary to reveal some details of the complaint in order to find out what happened. Make sure the employee knows that you expect him or her to keep the complaint confidential, as well.
- Explain what retaliation is and that the company prohibits it. Ask the employee to come to you immediately with any retaliation concerns.
- Ask whether the employee has any questions or concerns about the process.

You can provide some of this information in writing as well. For example, some investigators routinely provide written notice to everyone they interview explaining the importance of cooperating with the investigation, maintaining confidentiality, and reporting any retaliation immediately. This isn't strictly necessary, but it's a good way to underscore the witness's obligations and demonstrate that the company is taking the matter seriously. Appendix B (and the CD-ROM) contain a sample written notice that you can adapt for your own use.

> **TIP**
> **Follow up on employee concerns.** If an employee seems overly worried about confidentiality or other employees finding out who complained, find out why. Sometimes, these concerns indicate legitimate fears about retaliation. Ask whether anyone told the employee not to come forward or threatened to take some retaliatory action. If the employee claims to have been threatened or otherwise warned against complaining, add that to your list of things to be investigated, ask the employee to tell you immediately of any further threats, and monitor the workplace carefully for any sign of retaliation.

Don't compromise your impartiality. Make sure that the complaining employee feels comfortable coming forward, but don't sympathize so strongly that you lose your neutrality. Remember, you don't know what happened yet: The complaining employee may be a brave voice crying in the wilderness or may be the boy who cried wolf. Avoid statements implying that you believe the employee is telling the truth, like "What happened to you must have been awful" or "I'm so sorry for what you've been through."

Some investigators begin by thanking the complaining employee for coming forward. While this is an encouraging gesture that can get the interview off on the right foot (and convince the employee to answer your questions fully), it can also improperly signal that you believe the employee's story. If you choose to give thanks, say something like "Thank you for coming forward with this information. We plan to look into it right away."

Sample Questions

Once your introductory statements are out of the way, you'll start your questioning. Of course, the questions you ask will depend on the nature of the complaint. No matter what the complaint is about, however, you'll want to cover the basics: who, what, where, when, how, and (sometimes) why. Here are some sample questions to consider:

SAMPLE QUESTIONS

- What happened? If the complaint involves several incidents or a pattern of misconduct over a period of time, ask about each separately. Start with the most recent problem and work backwards.

- Who was involved? What did that person say or do?

- What was your response or reaction, if any?

- When and where did the incident(s) take place?

- Why did you decide to come forward now (if the incident took place quite a while before the complaint)?

- Did anyone witness the incident(s)?

- Did you tell anyone about the incident(s)?

- Do you know of anyone who might have information about these incidents?

- Have you been affected by the incident(s)? How?

- Do you know of any similar incidents involving other people?

- Do you know of any evidence—documents or otherwise—relating to your complaint?

- How would you like to see this problem resolved? (Make clear that the company will ultimately decide how to handle it, but you'd like to hear the employee's opinion.)

- Is there anything else you'd like to tell me?

Once you have finished your questions, go back through your notes with the employee to make sure you got everything down correctly. Double check dates, names, and times. If you plan to ask the employee to sign a statement rather than your notes, prepare that document now—you can let the employee take a break while you pull it together.

Conclude the interview by giving the employee some idea what to expect. Tell the employee that you plan to interview the accused worker and any other witnesses, review any additional evidence, and complete the investigation as soon as possible. Ask the employee not to tell anyone about the investigation or talk about the complaint with coworkers. Finally, ask to be contacted with any new or additional information about the complaint.

When Emotions Run High

Employees often find it difficult to come forward with a complaint, especially about discrimination or harassment. Many employees complain only as a last resort, after trying informally to stop the misconduct. An employee who complains may be wrestling with difficult feelings of embarrassment, anger, sadness, fear, and reluctance to come forward.

When an employee finally does decide to complain, these emotions may spill out during the interview. The worker may cry, become angry, or even try to "take back" the complaint. Your best response is to listen and be understanding. Assure the employee that you know this is difficult and emotional, and that you want to get to the bottom of things. If the complaining worker tries to rescind the complaint, explain that you will have to investigate anyway, and you would like the worker's cooperation. If the employee is afraid of the accused employee, think about immediate steps you can take to calm these fears, such as separating the workers.

Don't try so hard to sympathize that you lose your objectivity in the investigation, however. Remember, your job is to remain impartial, uncover all of the facts, and then make a reasoned, objective decision.

Interviewing the Accused Employee

Imagine what it's like to be accused of wrongdoing in the workplace. If you actually committed misconduct, you probably wouldn't be eager to admit it; if you were wrongly accused, you would likely be upset, even angry. Keep this in mind when interviewing the accused (or suspected) employee. As the investigator, you'll have to assure the employee that you'll make a fair decision while also trying to uncover the truth.

Getting Started

As in your interview with the complaining employee, you should start by explaining the process. Here are some topics you should cover at the outset:

- Let the employee know that a complaint has been made (or a problem has come to your attention) and that you will be investigating the situation.

- Assure the accused employee that you have not yet reached any conclusions and that you will listen carefully to everyone involved before taking any action.

- Explain that you expect the employee to give you complete, accurate information and to answer all of your questions truthfully.

- Explain that you will keep the investigation as confidential as possible and that the employee should not talk to coworkers about the investigation or the complaint.

- Tell the employee that retaliation is forbidden, and explain what retaliation is.

- Ask if the employee has any questions or concerns about the investigation.

Union Members Have the Right to Bring a Representative

Union members have the right to bring a union representative to any investigative interview that could result in disciplinary action against the employee. (This is referred to as the employee's "Weingarten" right, named after the case that decided the issue.) This right was extended to nonunion employees in 2000, but that extension was short-lived: The National Labor Relations Board (NLRB) overruled itself in 2004 and once again limited Weingarten rights to union members.

The employer has no obligation to inform the employee of this right. However, the employer must allow a representative, if requested by the accused employee, or forgo the interview altogether.

Sample Questions

The questions you ask the accused will, of course, depend on the nature of the complaint and the employee's responses. Remember to begin with the easy questions and background details, then work your way up to the harder issues. Here are some sample questions to consider:

SAMPLE QUESTIONS

- What is your typical workday like? What time do you arrive, what time do you leave, what are your responsibilities?

- Do you supervise any employees? What are their names and positions?

- [State the allegations one at a time.] Did this happen? What can you tell me about it?

- [If the accused employee says the allegations are false:] Could someone else have misunderstood your actions or statements? Have you had problems working with anyone? Do you think someone might have made up these incidents? Why?

- [If the accused employee does not completely deny the allegations:] What happened? When and where?

- Did anyone witness the incident(s)?

- Did you tell anyone about the incident(s)?

- Do you know of anyone who might have information about the incident(s)?

- Do you know of any documents or other evidence relating to this situation?

- Is there anything else you'd like to tell me?

> ### 💡 TIP
>
> **Silence is golden.** If you're having trouble digging information out of an accused employee, take a page from therapists and counselors—trained experts at getting others to talk about uncomfortable things—and try a little silence. If an employee is giving you short answers and holding back information, let the silence deepen. Instead of immediately asking another question, wait a bit. Look at the employee expectantly. (Those who really want to get into character might even try a "Hmmm" or "I see"). You'll be surprised at how often this prompts employees to add something to a previous answer or try a bit harder to explain their side of the story.

When you're through with your questions, review your notes with the employee; ask the employee to sign off on your notes or a written statement summarizing the interview.

Again, close the interview by telling the accused employee what will happen next. Explain that you will interview witnesses and review other evidence before reaching a final conclusion. Stress again that retaliation is strictly prohibited. And ask the employee to bring any new or additional information to your attention at once.

Interviewing Witnesses

There are many kinds of witnesses. Some have seen or heard, firsthand, the misconduct at issue, while others have only heard rumors. Some will be privy to an entire dispute, while others have only a bit of information to share. And some may have an axe to grind (or favor to curry) with either the complaining or the accused employee.

When you interview witnesses, your goal is to find out what they know without revealing any information unnecessarily. While the accused employee has the right to know what allegations have been made, third-party witnesses have no such right—and you have good reasons to maintain confidentiality. If the allegations turn out to be false, you could get into legal trouble for publicizing them unnecessarily. Even if no lawsuit is in the offing, you can cut down gossip by keeping a tight lid on the investigation.

It can be tough to figure out whom to interview as a witness, especially if the complaining employee and/or accused employee suggest a number of candidates. You'll want to interview anyone who allegedly heard or saw something important. Sometimes, however, an employee (particular one accused of wrongdoing) will suggest witnesses who can attest to his or her good character; "Ask Mary or Scott; they know I would never do anything like this!" Although witnesses like this won't add much to your investigation, you might decide to interview one or two, so the employee knows you are taking his or her suggestions seriously.

You shouldn't simply pick and choose, or decide to interview only a set number of witnesses, however. If you decide not to interview a witness suggested by another employee, you should have a good reason—and document it in your investigation report (see Chapter 4).

Getting Started

Once again, begin with an opening statement. Here are some topics to include:

- Explain that you are investigating a workplace problem and that you believe the witness might have information that will help you figure out what happened.

- Let the witness know that you have not come to any conclusions about what happened.

- Explain that you expect the witness to give you complete and accurate information and to answer all of your questions truthfully.

- Tell the employee not to talk to anyone at work about the investigation.

- Explain what retaliation is and that it's strictly prohibited. Ask the witness to come to you with any concerns about retaliation for participating in the investigation.

- Ask whether the employee has any questions or concerns about the investigation process. (You may find yourself having to explain that you cannot answer some of these questions, particularly if the witness asks who complained or who else is being interviewed.)

Sample Questions

When deciding what to ask a witness, think about who suggested the witness and why. Did the complaining employee tell you that the witness saw the misconduct? Did the accused employee tell you that he or she confided in the witness after an incident? Sticking to the facts the witness is supposed to know will help you keep things confidential. Here are some questions to consider for third-party witnesses:

SAMPLE QUESTIONS

- Do you work with [the complaining employee or accused employee]?

- If the person may have witnessed the incident, ask what the witness saw or heard. For example, "Were you in the lunch room last Friday? What time? Who else was there? Did you hear Mark and Sarah talking to each other? What did each of them say?"

- When and where did this take place?

- Did you tell anyone about the incident?

- Did [the complaining employee] tell you anything about the incident?

- Did [the accused employee] tell you anything about the incident?

- Have you personally witnessed any other incidents between [the complaining employee] and [the accused employee]?

- Have you heard these issues discussed in the workplace? When, where, and by whom?

- Have you ever had any problems working with [the complaining employee or the accused employee]?

- Is there anything else you'd like to tell me?

As with all interviews, review your notes with the witness when you are through with your questions. Make sure you wrote everything down correctly and that your notes include all of the important details. If you plan to ask the employee to sign a statement rather than your notes, prepare that document now.

When your questions have been answered, thank the witness for participating. Stress that the interview and the investigation must remain confidential; tell the witness not to discuss either with coworkers. And ask the witness to return to you with any further information.

Interviewing Nonemployees

In some situations, you might want to interview someone who doesn't work for the company: a customer who overheard racist comments, a bystander who saw some employees fighting on the street, or a friend or partner in whom an employee confided. Handle these interviews with special care. Talking to someone outside the company can lead to problems. From a legal standpoint, an accused employee is more likely to take offense—and possibly contemplate a defamation lawsuit—if people outside the company learn of the allegations. On the practical side, unless the witness is willing to sign a confidentiality agreement, the company has no way to enforce its confidentiality rules against outsiders, which means your company's dirty laundry might get aired in public.

You may have to run these risks if the witness is crucial to the investigation. For example, if a customer is the only witness to an employee theft or a sexual harassment incident, you need to find out what that person saw. If you find yourself in this situation, stay on your best behavior. Remember, you will be representing the company to the outside world, and you'll want to make it look good. And the witness is under no obligation to talk to you—you're really asking for this person's help, and you should make that clear from the start.

When interviewing an outside witness, confidentiality is especially important. Conduct the interview offsite, at a place that's convenient for the witness. Don't reveal anything unnecessarily—including the names of the employees involved or what you suspect might have happened. And be sure to thank the witness for helping you get to the bottom of things.

Gathering Other Evidence

In some cases, there will be no evidence of wrongdoing other than witness statements. Much workplace misconduct is interpersonal—conducted face to face, rather than in writing. If the alleged misconduct consists of verbal or physical harassment, threats, or violence, there may be no document or other tangible piece of evidence related to the incident.

Sometimes, however, documents and other physical evidence play an important role in the investigation. If one employee accuses the other of sending threatening emails, for example, you'll want to get your hands on those messages. Or if an employee is accused of bringing a weapon to work or drinking on the job, you'll want to look for the "smoking gun" (or the empty bottle).

And in some cases, you might want to pay a visit to the scene of the alleged misconduct. This could give you important clues about who's telling the truth, what questions to ask, and which witnesses to interview.

> **CAUTION**
>
> **Don't pretend to be someone you're not.** As the Hewlett Packard "pretexting" incident has made abundantly clear, investigators who use a false identity to try to gather information can get in a lot of trouble. In HP's case, an outside investigator allegedly got a board member's phone records by calling the telephone company and pretending to be the member. (The investigator was trying to figure out who was leaking confidential information.) This type of investigating can lead to legal problems and very harmful publicity.

Documents

In every investigation, stop and ask yourself, "What documents could help me figure out what happened?" Think about the types of records your company keeps—in personnel files, attendance reports, inventories, computer records, and so on.

In some investigations, documents play a starring role. For example, if an employee claims that her coworkers sexually harassed her by sending X-rated messages and images over the office email system, those messages might be the most important evidence you can gather.

> **TIP**
> **Get technical help to uncover the history of important electronic documents.** Sometimes, you'll need to know who sent an electronic document, when it was created, who else received it, and whether it was altered. In these situations, your company's technical staff may be able to help you get the information you need. If not, it might be worth the expense to hire outside help to recover this data.

More often, however, documents play a supporting role by providing important background information. For example, if an employee complains that a supervisor has discriminated against him, you might review the employee's personnel file to see how the supervisor has documented their exchanges. Or, if an employee is accused of stealing company equipment, inventory records can help you figure out exactly when the goods disappeared.

Documents might also help you pin down crucial details. For example, attendance records can corroborate (or contradict) an employee who claims to have been out of the office on a particular day. Or, if an employee accuses a supervisor of changing her performance review after she complained of harassment, you can use documents to find out when the complaint was made, when the performance review was drafted, and whether the review was changed at any time.

Here is a checklist of documents that may figure into your investigation. Of course, not every workplace will use all of these types of documents—and not every document on the list will be relevant to a given investigation. But this list will give you a starting point when you start considering which documents might be helpful:

Document Checklist

- ☐ Company policies
- ☐ Email messages
- ☐ Postings to company bulletin boards (electronic or corkboard)
- ☐ Correspondence
- ☐ Performance evaluations
- ☐ Work samples
- ☐ Written warnings and other disciplinary records
- ☐ Customer complaints or comments
- ☐ Commendations
- ☐ Documents signed by the employees involved (such as hiring agreements, employment contracts, and other agreements)
- ☐ Attendance records (for work generally, required meetings, or training sessions, for example)
- ☐ Payroll records
- ☐ Time cards or other records showing hours worked
- ☐ Work schedules
- ☐ Inventory records
- ☐ Expense reports
- ☐ Computer records (of Internet sites visited, productivity, and so on)
- ☐ Cash register receipts
- ☐ Purchase orders
- ☐ Productivity reports (such as records of sales completed, deadlines met, or projects finished)
- ☐ Sales receipts
- ☐ Equipment logs
- ☐ Notes taken by an employee involved (for example, if an employee made a record of threatening or harassing comments by another employee, or kept a diary or journal of workplace incidents)
- ☐ Files from any previous investigations of the same employees or same types of incidents

TIP

Look for documents that are not in official personnel files.
Many supervisors make a habit of keeping their own working files on the employees who report to them. These files often contain documents that never find their way to the employees' official personnel files. For example, a supervisor will probably give an employee's final performance review to the human resources department to place in the employee's personnel file. However, the supervisor might keep old drafts of the review, the employee's comments on the review, and informal notes on the employee's performance in a working file. To make sure that you get your hands on every important document, ask supervisors for all documents they have on the employees involved in the incident, whether or not those documents appear in the employees' personnel files.

If you decide a document is relevant to your investigation, take good care of it. Make a record of where you found it and store it in a secure location. If you plan to use the document in your interviews (for example, to show to the accused employee), don't bring the original—make a copy. That way, you won't have to worry about writing on the document or losing it. If your company later faces a lawsuit relating to the investigation, you will want to be able to show where important documents came from and, more important, that they have not been altered.

EXAMPLE: Sanjiv is accused of sexually harassing a coworker, Linda. During your investigation, Linda gives you several handwritten notes that Sanjiv gave to her. These notes include sexually explicit comments and threats to harm Linda if she doesn't agree to have a relationship with him. As a result of your investigation, Sanjiv is fired.

Sanjiv sues the company for wrongful termination, claiming that he never harassed Linda and that the company really fired him for complaining about health and safety violations. He claims that the investigation was biased and that the notes were doctored to give the company a reason to fire him. He agrees that he wrote part of the notes but claims that the offensive language and threats were added by someone else. You should be able to defeat these arguments if you can show that you recorded the date you received them, noted that Linda gave them to you, placed them in a secure location, and did not remove them from that location until you were asked to hand them over in the lawsuit.

Other Evidence

Misconduct doesn't always leave a paper trail. Sometimes, the path is cluttered with bulkier objects, such as discarded plastic baggies, a knife hidden in a desk drawer, or confidential company data stored on a CD-ROM. In the most extreme cases, you might need to test this evidence to determine its relevance. For example, you may need to check for fingerprints or test for the presence of illegal drugs.

Always consider the range of possible evidence that might exist. If you find evidence like this, store and label it carefully. Indicate when and where you found the evidence, then place it in a secure location. This could prove important later, if you must prove that the evidence has not been tampered with.

CAUTION

Give contraband to the authorities. If you come across illegal evidence, such as controlled substances or an unregistered or illegal weapon, contact a lawyer right away to find out whether you should report it to the police. If you hang on to items that are illegal to possess, you could find yourself facing criminal liability.

Clues From the Scene

It's often a good idea to visit the place where the alleged misconduct took place. This will give you a better understanding of what the witnesses are describing and give you ideas for additional witnesses or follow-up interview questions. It might even convince you that someone is—or is not—telling the truth.

For example, imagine that an employee has complained that another employee raised his voice to her and threatened to harm her one morning in the hallway outside her office. You go to the hallway at about the time when the incident allegedly happened. You notice that the employee's office is next door to a kitchenette, which employees are allowed to use. During the five minutes you spend there, you see 20 different employees come to get coffee, put their lunches in the refrigerator, or just talk to their coworkers. These are all potential witnesses to the incident—and you should ask the complaining employee if she noticed any of them nearby when she was threatened. If nobody heard the threats, despite all of this traffic, the complaining employee's story starts to sound a bit far-fetched.

On the other hand, imagine that you went to the hallway and noticed that the complaining employee's office was next door not to a kitchenette, but to an equipment room full of noisy machinery. You don't see anyone else while you're investigating. In this situation, it wouldn't hurt the complaining employee's credibility a bit if there were no witnesses to the threats.

Follow-Up Interviews

Once you complete your interviews and review any other available evidence, consider setting up another interview with the accused employee—especially if you have heard new allegations or information since your last interview. If witnesses have added significant details or documents supporting the complaining employee have surfaced, it is probably a good idea to get the accused employee's response to these additional facts. Courts are more likely to find an investigation was fair and thorough—and its outcome reliable—if the accused employee is given the opportunity to respond to all the evidence before the company makes a final decision.

You should also consider another interview with the complaining employee. If the accused employee or witnesses have denied the complaining employee's allegations or offered reasons why the complaining employee might not be telling the truth, you should let the complaining employee respond.

Make and Document Your Decision

N ow you're facing what may be the hardest part of your job as investigator: reaching a conclusion about what happened and what to do about it. You have interviewed all the witnesses. You have gathered relevant evidence. But how do you decide who is telling the truth and who is lying? How do you figure out what actually occurred and why?

Because every investigation—and every person involved in an investigation—is a little bit different, there's no single formula to apply or test to use that will always lead you to the right answers. However, there are some guidelines that will help you sort through conflicting stories. This chapter offers some tried and true strategies for evaluating the results of your investigation and reaching a decision.

After you have made your assessments, you must decide whether wrongdoing occurred and what, if any, corrective action to take (if that's part of your job). You must document your investigation and decisions. And, even after the investigation is written up and filed away, you'll want to take a few steps to make sure that you've really dealt with the underlying problem—by following up with the affected employees and thinking about whether any workplace changes are necessary to avoid similar problems in the future.

Evaluate the Evidence

If there is no dispute about what actually happened, you can skip right to "Decide Whether Misconduct Occurred," below. However, if there are important disagreements among the witnesses—and particularly if the accused worker denies the facts of the complaint—you will have to figure out where the truth lies.

Look at the Facts

To begin, review the evidence you have gathered and your notes from interviews. If there are multiple allegations, go through each one separately. Are there any facts to which everyone agrees? What are the major points of contention? As to each of these disputes, what did the witnesses say? Are there any documents supporting one version or the other?

Some investigators find it helpful to group the evidence into two categories: disputed facts and undisputed facts. If you can make a decision based solely on the undisputed facts, then you don't really have to decide which witness(es) you believe; they've all agreed on the important points. If the undisputed facts don't give you enough to go on, think about which disputed facts will have to be resolved in order to reach a conclusion. Focus on these facts—and on each witness's version of these facts—as you consider credibility issues (discussed below).

> **EXAMPLE:** Mimi is evaluating the evidence she has gathered in her investigation of products missing from an electronics store. Here are the undisputed facts her investigation has revealed:
>
> 1. The missing products are all high-ticket items—each is worth several hundred dollars or more.
> 2. The products were signed for by the receiving department but could not be located on the stockroom shelves when customers sought to purchase the items. In other words, the items disappeared from the stockroom, not from the showroom floor or in transit between the manufacturer and the electronics store.
> 3. Franklin and Debbie are the only two employees who were working in the stockroom when each of the thefts occurred.
> 4. Franklin recently bought a new Land Rover and took a cruise to the Bahamas.
>
> Is this enough information for Mimi to decide what happened? Nope. The only fact that points to Franklin as the culprit is his recent change in spending habits, and there could be lots of reasons for that. So Mimi has to move on to consider the disputed facts. She realizes that these disputed facts are the most important:

1. Debbie claims that Franklin disappeared for an hour or so during each shift when items were taken. Franklin claims that he is frequently asked to work in other areas of the store, and was probably working elsewhere at the time.

2. Franklin claims that his wife recently inherited a large sum of money from her deceased grandfather, which paid for their new car and cruise.

3. Several employees claim to have seen Franklin's car parked at the loading dock (which backs onto the stockroom) on occasion. Franklin denies that he has ever parked near the loading dock and says these employees must be mistaken.

Mimi can now focus her energy on assessing these key disputed facts. As sometimes happens, Mimi realizes that she might have to gather some more information to make a final decision. For example, she might briefly interview the managers who were working when Franklin claims to have been asked to work in a different part of the store, to find out if anyone reassigned Franklin. She might also perform a quick public records search online to see what she can find out about Franklin's grandfather-in-law.

Assess Credibility

When you're faced with conflicting stories—as happens in many investigations—you will have to consider each person's version of the facts. Evaluating credibility and determining who's telling the truth can be difficult, but the following guidelines will help you sift through the evidence:

- **Plausibility.** Whose story makes the most sense? Does one person's version of events defy logic or common sense? Based on your visit to the scene (see Chapter 3), could the employees involved have heard and seen what they claimed to have witnessed? Should they have heard and seen things that they did not admit?

- **Source of information.** Did the witness see or hear the event directly? Did the witness report firsthand knowledge, or rely on secondhand statements from other employees or rumors?

- **Detail.** How general or specific was each person's statement? If a witness gave a detailed statement, were those details supported by other evidence? Did the accused or suspected employee deny the allegations in detail or only generally?

- **Corroboration and conflicting testimony.** Are there witnesses or documents that support one side of the story? Does the evidence contradict one person's statements? Do the witnesses support the person who suggested you interview them? If there are conflicts, are they over minor or significant issues?

- **Contradictions.** Was each person's story consistent throughout your questioning or on a second telling? Did any of the witnesses contradict themselves during your interview? If so, did the change involve a minor issue or a matter of substance?

- **Demeanor.** How did the witnesses act during the interview? Did the accused employee have a strong reaction to the complaint or no reaction at all? Did the complaining employee seem genuinely upset? Were any witnesses' reactions unusual, based on their typical demeanor or behavior? Judging demeanor should be tough—even for the experts—and you certainly shouldn't base your conclusions on demeanor alone. But you should consider any reactions that are particularly strong or unexpected.

- **Omissions.** Did anyone leave out important information during the interview? Is there a sensible explanation for the omission? Did an accused or suspected employee admit an important detail only after being confronted with it?

- **Prior incidents.** Does the accused employee have a documented history of this type of misconduct? Has the complaining employee made previous complaints? Have there been other incidents between the complaining and the accused employee?

- **Motive.** Does either the complaining worker or the accused worker have a motive to lie about, exaggerate, or deny the incident? Is there any history between these employees that affects their credibility? Do any of the witnesses have a special loyalty to—or a grudge against—any of the employees involved?

TIP

Reopen the investigation, if necessary. Sometimes, your evaluation of the facts and credibility assessments will lead you to only one definite conclusion: You need more information. This is not uncommon. You might not see important lines of questioning or additional evidence to gather until you analyze all of the facts. If you think you need more information, it's much better to continue the investigation than to make a decision that might later be called into question.

Put It All Together

Once you've examined all of the facts and weighed each witness's credibility, you will probably begin to see the real story—or at least, the way that things are most likely to have played out. Often, investigators find that one version of events is really implausible or that it makes a lot less sense than the other. In investigations as in science, the adage holds true: The most obvious explanation is often correct.

However, the web may remain hopelessly tangled even after you've considered every angle. In that case, you might have to end the investigation by admitting that you cannot figure out what really happened. If there is evidence on both sides and it really could have happened either way, it's better to throw up your hands than to take disciplinary action that isn't supported by the evidence. See "Take Action," below, for more on how to handle these situations.

EXAMPLE: Stuart complained that Marcus threatened to fire him for taking time off to report to jury duty. Stuart said that Marcus made this threat in the lunch room on April 28. Marcus seemed very surprised by this allegation; he agreed that he spoke to Stuart in the lunch room about his jury summons but said only that he hoped Stuart didn't get picked to sit on a jury because jury duty can be so boring. Marcus suggested that the investigator speak to several witnesses, all of whom confirmed his side of the story. Marcus also said that Stuart had seemed upset since his last performance review, when Marcus noted that Stuart hadn't met several of his performance goals for the year. When the investigator interviewed Stuart a second time to get his reaction to this, Stuart admitted that the witnesses were there but insisted that they must have misunderstood what Marcus said. He also admitted his bad feelings about the performance review.

In this case, the investigator can conclude that there was no wrongdoing. All of the witnesses support Marcus's version of events. Stuart cannot explain this discrepancy. Marcus has also offered a reason for Stuart's complaint, which Stuart has not denied.

Get a Second Opinion

Except in the most clear-cut situations, it's a good idea to ask someone else to review your investigation and the conclusions you've reached. This will help you make sure that you've considered all the angles, documented everything properly, and made an objective decision based on the evidence.

If possible, choose someone who is fairly high up in the company and has some distance from the situation—for example, a human resources director for a different region. Give this person all of your investigative documents and evidence, then ask whether your decision seems justified. This person may point out gaps in your documentation or ask questions that you hadn't considered. A lawyer can also help you make sure that your investigation and conclusions are sound.

EXAMPLE: Same as above, but one witness (a friend of Marcus's) confirms Marcus's version of the conversation and one witness (a coworker with whom Stuart often eats lunch) confirms Stuart's version. Although Stuart admits his bad feelings about the performance review, he points out that he went to Marcus's manager shortly after his evaluation to talk about the review. The manager confirmed Marcus's opinion of Stuart's performance and explained how Stuart could improve. Stuart says that he felt more comfortable with the evaluation after this conversation, although Marcus was upset that Stuart went over his head and complained. Marcus denies being upset about this.

What should the investigator do now? Without more evidence, the investigator cannot reach a conclusion. Both Stuart and Marcus claim that the other had a motive to lie, and both claim to be telling the truth. In short, this one could go either way.

Decide Whether Misconduct Occurred

Once you have evaluated the evidence and reached some factual conclusions, you will have to decide whether company policies were violated or misconduct occurred. This decision will dictate what further actions you should take and what you should tell the employees involved.

Misconduct and Discipline: Who Decides?

You may not be responsible for deciding whether discipline should be imposed. In many larger companies with dedicated human resources departments, the investigator is responsible only for reaching factual conclusions about the situation under investigation—that is, for deciding what probably happened—not for making decisions about discipline. Even in smaller companies, the investigator won't always be responsible for discipline, depending on where he or she ranks on the company ladder. Tailor your report and conclusions to your responsibilities: If you don't make disciplinary decisions, limit yourself to deciding (and writing down) your conclusions about what happened, not what should be done about it.

At this point, you may be wondering what, exactly, constitutes misconduct. For the most part, it isn't hard to tell whether an employee has crossed the line that separates eccentric behavior, jokes, or silliness from actions that are worthy of discipline. However, there are some gray areas—situations in which it's tough to distinguish misconduct from a misunderstanding.

EXAMPLE: Over the course of several months, $300 has gone missing from petty cash. Numerous employees saw Claude taking money from the petty cash drawer on three separate occasions. When you ask Claude about it, he denies taking the money and calls his coworkers liars. Based on these facts, it looks like Claude has committed misconduct.

Now assume that employees have seen Claude taking the money, but they've also seen Claude putting money back into the drawer. No money is missing from the petty cash account. When you ask Claude about it, he immediately admits taking the money but says that he always paid it back. He assumed that this was OK because his supervisor also borrows from petty cash. Now, the situation is less clear. Claude hasn't lied, and technically he hasn't stolen. He may have exercised poor judgment, but his supervisor's actions led him to believe his actions were OK. He should be told that he has violated company policy and perhaps given a warning, but severe disciplinary measures aren't called for. His supervisor should also be warned and, perhaps, disciplined for violating company policy.

In "Take Action," you'll find information on what to do once you've decided that wrongdoing did or did not occur, or you've decided that you can't reach a conclusion. If you're having trouble making these distinctions, however, here are some guidelines that may help:

- **The law.** Are the employee's actions illegal? Has the employee committed actionable harassment, stolen from the company or its customers, or threatened to harm someone?

- **Written company policies.** Does the employee's conduct violate company policies, as expressed in the employee handbook or in other documents that are distributed to employees?

- **Company practices and procedures.** Did the employee violate a rule that is known in the workplace, even if it isn't written down?

- **Common sense.** Was the employee's action obviously inappropriate or dangerous, even if it isn't illegal or explicitly prohibited by company policies? For example, an employee decides to play a prank on the supervisor who just gave him a bad review by disassembling the supervisor's car and reassembling it on the factory floor, which disrupts an entire shift of work and creates a hazard for employees on the floor. It's not clear that this is illegal, and many companies won't have had the foresight to explicitly prohibit car assembly in the workspace, but this employee's conduct is deserving of discipline.

What these criteria have in common is that, in each case, employees have fair notice of what constitutes misconduct. If actions are prohibited by law, violate written or understood company policy, or don't pass the blush test ("I didn't know I'd get in trouble for calling in a false fire alarm when our biggest client was here—that's not in the company handbook!"), then it's fair to label those actions misconduct and take appropriate corrective action. On the other hand, if an employee's actions are not illegal, against company policy, or obviously inappropriate (like Claude's loans from the petty cash drawer, in the example above), it might not be fair to take action against the employee. Instead, this might be an opportunity to create or revise company policies, inform employees about the company's expectations, or perhaps provide some training.

Take Action

After you have decided whether wrongdoing occurred, you will have to take action based on your findings. This section describes how to handle each of the three conclusions you might reach:

- no misconduct occurred
- you can't decide whether misconduct occurred, or
- misconduct occurred.

No Misconduct

There are several types of situations in which you might find that no misconduct occurred. If there was some incident between the complaining and the accused employee, but nothing happened that is illegal or prohibited by company policies, you might find that no misconduct occurred. In these situations, you should consider whether the accused employee's behavior (and/or the complaining worker's conduct) warrants counseling or warning.

> **EXAMPLE:** Sabine complains that Henry, a coworker, asked her to go out on a date with him, then seemed unhappy when she turned him down. Henry agrees that this happened, acknowledges that he was disappointed when Sabine declined, but says that he has not asked her out or had any social interaction with her since. Both agree that the incident has not affected their ability to work together. This is not misconduct, but you might want to make sure Henry knows that any further advances towards Sabine could violate company policies on harassment.

In rare cases, you might conclude that the complaint was false. If the complaining employee acted in good faith but was mistaken (for example, if he or she misunderstood an incident or was confused about the accused employee's actions), you probably won't have to take any further action once the misunderstanding is cleared up. On the other hand, if the complaining employee acted maliciously—that is, the employee lied rather than making a mistake—discipline against the complaining worker is in order. Consider the employee's motives, how serious the allegations were, and the disruptions to your company in determining an appropriate response.

Handling False Complaints

Sometimes, an employee makes a complaint that turns out, after a thorough investigation, to be false or unfounded. Some employers are tempted to punish the complaining employee in this situation—after all, investigations disrupt the workplace, cost time and money, and can cause considerable stress for employees wrongly accused of bad conduct. But think twice before taking action against an employee who brings a complaint. If the employee had a good-faith reason for complaining, any disciplinary action against that employee might constitute retaliation.

A complaint is in good faith if the employee honestly and reasonably believes the complaint to be true. Even if an investigation proves that the employee was mistaken, you cannot take action unless the complaining employee acted maliciously or recklessly. For example, imagine that Sarah accuses Bernice of stealing from the cash register. If Sarah made up the allegation to get back at Bernice for dating Sarah's former boyfriend, Sarah should be disciplined for making the complaint. However, if Sarah saw Bernice taking money from the register and reasonably believed that Bernice was stealing, Sarah should not be disciplined if it turns out that Bernice had permission to take the money to purchase company supplies.

Savvy employers discipline complaining employees only when they can prove that the complaint was false, was motivated by bad intentions, and caused the company or another employee harm (including damage to a falsely accused employee's reputation). And they do so only after consulting with an experienced lawyer. An employee who is disciplined for complaining might turn around and sue for retaliation. Even if you believe you had good reason for imposing discipline, a jury might see it otherwise. And juries are quite willing to make employers pay in these situations—some of the highest damages awards in employment cases go to employees claiming retaliation.

Inconclusive Results

In some cases, you may be unable to figure out what happened. If the results of your investigation are inconclusive, you should tell both the complaining and the accused employee that you hit a dead end.

If your investigation uncovered confusion about a particular policy (such as what constitutes sexual harassment or what is required under a safety rule), some workplace training might be in order. If you can't figure out whether company policy was violated or who is behind a problem, at least you can take steps to prevent future misconduct.

> **EXAMPLE:** Jon claims that his boss, Maureen, said she wouldn't give him a raise because he refused to clock her in each morning at 8 a.m. (when she sometimes arrived at work ten to fifteen minutes late). Maureen denies Jon's claims but admits that she has been warned about her tardiness and that she has joked with Jon about clocking her in. Maureen also says that she does not plan to give Jon a raise because his work performance has been slipping—her statement is supported by productivity records. No witnesses have seen or heard anything relevant. In this situation, it's not clear what happened. You might want to warn Maureen that having another worker clock her in is a violation of company policy that will result in discipline, but otherwise there isn't much you can do.

Misconduct

You may find that the accused employee engaged in misconduct that requires discipline. If so, and if you are responsible for determining disciplinary measures, choose a corrective action that will be effective in ending the wrongdoing—and in signaling that the company takes it seriously. And no matter what disciplinary measures you come up with, implement them immediately.

Here are some factors to consider when trying to decide on an appropriate corrective action:

- **Severity.** How serious was the misconduct? If there was a victim (for example, an employee who was harassed or threatened), how was the victim affected by the accused employee's actions? What effect did the accused employee's actions have on the workplace?

- **Consistency.** Have other employees committed similar types of misconduct in the past? How were these incidents handled? Being consistent when you discipline employees will help you avoid charges of discrimination and unfair treatment.

- **Policy.** Does the company have a progressive discipline policy? Where does this misconduct—and this employee—fall on your company's scale?

- **History.** Have there been any similar prior incidents involving this employee? Does the employee have a history of disciplinary problems?

- **Knowledge.** Did the employee know that his or her conduct was prohibited? Did workplace rules and policies clearly spell out the company's expectations? An employee who knowingly violates a rule often deserves harsher discipline that an employee who wasn't aware of his or her transgression.

- **Evidence.** How strong is the evidence of wrongdoing? Remember, your company may have to defend whatever action you take in court. Do you have strong, first-hand, corroborated evidence of wrongdoing? If you are going to take harsh disciplinary measures, make sure the evidence you've gathered will support your decision.

Once you have decided how to discipline the wrongdoer, take care of it immediately. Meet with the employee to inform him or her of the results of the investigation and the discipline that will be imposed. Follow your company's policies on discipline, including documenting your decision.

CAUTION

If you discipline an employee based on findings by an outside investigator, you must provide a summary to the employee. As noted in Chapter 2, using an outside investigator brings some of the provisions of the Fair Credit Reporting Act into play. If you decide, based on the investigator's report, to impose discipline, you must provide a summary of the nature and substance of the report to the disciplined employee. This requirement doesn't apply if you investigate in-house. Appendix B includes a sample form you can complete and provide to the employee.

If the Complaining Employee Is Unhappy

Even if you take immediate and effective action against the wrongdoer, the complaining employee may be upset. Perhaps the complaining employee believes a harsher punishment should have been imposed, has suffered damage to reputation and/or work opportunities because of the complaint, or does not believe the wrongdoer will shape up.

Your company is under no obligation to impose the punishment your complaining employee favors. Your obligation is to the company, the accused employee, and the rest of your workforce to be fair and reasonable. However, you should listen carefully to the complaining employee's concerns. Perhaps the employee who claims that the wrongdoer will never change is worried about retaliation or further misconduct. If so, you can assure the complaining employee that you will deal swiftly with any such behavior. An employee who claims to have suffered because of the misconduct may have a point: If the employee was unfairly denied a promotion, raise, or time off, for example, you should consider conferring these benefits retroactively.

Although complaining employees may well have their own axes to grind, they can also help you figure out whether you have chosen an effective remedy. If the resolution you've chosen isn't going to work, better to hear about it now when you can fix the problem than later in a lawsuit.

You must also meet with the complaining employee. Explain that the wrongdoer has been disciplined and describe any steps you will take to prevent further problems. Give assurances that the employee can come to you with any concerns about the situation.

Some employers apologize to the complaining employee for the misconduct. This is a nice gesture, and one that can go a long way towards making employees feel that their concerns—and suffering—were taken seriously. However, if you offer an apology, choose your words with care. Avoid saying things that could be construed as admitting that what happened is the company's fault. There is a world of difference between "We're so sorry that this happened" and "We're so sorry that we allowed this to happen."

Document Your Decision

If you've followed the advice in this book, you've already documented every step of your investigation. At this point, you should have:

- a written complaint or your notes from meeting with the complaining employee, if there is one (if the investigation was based on something other than a complaint—for example, an audit revealed missing funds or sexist graffiti appeared at a worksite—you should have notes about the incident)
- notes from your other interviews, and
- copies of any relevant documents, policies, or other physical evidence relating to the investigation.

You should also make a note of any proposed witness who was not interviewed and the reasons why no interview was conducted. For example, if an employee accused of sexual harassment suggests that you speak to his friend and coworker, who can attest that he "wouldn't sexually harass anyone," you could reasonably choose to save your interviews for those who actually know something about the incident.

Some investigators, particularly consultants who specialize in conducting investigations, prepare formal investigative records. Although you don't have to prepare a formal document with index tabs and footnotes, you should preserve your notes from the investigation and write a brief report of what you did and why. Remember, you might have to prove to a jury that you acted reasonably and your conclusions were sound. If you have documented the reasons for your decision, you will have an easier time remembering the details—and convincing the jury that you considered all the angles before taking action. You will also have a contemporaneous record (that is, one made at the time of the investigation) of what you did and why. This type of document is much more persuasive to a jury than one created after the fact to present in a courtroom.

Prepare an Investigation Report

When you sit down to write your investigation report, remember your audience. If your company is sued for anything related to the investigation—for example, because of the underlying incident or because of the punishment imposed on the wrongdoer—the document you write today could end up in the hands of a lawyer suing your company (and later, in the hands of a judge or jury). If this worst-case scenario comes to pass, your report will be put under a microscope. Any important omissions, inappropriate comments, or random musings could come back to haunt you.

Because of the unfortunate possibility that your report might be evidence in a lawsuit someday, it can be hard to figure out how much detail to include. Your documentation doesn't have to memorialize every thought that crossed your mind during the investigation—nor should it. If you include a lot of extraneous detail, the jury might have trouble following your decision-making process. But make sure to write down all of the major decisions you made and why.

For example, if you did not believe a witness's statement, make a note of that and the reasons for your skepticism. Similarly, if you concluded that no misconduct occurred, write down all of the reasons for your decision. If you write extensive notes but later claim to have left out an important detail, the jury may well believe that you are trying to build a case after the fact.

If you conclude that the employee committed misconduct, you should certainly say so. However, you should avoid saying that the employee broke the law or committed a legal violation (for example, that the employee sexually harassed someone). The reason is simple: In many cases, the company can be liable for an employee's illegal conduct. If you state, in an investigation report, that an employee committed an illegal act, you have conceded your company's liability. Even if it later turns out that you were wrong, that other facts mitigate your company's responsibility, or that your company may have a valid defense, this admission will be very hard to undo. You're far better off simply saying that the employee committed misconduct, violated company policies, acted inappropriately, or used poor judgment.

If the results of your investigation were inconclusive, you should document the reasons why you were unable to sort things out. Note the conflicting evidence carefully. This documentation will be invaluable if similar allegations are later made against the accused employee. You will have a record of previous problems to support any discipline you might impose.

Your documents should include a notation of the discipline (if any) you imposed on the wrongdoer. This information should also go in the wrongdoer's personnel file. If your meeting with either the wrongdoer or the complaining employee was eventful (for example, there was heated argument or significant commentary), you might want to include some notes from that meeting as well.

Investigation Report Checklist

Here are some important facts your investigation report should include, if applicable:

- ☐ the date of the incident(s) under investigation
- ☐ if there is a complaint, the date of the complaint and name of the employee who complained
- ☐ why the investigation was initiated (for example, an employee complained, a fight broke out, or an employee was suspected of being under the influence of drugs at work) and the basic facts to be investigated
- ☐ who conducted the investigation
- ☐ when the investigation began
- ☐ what documents or other evidence were gathered
- ☐ where documents or evidence were found (for example, in an employee's personnel file, pinned to the company bulletin board, or in an employee's desk drawer)
- ☐ when documents or evidence were gathered
- ☐ any company policies that are relevant to the incident under investigation
- ☐ who was interviewed
- ☐ the date of each interview
- ☐ a summary of each witness's statement
- ☐ a summary of any other important facts (for example, things you may have noticed when visiting the scene of the incident)
- ☐ your conclusions and how you came to them
- ☐ any important issues left unresolved
- ☐ any action taken in the workplace (for example, discipline against the wrongdoer or workplace training)

You'll find a sample investigation report in Appendix C; a blank form you can use for your investigation reports is in Appendix B and on the CD-ROM at the back of this book.

Where to Keep Investigation Records

Now that you've written your investigation report, what should you do with it—and with your notes and other documents from the investigation? Create a separate investigation file to be kept with the company's other confidential records. The investigation file should be treated like an employee's medical records—it should be kept confidential and revealed only on a strict need-to-know basis. Don't put the investigation report in any employee's personnel file—in most states, employees have the right to inspect the contents of their personnel files.

What Goes in the Investigation File

Put all documents relating to the investigation in the confidential investigation file, including:

- The complaint, if there is one.
- Copies of any company policies pertaining to the incident(s) investigated.
- Copies of any documents you considered in reaching your conclusion.
- Photos, diagrams, notes, and other evidence relating to the investigation.
- Copies of the written instructions you gave to witnesses regarding cooperation, retaliation, and confidentiality (see Chapter 3).
- Your notes from interviews, signed by the witness.
- Your investigative report.
- Copies of any disciplinary action taken as a result of the investigation.

Appendix C includes a sample investigation file for a sexual harassment case.

If you took corrective action against an employee, that employee's personnel file should include a memo or other documentation of the discipline imposed. It should also indicate that a separate investigation file exists on the incident. That way, if another incident arises involving the same employee, the investigator will know to look in the confidential files for information on the previous problem.

> **CAUTION**
>
> **Don't toss documents without speaking to a lawyer.** Some investigators throw away their notes once they have written a final investigation report. However, this can be very risky. If the incident under investigation—or the investigation itself—turns into a lawsuit, you might be accused of destroying evidence. If you have a lot of extraneous paper you'd like to get rid of or you're concerned about a particular document, get some advice from a lawyer before you throw it away.

Follow Up

You've finished your investigation, taken action if you've found workplace wrongdoing, written your report, and filed it away. So now you can rest on your laurels, right? Not yet. There are still a few things you should do to make sure that you've effectively dealt with the underlying problem.

Meet With Employees

Check in periodically with the complaining employee, if there is one. Make sure that the misconduct has stopped, no retaliation has taken place, and the employee is comfortable in the workplace. If you learn of any problems during these conversations, take action right away.

In some cases, you may also want to follow up with the accused employee, if that employee is still with the company. Ask whether the employee has any concerns relating to the investigation, and whether things are getting back to normal.

Verify Corrective Actions

You'll want to make sure that any corrective actions you recommended were taken. Was the wrongdoer actually disciplined—for example, was a written warning placed in the personnel file, or did the employee actually serve a recommended suspension? If the wrongdoer was told to complete a training program, a rehabilitation program, or counseling (for example, on anger management), has it happened? If you recommended a change in reporting relationships, has that taken place?

Consider the Big Picture

Some investigations reveal companywide problems that should be addressed. Did your investigation turn up significant confusion about company rules or appropriate workplace behavior? Are managers in need of some advice about dealing with employees and employee problems? Did you discover that previous incidents had been swept under the rug or improperly documented? If you answer "yes" to any of these questions, you need to take some action. Your company's employees may need training on company policies, proper management practices, record keeping, or legal requirements. ●

PART

II

Investigating Common Workplace Problems

Investigating Discrimination

Investigating claims of discrimination can be complicated. Because the essence of most discrimination claims is that the complaining employee was treated differently from other employees because of his or her protected characteristic (race, gender, religion, and so on), a thorough investigation will require you to look not only at how the complaining worker was treated but also at how other workers were treated, how the employee accused of discrimination has acted in the past, and whether the reasons the accused employee gives for the challenged decision or action are consistent and legitimate.

Because you will need to gather potentially sensitive information about a number of employees, these investigations can easily mushroom. To handle a discrimination investigation successfully, you'll need to figure out exactly what information you need and how to get it. If you aren't thorough enough, the investigation might not hold up in court—or convince complaining employees that their concerns have been taken seriously. If you go overboard in your information gathering, however, you could create unnecessary delays and risk compromising the confidentiality of the investigation.

An investigation of discrimination is likely to trigger an emotional response, as well. Employees who feel they are being judged based on a protected characteristic rather than their skills and performance are likely to be angry, particularly if they are members of a group that has historically been mistreated in this country. An employee accused of discrimination will probably have a very strong reaction as well; being labeled as a bigot does not sit well with anyone.

This chapter will give you the information and strategies you need to conduct a thorough and effective discrimination investigation. First, it explains the law of discrimination, including common types of discrimination claims. Then, it describes how the ten steps to an effective investigation (as explained in Part I) apply to discrimination, paying special attention to the unique considerations that arise in these investigations.

What Is Discrimination?

It is illegal for an employer to make job decisions based on a person's race, religion, or other "protected characteristic" (as explained below) rather than on that person's ability to do the job. This rule applies to every aspect of the employment relationship, from hiring to promotions, job assignments, pay raises, leaves of absence, working conditions, performance evaluations, demotions, discipline, and firing.

Discrimination is prohibited by federal, state, and some local laws. These laws are enforced by government agencies, including the Equal Employment Opportunity Commission (EEOC), which enforces federal antidiscrimination laws, and state fair employment practices agencies, which handle violations of state law. Appendix D includes a list of EEOC offices and contact information for state fair employment practices agencies.

Protected Characteristics

Federal, state, and local laws determine which characteristics are protected and which are not. Under federal law, employers may not make job decisions based on an employee's race, color, national origin, religion, gender (including pregnancy), disability, citizenship status, or age (if the employee is at least 40 years old). Virtually every state and some localities also outlaw discrimination on these bases, and many protect employees from discrimination on bases not covered by federal law, such as sexual orientation or marital status. You can find information on your state's antidiscrimination laws in Appendix D.

Race and Color

Discrimination on the basis of race or color might include segregating employees of a particular race in certain jobs, making decisions based on stereotypes about race, treating an employee differently for associating with people of a particular race, making decisions based on conditions that correlate to race, or making distinctions based on skin color.

Here are some examples:

- A department store chain routinely channels white employees to sales jobs, while Latino employees are placed mostly in restocking and warehouse positions.

- A delivery company refuses to hire Asian applicants as truck drivers; the hiring committee believes Asians are poor drivers and are more likely to get in accidents.

- A consulting firm doesn't promote a white employee whose husband is Lebanese; the firm's principals often bring their spouses when they entertain important clients, and they are afraid their clients will feel uncomfortable around an Arab-American.

- A restaurant chain has many African-American employees; however, the chain routinely assigns lighter-skinned African-Americans to wait tables and seat customers, while African-Americans with darker skin are channeled to jobs washing dishes and bussing tables.

Discrimination Statistics

The Equal Employment Opportunity Commission (EEOC), the federal agency responsible for administering and enforcing laws that prohibit discrimination, collects statistics on how many discrimination charges are filed with the agency each year, and on what basis. In every year of the last decade, there have been more charges filed alleging race discrimination than any other type. Charges of sex discrimination run a close second, with age and disability discrimination not far behind. Although there have been more charges of discrimination based on national origin and religion filed in recent years (in the wake of the World Trade Center attack of 9/11, many commentators believe), these charges still make up a relatively small portion of the EEOC's total docket.

Which Antidiscrimination Laws Apply to Your Company

Not every antidiscrimination law applies to every employer. For the most part, whether your company has to follow these laws depends on its size and location. Federal antidiscrimination laws (listed below) apply only to employers with more than a minimum number of employees—and this minimum number is different for each law.

Name of Law:	Discrimination Prohibited on the Basis of:	Applies to:
Title VII	Race, color, national origin, religion, sex	Employers with 15 or more employees
Age Discrimination in Employment Act	Age (against employees age 40 and older only)	Employers with 20 or more employees
Americans With Disabilities Act	Physical or mental disability	Employers with 15 or more employees
Equal Pay Act	Sex (applies only to wage discrimination)	All employers
Civil Rights Act of 1866	Race	All employers
Immigration Reform and Control Act	Citizenship status, national origin	Employers with four or more employees

States also have antidiscrimination laws; some apply to smaller employers, and many outlaw additional types of discrimination. Your company must follow all laws that apply to it, whether federal, state, or local. To find out what types of discrimination are prohibited in the state(s) where your company does business, see the chart "State Laws Prohibiting Discrimination in Employment," in Appendix D.

English-Only Rules

Some employers have adopted "English-only" rules that require employees to speak only English in the workplace. Sometimes, these rules are justified—for example, if a team of employees is working together and English is their only common language, or if safety or customer service requires it. An English-only rule will not be considered discriminatory as long as there is a legitimate business justification for the rule.

EXAMPLE: An auto parts factory imposes an English-only rule for its line workers, who must work together using heavy machinery. Such a rule is probably justified by safety concerns. However, if the factory prohibited workers from speaking other languages even on breaks and while making personal telephone calls, that would be a tougher sell. Similarly, if the company imposed a rule that prohibited workers from speaking only certain languages (such as a "no Spanish" rule), that would be discriminatory.

National Origin

An employer discriminates based on national origin when it treats an employee differently because of ethnicity or country of ancestry, or because of traits closely linked to ethnicity (such as surname, accent, cultural identity, and so on).

Examples of national origin discrimination include:

- An airline doesn't allow anyone who appears to be from the Middle East to work in any position that involves dealing with passengers.

- A hardware store that serves a predominantly white neighborhood refuses to promote an employee who has adopted a traditional African style of dress.

- A Chinese restaurant hires only people with Asian features and surnames to wait on customers.

- An automotive supply store disciplines Latino employees more severely than white employees for unexcused absences and tardiness.

Employers can legitimately make job decisions based on an employee's accent only if the accent significantly interferes with the employee's ability to do the job. For example, a business might transfer an employee with a heavy Indian accent from a software help desk position to a job that doesn't require customer contact. Such a transfer would be legitimate if customers had complained that they could not understand his instructions; the same transfer would be illegal if the employee was transferred simply because he had an accent or a particular type of accent, not because the accent impaired his ability to do the job.

Gender

An employer discriminates based on gender when it makes decisions based on an employee's sex, stereotypes about men and women, or pregnancy. Here are some examples:

- A consulting business does not assign women to positions that require significant travel; the company owner believes that women have greater responsibilities at home and will be reluctant to leave their families.

- A manager refuses to promote a pregnant woman to a position for which she will need substantial training; the manager thinks, "we'll just spend all that money to get her up to speed, then she'll quit to stay home with her kids."

- The manager of a sporting goods store assigns only men to work in its golf section, assuming that its customers for golf equipment—who are mostly male—will be less inclined to listen to a woman's advice about clubs and shoes.

An employer must treat pregnant women just as it treats other workers who are temporarily disabled. For example, if a pregnant woman is medically restricted from lifting more than ten pounds during her pregnancy, the employer must treat her like it would any other worker who had such a temporary restriction. However, employers may not impose special rules only on pregnant women—for example, an employer may not prohibit a woman from working past a certain point in her pregnancy or require a woman to take a certain period of time off work after having a baby.

Age

It is illegal to base employment decisions on a worker's age, but only if the worker is at least 40 years old (this is the federal law—some states protect all workers, regardless of age, from age discrimination). A company discriminates based on age by, for example, excluding older workers from certain job opportunities, refusing to hire or promote older workers, making decisions based on stereotypes about age, or providing more expensive benefits to younger workers.

Here are some examples:

- A computer software company hires mostly younger workers as programmers; although older workers apply, the hiring team assumes that they will have a harder time mastering the technology and staying on top of new developments.

- A company that provides human resources training has a team of trainers who are mostly in their 20s and 30s; the company wants a dynamic, energetic group of trainers, and so has screened out most of the older workers who have applied for training positions.

- A publishing company automatically stops paying for its workers' health insurance when they reach the age of 50. Because older workers are more likely to use their health benefits and therefore more expensive to insure, the company simply cuts them off the plan.

CAUTION

Benefits issues can be complicated. The law recognizes that certain benefits become more expensive as workers age (and become more likely to take advantage of them). Although employers cannot discriminate against older workers by offering them less-expensive benefits, they can often give older workers a different benefit plan, as long as the employer spends the same amount on benefits for older and younger workers. The rules on age discrimination in benefits are fairly complex; if you have questions about your company's benefits programs, talk to a lawyer.

Disability

Disability discrimination occurs when an employer makes job decisions based on an employee's disability, the fact that an employee has had a disability in the past, or the employer's perception that the employee is disabled. A disability is a physical or mental impairment that substantially limits a major life activity (such as the ability to walk, talk, see, hear, breathe, work, or take care of oneself), despite any medications or other measures the employee is using (such as a prosthetic limb or hearing aid) to remedy the effects of the condition. Courts tend not to categorically characterize certain conditions as disabilities; instead, they consider the effect of the particular condition on the particular employee.

EXAMPLE 1: Gerard has suffered from depression. Before he started taking medication, he was often unable to get out of bed in the morning and could not take care of himself. Once he began treatment, Gerard improved to the point where he now has a fairly active schedule and enjoys his life again. Because Gerard is not currently limited in his major life activities, he is probably not disabled under the law. However, if his employer decided not to promote him because he has suffered from depression in the past, that would be illegal discrimination based on the fact that Gerard has a history of disability.

EXAMPLE 2: Jamal sometimes stutters when he talks. Although the stutter is noticeable, Jamal can easily be understood when he speaks. Jamal probably doesn't have a legally recognized disability. However, if his employer decided not to promote him to a position that involved dealing with customers because of his stutter, that could be discrimination. Although Jamal does not have a disability, his employer is treating him as though he is substantially limited in his ability to speak.

Although a company may not discriminate based on an employee's disability, it is not legally required to hire or keep on employees who cannot do the job. If the employee cannot perform the job's basic functions, even with an accommodation, the employer is not required to hire or retain that employee.

Alcohol and Drugs

Scientists disagree over whether alcoholism and drug use are disabilities, diseases, habits, or something else entirely. As a legal matter, the issue is almost as murky. Here are the rules:

- **Alcohol.** Alcoholism is a legally recognized disability, which means that employers cannot fire or discipline workers simply because they are alcoholics (for example, because they attend Alcoholics Anonymous meetings or take medication to help control the urge to drink). However, an employer can fire or discipline an alcoholic worker for failing to meet work-related performance and behavior standards, even if the worker fails to meet these standards because of drinking. For example, a worker who shows up at the job inebriated or is habitually late to work because of heavy drinking the night before can be disciplined or fired.

- **Drugs.** Employees who currently use illegal drugs are not considered disabled. Nor are employees who misuse legal drugs, such as prescription painkillers or sleep aids. However, a worker who no longer uses drugs and has successfully completed (or is currently participating in) a supervised drug rehabilitation program is considered a person with a disability—which means that an employer may not make employment decisions based on the fact that a worker is or has been in rehab.

EXAMPLE: Jean suffered a spinal cord injury in a car accident and is paralyzed from the waist down. She uses a wheelchair to get around. Because Jean is substantially limited in the major life activity of walking, she has a legally recognized disability. Jean applies to work as a secretary in a law firm. She can perform all of the job's essential elements—typing, transcribing, answering phones, and so on—but her wheelchair won't fit under the desk. Raising the height of the desk is a reasonable accommodation that will allow her to do the job. Because Jean is qualified and can do the job with an accommodation, she is protected from discrimination.

Now suppose Jean applies to oversee a private campground. The job responsibilities include traveling through the campground twice a day to collect fees and check on campers, providing emergency first aid treatment to campers as necessary, and helping campers with problems that may arise (for example, getting a car out of a ditch or helping to pitch a tent). Jean may not be qualified for this job—her wheelchair cannot travel over the forested and rocky campground trails, and her ability to assist campers will be limited. The employer could legally decide not to hire Jean because she cannot perform the job's essential functions.

Religion

An employer may not make job decisions based on an employee's religious beliefs or practices. (Employers also have to make reasonable accommodations for employees' religious beliefs, in certain circumstances—see "Reasonable Accommodation," below.) Here are a few examples of religious discrimination:

- A group of friends who attend the same evangelical church go into business together; they refuse to hire anyone who does not share their faith.

- A company owner who is a self-proclaimed atheist tends not to promote religious employees to managerial positions; he believes that those who are religious have trouble exercising authority and thinking for themselves.

- A company that manufactures and distributes organic health supplies has a monthly company meeting, during which all employees must participate in a traditional Native American blessing ceremony.

Citizenship Status

An employer may not discriminate against employees based on their citizenship status, as long as they are legally authorized to work in the United States. Those who are legally authorized to work in this country include:

- citizens or nationals of the United States

- aliens lawfully admitted for permanent or temporary residence

- aliens admitted as refugees, and
- aliens granted asylum.

However, there are a couple of exceptions to this general rule. First, an employer may make job decisions based on an employee's citizenship status if federal law explicitly allows it (this exception generally applies only to government employers and some federal contractors). Second, an employer may give preference to a citizen or national of the United States over an equally qualified alien.

> **EXAMPLE:** Khalid, a refugee from Afghanistan, and Judy, a United States citizen, apply for a position at a blood bank. If both are equally qualified, the blood bank may hire Judy rather than Khalid simply because she is a citizen. However, if Khalid has better qualifications, the bank may not hire Judy based on its preference for a U.S. citizen.

Legal Claims of Discrimination

The classic legal theory of discrimination—sometimes called "disparate treatment"—is that an employer made a job decision based on a person's race, religion, or other protected characteristic. Most of the examples and the discussion above focus on disparate treatment discrimination, because it is by far the most common type of discrimination claim employees might make. You'll find more information on disparate treatment claims below.

However, there are two other types of discrimination claims:

- An employee who makes a "disparate impact" claim alleges that a company policy, practice, or requirement had the effect of discriminating against a protected group. For example, a woman might claim that an employer's failure to hire anyone who could not lift 60 pounds had the effect of discriminating against women. These claims are described in "Disparate Impact," below.

- An employee who brings a "reasonable accommodation" claim argues that the employer failed to make reasonable changes in work rules, schedules, practices, equipment, or the physical layout of the workplace that would have allowed him or her to do the job. For example, an employee who is hard of hearing might claim that an employer's failure to purchase TTY communications equipment made it impossible for her to be promoted to a sales position. These claims, which only apply in cases of disability or religious discrimination, are explained in "Reasonable Accommodation," below.

It's important to learn the legal standards for each of these theories so you can recognize when an employee is complaining about something that might be illegal. Keep in mind, however, that you may want to take some corrective action even if your investigation reveals that an employee might not be able to prove discrimination in court. For example, if your investigation reveals that a manager accused of race discrimination is not making decisions based on race, but is favoring employees who are his friends outside of work over their coworkers, you will probably want to address that manager's behavior.

Disparate Treatment

In a disparate treatment case, an employee claims to have been denied a job benefit or treated negatively because of a protected characteristic. Most disparate treatment claims involve firing, discipline, failure to promote, or inconsistent application of work rules.

The elements of a disparate treatment claim—what an employee must prove to win a lawsuit—depend on the employee's allegations. However, an employee usually has to start by showing that:

- he or she has a protected characteristic
- he or she was denied a job benefit or subjected to a negative job action (for example, did not receive a promotion, was not allowed to take time off, was disciplined more harshly than other employees, or was fired)
- he or she was qualified for the benefit (for example, the employee met the requirements for the promotion) or was undeserving of the negative job action (for example, the employee received a negative evaluation despite good performance), and

- employees who do not share the complaining employee's protected characteristic received the benefit or were not subjected to the negative job action (for example, male employees were not fired or a white person got the promotion).

Once the employee makes this showing, the employer must give a legitimate, nondiscriminatory reason for the decision the employee is challenging. To win the lawsuit, the employee must then show that the employer actually acted out of discriminatory motives (lawyers call this "pretext," because the employee must show that the employer's stated reason is just an excuse or pretext for discrimination).

Most of the disputes in discrimination lawsuits are over this last issue—why the employee was treated differently. To show that the company was motivated by bias, an employee generally must come up with something more than the simple fact of different treatment. For example, it isn't enough to show that a woman didn't get a promotion that went to a man: The female candidate must also show some evidence that the decision was motivated by discrimination.

Often, this evidence takes the form of comments by decision makers—for example, the supervisor who says, "I'd like to bring in a more youthful, dynamic group of salespeople" before choosing a younger employee over an older employee, or the manager who makes frequent sexist jokes, then promotes only men to be in charge of accounts.

An employee can also try to prove discrimination by showing that the company's explanation for an employment decision doesn't hold water. For example, a company promotes a white employee to a managerial position, stating that he had more supervisory experience than a Chinese-American employee who was not promoted. If the Chinese-American employee can show that he actually had more years of supervisory experience and better qualifications for the job, the company's rationale starts to look a little suspect.

If the employer's rationale is really weak and the evidence of different treatment is strong enough, an employee can win a discrimination lawsuit, even without any direct proof (such as discriminatory statements) that the employer was motivated by bias.

EXAMPLE: Curtis, who is African-American, claims that he was disciplined more harshly for horseplay than white employees. Curtis says that white employees who engaged in the same behavior received a verbal warning, while he was fired. The company contends that Curtis's behavior merited harsher discipline because he damaged company equipment (he accidentally knocked a postage meter off of a table and broke it), while the white employees to whom he compared himself did not.

However, Curtis's lawyer reviews company records and discovers that each of the four employees who have been fired for horseplay is African-American—and that the company has relatively few (about 5%) African-American employees. The lawyer also discovers that ten white employees have been disciplined for horseplay, but none received any discipline harsher than a verbal reprimand. What's more, three of these white employees damaged company equipment—one pushed a forklift off the loading dock in a drunken rampage after the company holiday party! In this situation, Curtis might win a discrimination claim, even without any evidence that his supervisor has made racist remarks or that the company has an explicit policy of only firing African-Americans. The company's explanation doesn't pass the blush test—and the numbers are pretty powerful evidence that something else is going on.

Disparate Impact

An employer may commit illegal discrimination even if it didn't intend to make job decisions based on race, gender, or another protected characteristic. Under the theory of disparate impact, an employer discriminates if it adopts a neutral policy that has a disproportionately negative effect on a protected group. For example, an employer that requires all employees to have a college degree may exclude more employees of certain races. Similarly, an employer that imposes a height or strength requirement for some positions may screen out disproportionately large numbers of women.

Of course, these types of requirements may be perfectly legitimate—for example, a person who works loading and unloading heavy packages in a warehouse, felling trees, or rescuing people from burning buildings must have some strength to do the job. Recognizing this, the law allows employers to defend against a disparate impact claim by showing that the rule or requirement is job related and necessary to the business.

EXAMPLE 1: Delivery Co. delivers packages across the country for its customers. Delivery Co. requires all of its warehouse workers to be able to lift and carry 50-pound packages. Because the warehouse workers spend a large portion of their day carrying heavy packages, this requirement is job related and necessary to the business, even if it screens out disproportionate numbers of women.

EXAMPLE 2: Delivery Co. also delivers letters, contracts, and blueprints for business clients. Some warehouse workers deal exclusively with these documents, while others handle the packages. If Delivery Co. applied its "50-pound rule" to all warehouse workers, it could face a sex discrimination claim. The document handlers don't have to lift heavy packages, so the rule is neither job related nor necessary to the business as applied to them.

Disparate impact claims arise often in the hiring context—for example, an employer that requires all applicants to take a written, standardized test might screen out disproportionate numbers of minority applicants, which could result in a disparate impact claim. Layoffs and other group firings could also result in a disparate impact claim if the employer uses firing criteria that result in a disproportionate number of protected workers losing their jobs. Generally, however, disparate impact claims are much less common than disparate treatment claims.

Slightly Different Rules Apply to Age Discrimination

Until the Supreme Court decided the case of *Smith v. City of Jackson,* 544 U.S. 228 (2005), it wasn't clear whether employees could sue for age discrimination based on disparate impact. The Supreme Court decided that these claims are allowed, but what the employer and employee have to prove is a bit different than for other types of discrimination claims.

In a disparate impact age discrimination case, the employee must point to a specific employment practice (such as a policy, screening test, or job requirement) that led to the disparate impact. And, the employer can escape liability if it can show that its practice was based on a reasonable factor other than age—even a factor that often correlates largely with age, such as seniority. Because of these different standards, it is generally thought to be more difficult for employees to win disparate impact claims based on age.

Reasonable Accommodation

In some situations, an employer may be required to take action based on an employee's protected characteristic in order to avoid discriminating. For example, in order to avoid discriminating against a disabled worker, an employer may need to install a handrail in the bathroom. This may sound counterintuitive—isn't it discriminatory to make decisions based on an employee's protected characteristic? Usually, the answer is yes. However, the law recognizes an exception to this general rule when an employee, because of religious beliefs or a disability, needs some changes to workplace rules or equipment in order to do the job.

Religion

Employers are legally required to reasonably accommodate an employee's religious practices unless doing so would create an "undue hardship." These claims often come up in regard to scheduling. For example, an employee whose religion prohibits working on the Sabbath might request a schedule change to take that day off. Religious accommodation claims might also involve dress codes—for example, an employee whose religion requires a particular style of dress might ask the employer to make an exception to its usual rules about employee grooming and attire.

> **EXAMPLE:** Alicia is a Seventh Day Adventist. She works as a hygienist in a large dental practice. Her employer has informed her that it plans to begin staying open on weekends in order to attract more clients. The employer says that every hygienist will be required to work either Saturday or Sunday each week. Alicia tells her employer that her religious beliefs prevent her from working on Saturdays. As an accommodation, the employer agrees that Alicia can work on Sundays and have Saturdays off every week.

An employer does not have to accommodate an employee if doing so would cause an undue hardship. Although the law isn't entirely clear about what constitutes an undue hardship, there are a few rules. If the accommodation would require more than ordinary administrative costs (for example, the cost of making a payroll or scheduling change), then the employer doesn't have to provide it. Similarly, an employer cannot be required to override a seniority system to accommodate an employee's religion—if granting the accommodation would deprive another employee of a transfer, shift preference, or other benefit, the employer doesn't have to provide it.

> **EXAMPLE 1:** Rory is a salesperson for an upscale furniture store. His employer institutes a dress code requiring all employees to wear professional attire and requiring male employees to wear their hair no longer than their shirt collars. Rory's religious beliefs prohibit him from cutting his hair. As long as Rory is neat and clean, his employer can't claim that accommodating his request for an exception to the dress code is an undue burden. It won't cost anything, and the employer will have a tough time proving that Rory's long hair will prevent him from presenting a professional image to customers.

EXAMPLE 2: Rachel works as a salesperson in a small antique store. During her shifts, she works with one other employee for most of the day; each works alone when the other takes a lunch break. She joins a religious group that believes in strict gender separation. The group's adherents are prohibited from interacting with persons of the opposite sex other than their spouse, their family, or clergy members. Rachel asks her employer to accommodate her religious beliefs by allowing her to serve only female customers. This accommodation would create an undue hardship: Her employer would have to either lose customers or hire another employee for the lunch hour, and Rachel's coworker would have to take on extra work.

Disability

Accommodating a disabled worker means providing assistance or making changes in the job or workplace that will enable the worker to do the job. For example, an employer might provide an accessible parking space, install ramps, or change the height of desktops and other facilities to accommodate a worker in a wheelchair; provide a quiet, distraction-free workspace for a worker with attention deficit disorder; or allow a worker who is fatigued from chemotherapy sessions to take more frequent breaks during the day.

It is the employee's responsibility to inform the employer of the disability and request a reasonable accommodation—the employer need not guess at what might help an employee do the job. Once an employee starts this conversation, however, the employer is legally required to brainstorm with the employee to figure out what kinds of accommodations might be effective and practical (the law calls this an employer's duty to engage in a "flexible interactive process"). Although an employer is not required to provide the precise accommodation a worker requests, it must work with the employee to try to come up with a reasonable solution.

However, your company is not required to provide an accommodation if doing so would cause the business "undue hardship." The law imposes more responsibility on employers to accommodate disabilities than religious beliefs—while any cost beyond an administrative burden creates an undue hardship in a religious accommodation claim, an employer can be legally obligated to shell out some money to accommodate a worker with a disability. In determining whether a particular accommodation creates an undue burden, courts consider:

- the cost of the accommodation
- the size and financial resources of the business
- the structure of the business, and
- the effect the accommodation would have on the business.

If the cost of the accommodation is significant when compared to the business's resources, the employer probably doesn't have to provide it. Similarly, if providing an accommodation would impose significant changes on the way the company does business, it isn't required.

EXAMPLE 1: Jon has attention deficit disorder. He finds it difficult to concentrate on a project if there is any background noise or activity. Jon works in the financing department of a large car dealership. He tells his employer of his disability and requests to be moved out of his cubicle near the showroom floor to an office with a door that closes, farther away from the wheeling and dealing. The company has some unused space upstairs and agrees to convert some of it into an office for Jon. This is a reasonable accommodation.

EXAMPLE 2: Gerrie works as a route supervisor for a company that sells and delivers bottled water. She arrives at work before anyone else, reviews the schedule for the day, and determines which driver will make each pickup and delivery. She then creates a route assignment for each driver, which the drivers receive when they arrive at work. Gerrie tells her employer that she suffers from depression and that the medication she takes for her condition makes her groggy in the morning. She asks if she can change her schedule and come in several hours later. Because the customers expect their water on time, and because the drivers cannot begin their deliveries until Gerrie gives them their route assignments, her requested accommodation probably poses an undue hardship. Allowing Gerrie to come in late would substantially disrupt the company's business.

Ten Steps to an Effective Discrimination Investigation

In discrimination cases, your investigation will almost always begin with an employee complaint. Unlike harassment or employee theft, discrimination cannot really be anonymous—and it always has a victim. You are most likely to hear about discrimination directly from the employee who feels mistreated. If that employee doesn't come forward, you may hear a complaint from another employee—for example, a coworker or supervisor who feels that an unfair decision was made.

CROSS-REFERENCE

Read Part I first. This section explains how to apply the basic investigation steps covered in Part I of this book to a discrimination investigation. If you haven't read Part I, you should do so before getting into this more specific material—the discussion that follows assumes that you are already familiar with basic investigation procedures.

Here are some of the ways you may learn of a discrimination claim:

- **Formal complaint.** An employee may use your company's complaint policy (see Appendix A) to complain of discrimination.

- **Performance evaluation.** An employee may raise a discrimination issue during a performance review. For example, the employee might believe that the evaluation itself is discriminatory ("I got rated poorly because my project was three days late, but my white coworker turned in his project three weeks late, and he was rated higher than me"). Or the employee might use the performance evaluation as a forum to raise discrimination concerns ("I'm wondering why I always seem to get the projects that don't involve client contact—and I'm concerned that it might have something to do with the fact that I'm older than the other account managers").

- **Exit interview.** An employee leaving the company may be more willing to be frank about problems within the company. For example, the employee might say that he is leaving because he believes he is discriminated against. Or, he may raise a more systemic issue—an African-American employee might say, "I finally decided to take another job offer because I noticed that only white employees are promoted to management positions, no matter how many employees of color apply. I felt that I would never move up the ladder here."

- **Administrative charge.** Before an employee can bring a lawsuit alleging discrimination, he or she must file charges with the EEOC or a similar state fair employment practices agency. If an employee (or former employee) files an administrative charge, your company will be notified and receive a copy of the charge. In most cases, your company will also be asked to respond to the charge and give its side of the story. This means you'll have to investigate, so you'll know whether you need to take action and what to tell the agency.

The Government May Investigate, Too

If an employee files a charge of discrimination with a government agency, that agency may perform its own investigation. The agency will almost always ask your company to respond to the charge. However, the agency may also ask you to hand over personnel files, performance evaluations, and other documents; to allow the agency investigator to visit your company; and to make employees available for interviews with the agency investigator. If your company is embroiled in an agency investigation—especially one that involves more than one complaining employee—you should consult with an attorney. What you do and say during the investigation should be carefully choreographed, to avoid giving the complaining employee fodder for a lawsuit.

To learn more about agency investigations, check out the EEOC's fact sheet, "EEOC Investigations—What an Employer Should Know." You can find it—as well as many other helpful resources on discrimination and harassment—on the EEOC's website, www.eeoc.gov.

- **Letter from an attorney.** This is possibly the least popular way to find out about a discrimination claim. If an employee asks a lawyer for help in dealing with potential discrimination, your first notice of the problem may come in an envelope with an "Esquire" in the return address. Many lawyers will recount the facts as their clients have related them, then ask your company to respond within a certain period of time. If your company is the unfortunate recipient of one of these letters, investigating is a must; you should also bring in your company's lawyer to help you decide how to respond.

Once your company is aware of a claim of workplace discrimination, you are ready to use the ten basic investigation steps, as described below.

Decide Whether to Investigate

When dealing with discrimination claims, an employer should generally err on the side of investigating. The Supreme Court has held, in the case of *Kolstad v. American Dental Association*, 527 U.S. 526 (1999), that an employer may not be liable for punitive damages for discrimination by managers and supervisors, as long as the employer makes good-faith efforts to prevent discrimination. (Punitive damages are damages intended to punish the employer for especially egregious conduct, to deter future discrimination—they often make up the largest part of a damages award in a discrimination case, sometimes totaling two, three, or ten times the amount of other damages awarded in a case.)

The Court didn't specify exactly what constitutes good-faith efforts, but it suggested that having an antidiscrimination policy and responding appropriately to complaints of discrimination—by performing an investigation and taking disciplinary action against wrongdoers—could protect an employer from these types of damages. In light of this decision, it makes sense to investigate most claims of discrimination.

However, not every claim of discrimination is a claim of *illegal* discrimination. Discrimination is only illegal if it is based on a protected characteristic, as explained above. Discrimination on other bases—for example, because of an employee's hair color, fashion sense, or sense of humor—is not illegal.

Discrimination or Harassment?

Sometimes, it can be hard to tell whether an employee is complaining of discrimination or harassment. As a legal matter, harassment is a form of discrimination. Like discrimination, harassment is mistreatment based on a person's protected characteristic. While discrimination most often results in a negative job action (such as losing a promotion, getting fired, or being denied a job benefit), harassment can consist solely of demeaning behavior—for example, racist jokes, sexual innuendo, or repeated negative comments about an employee's disability or ethnicity.

In some harassment cases, however, an employee complains that the harassment resulted in a negative job action. For example, in a sexual harassment case, an employee may allege that she was denied a promotion or fired because she refused to submit to sexual demands.

If you get confused about whether an employee is complaining about discrimination or harassment, take heart: The way you classify the claim is not as important as what you do about it. In either situation, you will be looking at whether an employee was mistreated because of a protected characteristic. And in either case, your job will be to figure out what happened, document your findings, and take action to make sure that the mistreatment stops.

EXAMPLE: Yvonne claims that she wasn't promoted to a customer service position because she favors outlandish outfits in loud colors. She says this is unfair because her attire has nothing to do with her ability to serve customers. Yvonne may be right and she may be wrong, but she has not been discriminated against. No law prohibits an employer from making decisions based on an employee's clothing style, per se.

However, if Yvonne claims that she didn't receive the promotion because she wears hijab (a body covering or head scarf worn by some Muslims), she could have a discrimination claim. Although the employer's decision was based on her clothing, that clothing is strongly associated with a particular religion and ethnicity. Therefore, the employer's decision could be discriminatory.

> **CAUTION**
>
> **Remember state laws.** Many states prohibit discrimination on bases that are not covered by federal law—such as sexual orientation, marital status, or weight. Check the chart in Appendix D—and contact your state fair employment practices agency—to find out your state's rules.

If you decide that an employee has not alleged illegal discrimination, you still might want to investigate. After all, you can't say for sure that a judge or jury will agree with you: Even if a decision looks legitimate to you, it might look like discrimination to someone else. And, even if you're fairly certain that your company is on safe ground from a legal perspective, you may still want to take some action. For example, say that an employee alleges that his manager allows workers who play or cheer for the company's softball team to leave early once a week to attend games, while everyone else has to be at their desks until five o'clock. Discrimination on the basis of softball? Not from a legal perspective, but it may be a poor management practice—one you'll want to look into and possibly stop.

Take Immediate Action, If Necessary

Before you start your inquiry, you will have to decide whether some immediate action is necessary to prevent further incidents and to protect the integrity of your investigation. You should consider taking action before the investigation if:

- **The accused employee continues to make managerial decisions.** For example, if the vice president who approves promotions is accused of discriminating against older workers, you might not want the VP to fill any new vacancies until the investigation is complete.

- **Tension between the accused employee and the complaining employee has escalated significantly.** In this situation, you may have to change reporting relationships until you sort things out.

- **The alleged victim and/or witnesses appear to be intimidated by the accused employee.** This might be the case, for example, if the complaining employee says that her supervisor threatened retaliation if she complained.

Whatever course you take, you must be very careful to avoid retaliation (or the appearance of retaliation). The Supreme Court recently clarified that any action that could deter a reasonable employee from complaining of discrimination may constitute retaliation, depending on the facts of the case. (*Burlington Northern & Santa Fe Railway Co. v. White*, 126 S. Ct. 2405 (2006).) If you separate employees by placing the worker who complained on administrative leave or by moving that worker to another shift or a different work area, you could be accused of retaliating.

Time Off for the Complaining Employee

If an employee who complains of discrimination wants to take some time off, find out why. If the employee has been threatened with retaliation or is being shunned by coworkers for making a complaint, these are facts you need to know. Also, make sure the employee doesn't feel forced to take time off—explain that retaliation is prohibited and that you will investigate as quickly as possible.

If an employee simply wants to take some time to catch his or her breath, you can arrange for a brief period of paid leave. However, make sure that the employee will be available to participate in the investigation.

Your safest strategy in these circumstances is to move the accused employee or suspend him or her with pay until you complete the investigation. When you tell the accused employee about the change, emphasize that it's temporary, that no conclusions have been made about the truth or falsity of the allegations, and that the company does not view the transfer or suspension as punitive. If you must take an immediate action like this, complete the investigation as quickly as possible to minimize workplace disruption.

> **CAUTION**
>
> **Don't suspend workers without pay.** From a legal standpoint, suspending exempt, salaried employees—those who are not entitled to overtime pay for working extra hours—without pay while you investigate violates wage and hour laws. And even though you can suspend hourly, nonexempt workers without pay, it's not a good idea. A suspension without pay is punitive: It improperly signals that you have made up your mind about the allegations before you've even begun to investigate. A worker who is suspended without pay will probably be angry about it—and if the allegations are false, that anger may well provide the fuel for a lawsuit. And unpaid suspensions can be an administrative hassle, as they require you to interrupt your usual payroll system. The wages you shell out to a temporarily suspended employee will be a small price to pay to avoid these problems.

Choose the Investigator

You can find tips on choosing the right investigator in Chapter 2. However, there are a couple of additional things to consider when choosing an investigator for a discrimination claim.

Impartiality

An employee who alleges discrimination believes that he or she was treated unfairly—that other workers were favored for illegitimate reasons. It follows, therefore, that the person who investigates such a claim must be objective and impartial—and be perceived in the workplace as objective and impartial.

Of course, this is an important consideration in any investigation, but it is especially crucial when investigating discrimination. Make sure you (or your chosen investigator) have no connection to the employees involved, no role in the alleged discriminatory acts, and no history of problems or controversy on issues of race, gender, and so on.

EXAMPLE: Fiona alleges that her employer does not promote women to higher levels of management; she says this "glass ceiling" has kept her from getting several promotions. The company is considering asking Brian to investigate Fiona's claims. Brian has no connection to Fiona or to the promoting supervisors, and he doesn't participate in promotion decisions. However, Brian sits on the board of directors of an exclusive, all-male country club, and has been interviewed in local papers defending the club's membership policy. Even if Brian could investigate Fiona's claims impartially, he is the wrong choice as an investigator. Fiona and other women he interviews could reasonably question his ability to look fairly at a sex discrimination claim, and he wouldn't have much credibility if the company had to defend his investigation in a lawsuit.

When to Use an Outside Investigator

In some situations, it makes sense to bring in an outside investigator. Consider hiring a professional in these situations:

- Widespread discrimination is alleged—for example, that the company never promotes women, fires disproportionate numbers of older workers, or bends the rules only for white workers.

- Discrimination by a high-ranking company official (such as the CEO, president, or chairman) is alleged.

- An employee challenges a company practice or policy as having a disparate impact on a particular group (see "Disparate Impact," above)—these cases require an investigator to review statistics and information about lots of workers and potentially affect a large number of people.

- The charges have been publicized in the community and/or media.

- An employee has filed a charge of discrimination with the EEOC or a similar state fair employment practices agency.

- An employee has hired a lawyer or filed a lawsuit.

Plan the Investigation

Because discrimination investigations almost always begin with an employee complaint, you'll have a natural starting point for your investigation planning. And because discrimination complaints will almost always require an investigator to dig deeply into personnel files and other written records, you should spend some time gathering the documents you will need to make your decisions.

Examine the Allegations

Your first planning step is to carefully review the complaint. Consider these issues:

- **Who complained?** What is the employee's protected characteristic? Did the employee allege that other employees were also discriminated against?

- **The nature of the complaint.** What type of discrimination is alleged? Does the employee claim that he or she was discriminated against, or is the employee challenging a company policy or practice that affects a group of employees? Did the employee request a reasonable accommodation for a disability or a religious practice? If so, what was the accommodation? What effect would the accommodation have had on the company, and what would it have cost?

- **Who is accused of discrimination?** Is it a high-ranking company official? Does the employee accuse this person of making bigoted comments and holding biased views, or is the employee complaining of a single personnel action? Is the employee accusing one person of discrimination, or is the charge leveled at a group of people or the entire company?

- **The employment decision at issue.** Is the employee alleging a failure to promote, improper firing, unfair application of workplace rules and procedures, or failure to accommodate a disability or religious practice? Who is responsible for making the decision complained of?

- **Has the employee named any witnesses?**

Based on your answers to these questions, you can begin to structure your investigation and determine what documents and other evidence to gather, whom to interview, and what questions to ask.

> ### ⓘ CAUTION
>
> **Courts caution employers to cast a wide net in discrimination investigations.** Some courts and juries have penalized employers for inadequate investigations of discrimination. The flaw in these investigations is often the employer's failure to look at the big picture: whether the company treats employees who share the complaining employee's characteristic differently than those who don't. If an employee alleges that Latinos are not promoted, or that women are denied work benefits (such as a company car) that are granted to men, for example, you will have to look beyond the complaining employee and the accused wrongdoer to examine company-wide practices. In these examples, your work might include examining which employees were promoted and which were not, or how many company cars have been issued and to whom.

Documents and Other Evidence

Discrimination investigations often rely heavily on documents. To adequately examine an employee's allegation that an unfair decision was made, you'll need to find out the basis for the decision and what information the decision maker relied on. Generally, this means you'll spend some time looking at personnel files, performance evaluations, employee qualifications, and other paperwork. Particularly if an employee alleges that another worker was unfairly selected for promotion, you will have to closely examine evaluations, recommendations, work samples, and other evidence of performance to figure out whether there was a legitimate, business-related reason for choosing one employee over the other.

In most situations, you will also want to look at similar employment decisions made by the accused employee in the past, to see if you can find a pattern (or lack of one). For example, if an employee alleges that he wasn't promoted because of his age, you should look at previous promotion decisions made by the same supervisor. Has the supervisor consistently promoted younger workers, or have older workers been promoted in the past?

Here are some documents that might be relevant in a discrimination investigation:

- Company policies, including policies on discrimination and policies on the specific job action in question. For example, if an employee alleges that he was unfairly denied a promotion, you'll want to examine any company policies or other written materials that describe how promotion decisions should be made. If an employee claims to have been disciplined unfairly, you'll want to look at company discipline procedures.

- Personnel files, including the files of the complaining employee and the accused employee. If the employee complains of being denied a benefit, you also may want to examine the personnel file of any employee who received the benefit, to figure out whether the decision was justified.

- Performance records, if the decision was (or should have been) based on employee performance. For example, in a promotion case, you'll need to examine the work records of the employee who was denied the promotion and the employee who received it.

- Attendance records or sign-in sheets from antidiscrimination training.

- Any other records related to the employment decision at issue. For example, if an employee complains that he was disciplined more harshly for unexcused absences than other employees, you will want to examine attendance records to find out how many times each employee was absent.

Interviews

Once you've finished your investigation planning, you'll have some ideas about which employees you should interview. Start by interviewing the employee who complained. Next, move on to the employee (often a supervisor or manager) accused of discrimination. Then, interview any witnesses, others who were involved in the contested decision, other employees who received the benefit the complaining employee was denied, and/or other employees who share the complaining employee's protected characteristic and report to the same supervisor (to find out whether they feel that they've been treated fairly).

Start every interview with some opening remarks to set the employee at ease, explain the process, and answer questions. You should also distribute a written notice regarding confidentiality and other issues (you'll find a copy in Appendix B and on the CD-ROM). Next, proceed to your specific questions, remembering to follow up on any new information raised by the witness's responses. Close the interview by letting the witness know what will happen next and inviting the witness to come to you with any concerns or additional information. And conduct follow-up interviews if any new information comes to light.

Getting Started

Some of your opening comments will be the same, no matter whom you're interviewing. Some of them will be geared more specifically towards a complaining employee, an accused employee, or a witness. The opening statement you make to every person you interview should cover these points:

- **The purpose of the meeting.** The information you give here will depend on whom you're interviewing. You can tell the complaining employee that the company will be investigating the complaint and that the purpose of the meeting is to gather as much information as possible. Tell the accused employee that a complaint has been made, that you're investigating, and that your role is to gather as much information as possible. A witness can simply be told that you're investigating a workplace problem and you believe the witness might have some relevant information.

- **The investigation process.** Explain that the company will be investigating the problem and interviewing other employees and will take appropriate steps if it finds that misconduct occurred.

- **Confidentiality.** Emphasize that you expect the employee to keep the investigation confidential and that talking about the investigation to other employees could be grounds for discipline. Explain that you will maintain confidentiality to the extent possible, although it will be necessary to reveal certain details in order to conduct thorough interviews and reach a decision.

- **Retaliation.** Explain that retaliation is prohibited and that the company will take immediate steps to discipline anyone who retaliates based on the complaint or investigation. Ask the employee to come to you with any concerns about retaliation.

- **Questions or concerns.** Ask whether the employee has any questions or concerns about the process.

When you interview the accused employee, emphasize that the company has not reached any decisions about what happened. Explain that you are interested in hearing what everyone has to say before making a decision or taking any action. Because you will probably have to reveal the name of the complaining employee (as explained below), spend some extra time discussing retaliation: what it is, that the company prohibits it, and that employees who engage in retaliation will be subject to discipline. Although the accused employee will probably want to know the allegations right away, you are better off postponing this discussion until later in the interview, after you have had a chance to gather some important background information. Explain that the accused employee will have the opportunity to hear and respond to the allegations before the interview is over.

For witnesses, your opening remarks can be brief. The witness doesn't need to know who complained, who is accused, or what the specific allegations are. Once you have explained that you are investigating a workplace problem and talked about confidentiality and retaliation, you can begin asking your questions.

Questions for the Complaining Employee

The questions you ask the complaining employee should focus on getting all of the details about the job action or decision at issue, as well as the employee's reasons for believing that the action was discriminatory. Your questions should be geared towards the specific employment decision in question. Here are some sample questions to consider when investigating a complaint that the employee was passed over for some job benefit, a complaint that the employee was fired or otherwise disciplined, and a reasonable accommodation complaint.

SAMPLE QUESTIONS

Employee Did Not Receive Benefit

- What benefit were you denied [for example, a promotion, a job transfer or schedule change, time off work, a raise]?

- Did you have to apply for the benefit? If so, when and how did you do so? If not, did you make it known that you wanted the benefit? How, when, and to whom?

- Do you know who made the decision to deny you this benefit? Do you report to this person? If so, when did you begin reporting to this person? Describe your work relationship to this person.

- How did you find out that you were denied the benefit? Who told you, if anyone? What did that person say? How did you respond? When did this happen?

- Have other employees received this benefit, either now or in the past? Did any employees receive this benefit instead of you? What are their names?

- [If the employee is alleging that another employee improperly received the benefit:] Do you believe that you should have received the benefit instead? Why?

- Why do you believe that this decision was based on your [protected characteristic] rather than your qualifications?

- Aside from this decision, is there anything else that leads you to believe you were discriminated against? Have you heard anyone make comments about [employee's protected characteristic]? If so, who made them, when, and what did they say?

- How has not receiving this benefit affected you? Have you had to spend any money, or lost potential income, because you did not receive the benefit?

- How would you like to see this situation resolved?

- Do you know of anyone who might have information about this decision?

- Do you know of any documents relating to your complaint?

- Is there anything else you'd like to tell me?

SAMPLE QUESTIONS

Employee Was Disciplined or Fired

- When were you fired or disciplined?

- Who told you about the firing or discipline? What reasons did that person give for the firing or discipline? What did you say in response, if anything? Do you know of any documents relating to this discussion?

- Do you know who made the decision to discipline or fire you? Is that person your supervisor? If so, for how long have you reported to that person? Describe your work relationship with that person.

- Do you know of anyone else who was involved in the decision to discipline or fire you? Describe your work relationship with that person.

- Were you told that you were fired or disciplined because of misconduct, performance problems, or other work-related reasons? Describe any incidents that were given as the basis for your firing or discipline. Are these allegations accurate? If not, why do you believe you were accused of these things?

- Do you know of others who were not fired or disciplined for the same misconduct or behavior? What are their names? When did these incidents occur?

- Why do you believe the decision to discipline or fire you was based on your [protected characteristic]?

- Aside from this decision, is there anything else that leads you to believe you were discriminated against? Have you heard anyone make comments about [employee's protected characteristic]? If so, who made them, when, and what did they say?

- How has being disciplined or fired affected you? Have you had to spend any money, or lost potential income, as a result?

- How would you like to see this situation resolved?

- Do you know of anyone who might have information about this decision?

- Do you know of any documents relating to this decision?

- Is there anything else you'd like to tell me?

SAMPLE QUESTIONS

Employee Was Denied an Accommodation

- Did you request an accommodation? If so, what did you request, when, and from whom? If not, did you make your need for an accommodation known in some other way? How, when, and to whom?

- Why did you request an accommodation? How would the accommodation you requested have assisted you?

- [If employee is disabled:] What is your disability? How does your disability affect your everyday activities? Describe the essential functions of your job. Are you able to perform these essential functions? How would the accommodation have helped you in this regard?

- [If employee requested an accommodation for religious reasons:] What is your religion? What are the religious beliefs or practices that require a modification to our usual work rules or practices? How would the accommodation have helped you in this regard?

- How did you find out that your request for an accommodation was denied? Did you receive written notice? If you were told in person, who told you? What did that person say? Do you report to this person? If so, for how long? Describe your work relationship to this person.

- Do you believe your requested accommodation was reasonable? What do you think the company would have had to do to provide the accommodation? If you know, approximately what would the accommodation have cost?

- How has the denial of your request affected you? Have you had to spend any money, or lost potential income, because you did not receive the accommodation?

- How would you like to see this situation resolved?

- Do you know of anyone who might have information about this decision?

- Do you know of any documents relating to this decision?

- Is there anything else you'd like to tell me?

Questions for the Accused Employee

The questions you ask the accused employee should focus on the reasons for the challenged decision. Because discrimination complaints usually challenge a job decision or action, the accused employee is almost always a manager (in other words, someone with the authority to make those decisions or take those actions). You will want to explore the accused employee's work history, treatment of other workers, and similar decisions or actions taken in the past. Here are some sample questions geared towards the type of discrimination alleged.

> **CAUTION**
>
> **You must allow the accused employee to respond to the allegations.** Some investigators are so eager to keep the interview civil—or to protect the complaining employee's privacy—that they never actually confront the accuser with the allegations. This is a big mistake, one that could undermine the legitimacy of the entire investigation. Courts have held that accused employees who never learn precisely what they are accused of haven't had a fair opportunity to tell their side of the story, to offer the names of relevant witnesses, or to explain why the complaining employees might have made the accusations. You don't necessarily have to say who complained, but you should say whom the employee is accused of discriminating against. And don't worry about privacy concerns—you have a very compelling business reason for revealing this information.

SAMPLE QUESTIONS

Employee Did Not Receive a Benefit

- Do you supervise any employees? What are their names? For how long have you been a supervisor/manager? Have you had any managerial training? If so, when, for what, and who conducted the training?

- Do your responsibilities include deciding who gets [the benefit at issue—for example, promotions, raises, time off]? How do you make these decisions? Are there company guidelines or policies on the topic? What criteria do you consider? How often do you decide whether to [promote someone, give someone a raise, grant a request for time off]?

- Do you supervise [the complaining employee]? For how long have you worked together, and in what positions? Describe your work relationship.

- Did you decide [the action at issue—for example, not to give the complaining employee a raise, who would be promoted to account manager, not to give the complaining employee time off]? If not, who made this decision? If you made the decision, did anyone else have input? Who?

- Explain the basis for your decision. What did you consider? Are there any documents that you looked at? Did you create any documents, notes, or memos in the process of making the decision?

- [If the complaining employee alleges failure to promote:] Who received the promotion? Why? Why did you decide not to promote [the complaining employee]?

- [If the complaining employee alleges denial of another benefit:] Have you given other employees this benefit [for example, time off, raises, or shift changes]? If so, what are their names, and why did they receive the benefit? Why did you deny [the complaining employee] the benefit? How is [the complaining employee]'s situation different from that of the employee(s) who received the benefit?

- Describe the qualifications for the position or the criteria for receiving the benefit. Did [the complaining employee] meet those criteria or qualifications? If not, in what ways?

SAMPLE QUESTIONS

Employee Did Not Receive a Benefit (cont'd.)

- Who told [the complaining employee] of your decision? If it was you, what did you say? How did [the complaining employee] respond? If someone else relayed your decision, who? Do you know what that person said? Why didn't you tell [the complaining employee] yourself?

- [The complaining employee] thinks [he or she] should have received the benefit because [state the complaining employee's reasons]. Did you consider that when making your decision? If so, why did [the complaining employee] not receive the benefit? If not, why not?

- [The complaining employee] thinks your decision was based, at least in part, on [complaining employee's protected characteristic]. What is your response to that? Can you think of any reason why [the complaining employee] might think that?

- Do you know of anyone who might have information about this decision?

- Do you know of any documents relating to this decision?

- Is there anything else you'd like to tell me?

SAMPLE QUESTIONS

Employee Was Disciplined or Fired

- Do you supervise any employees? What are their names? For how long have you been a supervisor/manager? Have you had any managerial training? If so, when, for what, and who conducted the training?

- Do your responsibilities include deciding whom to discipline and fire? How do you make these decisions? Are there company guidelines or policies on the topic? What criteria do you consider?

- [If the complaint is about a termination:] How many employees have you fired in the past few years? What are their names? Why were they fired? Were there other employees that you considered firing? If so, what are their names, and why did you decide not to fire them?

- [If the complaint is about discipline:] How many employees have you disciplined in the past few years? What are their names, and for what were they disciplined? Were there other employees that you considered disciplining? If so, what are their names, and why did you decide not to discipline them?

- Do you supervise [the complaining employee]? For how long have you worked together, and in what positions? Describe your work relationship.

- Who decided to fire or discipline [the complaining employee]? If it was your decision, did anyone else have input?

- Why did you fire or discipline [the complaining employee]? Tell me every factor you considered in reaching this decision. Did you rely on any documents in making your decision? Did you prepare any documents about the decision?

- Have you fired or disciplined other employees for similar conduct? Who, when, and for what reasons? Are there any documents relating to these decisions? What is the [complaining employee's protected characteristic—for example, race, age, or religion] of each of these employees?

- Did you tell [the complaining employee] that he or she would be disciplined or fired? If not, who did? Do you know what that person told [the complaining employee]? Why didn't you tell [the complaining employee] yourself? If so, what did you say? How did [the complaining employee] respond?

SAMPLE QUESTIONS

Employee Was Disciplined or Fired (cont'd.)

- Was the employee fired or disciplined for misconduct, poor performance, or other workplace problems? Does the employee have a history of these kinds of problems? Are these problems reflected in the employee's performance evaluations? Have you ever disciplined this employee before for the same problem? If so, when, what did you say, and how did the employee respond?

- [If the employee was fired:] Has the employee been replaced? By whom? What is this person's [complaining employee's protected characteristic—for example, race or national origin]?

- [The complaining employee] believes [he or she] should not have been disciplined or fired because [give the complaining employee's reasons]. Did you consider that in reaching your decision? Why or why not?

- [The complaining employee] believes that [complaining employee's protected characteristic] played a role in your decision. What is your response to that? Can you think of any reason why [the complaining employee] might think that?

- Do you know of anyone who might have information about this decision?

- Do you know of any documents relating to this decision?

- Is there anything else you'd like to tell me?

SAMPLE QUESTIONS

Employee Was Denied an Accommodation

- Do you supervise any employees? What are their names? For how long have you been a supervisor/manager? Have you had any managerial training? If so, when, for what, and who conducted the training?

- Do your responsibilities include deciding whether to change work rules, schedules, or other workplace issues to accommodate an employee's disability or religious practices? How do you make these decisions? Are there company guidelines or policies on the topic? What criteria do you consider? How often do you decide whether to accommodate an employee's disability or religious practice?

SAMPLE QUESTIONS

Employee Was Denied an Accommodation (cont'd.)

- Do you supervise [the complaining employee]? For how long have you worked together, and in what positions? Describe your work relationship.

- Did [the complaining employee] ever ask you to make a workplace change to accommodate a disability or religious practice? If so, what did the employee request? How did you respond? If not, has [the complaining employee] ever spoken to you about a disability or religious practice? What did [the complaining employee] say, and how did you respond? Has [the complaining employee] ever asked you to make a workplace change for any reason? What was the change? How did you respond?

- If a request for accommodation was made, did you deny the request? What did you consider in making your decision? What would the company have had to do in order to fulfill the request? What would the request have cost the company? Did you discuss the request with anyone else? Did you get input from anyone else in making your decision?

- Did you tell the employee that the request was denied? If so, what did you say, and how did the employee respond? If not, who told the employee? What did that person say, and how did the employee respond, if you know? Why didn't you tell the employee yourself?

- Did you offer the employee an alternative accommodation? If so, what did you offer, and how did the employee respond? What would the company have had to do in order to provide the alternative accommodation? What would the request have cost the company? If not, can you think of any other accommodations that would meet the employee's needs?

- Do you know of anyone who might have information about this decision?

- Do you know of any documents relating to this decision?

- Is there anything else you'd like to tell me?

Questions for Witnesses

When questioning witnesses, your goal is to gather information without giving too much away. To plan your questions, consider who suggested the witness and why. Did the witness play a role in the employment decision at issue? Did the witness see or hear allegedly discriminatory conduct or statements? Did the witness receive a benefit that was denied the complaining employee, or was the witness otherwise treated differently than the complaining employee? Is the witness another possible victim of discrimination?

Start by explaining, in very general terms, why the witness is being interviewed—that you are investigating a workplace problem and you believe the witness might have information that will help you figure out what happened. Then, move into questions that will help you figure out how the witness fits into the picture (if at all). Finally, find out what the witness knows. Start with general questions like these:

SAMPLE QUESTIONS

General questions:

- How long have you worked at the company? What positions have you held? What is your current position? What are your job responsibilities? To whom do you report? Who reports to you?

- Do you work with [the complaining employee] or [the accused employee]? How would you describe their work relationship with each other?

- [Your next questions will depend on what the witness said, did, or knows. Here are some examples.]

SAMPLE QUESTIONS

For a witness who played a role in the decision:

- Are you responsible for deciding or participating in decisions about [the decision at issue—for example, who gets promoted, who gets fired, whether the company will grant an employee's request for an accommodation]? How many such decisions do you make or participate in each year? What is the process for making these decisions? What do you consider in making these decisions?

- Were you involved in the decision to [fire, promote, deny time off to] [the complaining employee]? What was your role? What did you consider in making this decision? Whom did you talk to about the decision? Did you consider any documents in reaching this decision? Did you create any documents?

- Have you been involved in any previous decisions to [deny time off, promote, fire] an employee at the company? What are the names of these employees? What did you decide? Why?

- What role did [the accused employee] play in this decision?

- [The complaining employee] believes that [protected characteristic, such as race or age] played a role in this decision. How do you respond to that? Can you think of any reason why [the complaining employee] might think that?

- [The complaining employee] believes the decision was unfair because [give reason, such as he had more seniority than the employee who was promoted, or she was told she would receive a raise by February]. Did you consider that in making your decision? Why or why not?

SAMPLE QUESTIONS

For a witness who may have seen or heard something:

- Describe your typical workday.

- Has [the complaining employee] ever spoken to you about [the accused employee]? Has [the accused employee] ever spoken to you about [the complaining employee]?

- Have you seen any interactions between [the complaining employee] and [the accused employee] that made you uncomfortable? Describe them to me.

- [If the witness may have seen or heard the incident, ask questions to figure out whether the witness was there and what happened.]

- Have you ever heard [the accused employee] make any comment about [the complaining employee's protected characteristic, such as national origin or disability]? If so, what did the accused employee say?

SAMPLE QUESTIONS

For a witness who received the benefit:

- Did you recently [apply for a promotion, receive a raise]? When? Who made the decision? Did you have to apply? If so, what materials did you submit?

- Do you know of any other employees who applied for the benefit?

- When did you learn that you would receive the benefit? Who told you? What did that person say? How did you respond?

- Do you know what the qualifications or other criteria are for receiving this benefit? Do you meet those qualifications or criteria?

No matter what your reason for interviewing the witness, make sure to ask whether the witness knows of anyone else who might have information about the complaint or knows of any documents or other evidence relating to the complaint.

Closing the Interview

Once you have finished your questions, review your notes with the person you interviewed. Make sure you got everything right and that your notes include all of the important details; have the witness sign your notes or a written summary of the interview. Ask the employee not to discuss the complaint or the investigation with any coworkers. Remind the employee (especially the accused employee) that retaliation is prohibited. And, ask the employee to come to you immediately with any new information.

This is all you have to tell witnesses. When you close interviews with the complaining and accused employees, let them know what will happen next. Tell them that you'll interview them again if any important new information comes up.

Follow-Up Interviews

If any new information comes up during your investigation, you should conduct follow-up interviews with the complaining or accused employee. Both employees should have the opportunity to respond to new allegations or defenses to make sure that you have a complete understanding of the facts when you make your decision and to give you the opportunity to gauge credibility. It is especially important to let the accused employee know of any additional allegations that come up during the investigation. If you don't, the accused employee may claim, in court, that he or she was denied the opportunity to respond—and, therefore, that the investigation was not thorough or fair.

EXAMPLE: Roy claims that Anna unfairly denied him a promotion because of his race and national origin (Asian). You interview Roy and Anna, focusing primarily on the promotion decision. You also interview Rachel, a witness whom Roy suggests because she has told him that she believes Anna is biased against Asians. Rachel tells you that she and Anna used to be friends outside of work until one night when Anna, after a few drinks, made a number of racist comments about Asians and Asian-Americans, including Roy and other Asians who report to her. One of the comments, according to Rachel, was "Asians think they're better than everyone else—well, they're not going to get any positions of power in this company while I've got anything to say about it." Before you wrap up the investigation, you should go back to Anna to confront her with these allegations and allow her to respond.

Gather Documents and Other Evidence

Most discrimination claims allege that the employer made an unfair job decision—that is, a decision that was based on the employee's characteristic, rather than appropriate work considerations (such as performance, ability, skills, and so on). Your job as an investigator is to find out the real reason for the allegedly discriminatory decision, and this will require you to carefully review employment-related records to see whether they support—or contradict—the accused employee's stated rationale.

You should always start by gathering up any relevant policies (such as an antidiscrimination policy, or a policy relating to the job decision in question) and the personnel files of the complaining employee and the accused employee. These records should yield quite a bit of information, including:

- **Whether company policies spell out a procedure for making the decision in question.** For example, if an employee complains that she was unfairly denied an annual raise, examine workplace policies on raises (if there are any). Are employees promised an annual raise? Does the policy list the criteria for awarding or denying raises?

- **The complaining employee's work history at your company.** Has the employee had a history of performance problems? Has the employee been promoted repeatedly, received raises, or otherwise been rewarded? For how long has the employee reported to the accused employee? Examine the employee's evaluations and other work records during that time—are they generally consistent with the employee's work history, or do the records reveal a change in treatment? Has the employee complained of discrimination before? If so, how were those incidents handled?

- **The accused employee's history at your company.** Has anyone else ever accused this person of discrimination? If so, how were those situations resolved? What are the accused employee's qualifications as a supervisor? Has the employee received training or coaching in that area? Who else reports to the accused employee? What similar decisions has the accused employee made in the past—for example, who else has been promoted or denied a raise?

Once you have examined these records, you will want to look at documents relating to the employment decision in question. For example, if an employee complains that she was not promoted because of her gender, you should gather up any documents relating to the promotion decision—these might include the applications of everyone who applied for the position, any other written materials (such as performance evaluations, work samples, or written tests) the supervisor considered in deciding whom to promote, and any written notes the supervisor took when interviewing candidates.

After you've reviewed documents relating to the decision that is the subject of the complaint, you'll want to widen your net to look at similar decisions made by the same decision maker in the past. Using the same example, if a supervisor is accused of sex discrimination for failing to promote a woman, you'll want to look at other promotions by the same supervisor. If the supervisor has never promoted a woman even though plenty of qualified women have applied, you'll want to follow up on that. Similarly, if the supervisor has a history of promoting women, that might lead you to believe that the explanation lies in something other than the complaining employee's gender.

Evaluate the Evidence

In many discrimination cases, everyone agrees on what happened. Unlike a sexual harassment case, for example, in which the complaining employee and the accused employee may tell very different stories about what each said and did, a discrimination case is often based on some undisputed facts. An employee did not receive a promotion, was not granted time off work, was disciplined, was demoted, or was fired. The dispute in discrimination cases is often over the reasons for these actions—that is, everyone may agree about what happened, but they disagree about why.

In these situations, it can be tough to get to the bottom of things. Motivation—why a person does something—can be very difficult to gauge. You'll have to rely on outward indications of intent, including plausibility, corroboration, and consistency.

- **Plausibility.** Whose story makes the most sense? Does the employee's version of events ring true? What about the decision maker—has that person given a commonsense, nondiscriminatory reason for the challenged decision?

- **Corroboration.** If the complaining employee alleges that the decision maker made biased comments, did anyone else witness them? Do personnel files, performance evaluations, and other documents support the decision maker's rationale? Or do they support the complaint?

- **Consistency.** This is probably the most important factor to consider in many discrimination claims. A discrimination claim is, at its core, an allegation of inconsistent treatment. Does the evidence support the decision maker's stated reason for action? Has the decision maker been consistent in applying the rules? Has the decision maker used the same objective criteria to judge all employees? Have these criteria been used consistently over time?

EXAMPLE: Manuel requested a week off to attend his mother's funeral in Mexico and help his siblings wrap up her personal affairs. He complained that his request was denied because of his race and national origin; he tells you that white employees have been allowed to take time off for family matters. Manuel's supervisor agrees that he denied Manuel's request but claims that he was only following company policy, which requires employees to have worked for the company for at least one year before taking time off. After examining the attendance records of the other employees who report to this supervisor, you discover that two employees, both white, have taken time off during their first year of employment. When you ask the supervisor why they were allowed to take time off, he responds that they both had serious personal emergencies: One had to stay home to care for her child for a week while her nanny was in the hospital, and the other had a fire in his home, which required him to miss work for a week while he moved his family's belongings out and met with contractors and insurance adjusters.

Has this supervisor acted consistently? Not really. He has bent the rules for some employees and not others. Does he have a principled reason for distinguishing between Manuel's situation and that of the other two employees? Again, not really. A mother's death is a serious personal problem; although Manuel could miss her funeral, the employee with child care problems could have hired a temporary babysitter and the employee with the fire could have moved his family after work hours. The long and the short of it is that this supervisor has acted inconsistently, in a manner that—intentionally or not—has favored white employees. Whether or not Manuel could win a discrimination lawsuit, he has brought an important problem to light, which the company should deal with right away.

Of course, some discrimination cases involved disputed facts. If a supervisor is accused of making racist or sexist comments, the supervisor may deny the statements altogether or claim to have said something different. For example, if an employee claims that her supervisor told her that she should stop working after having her baby, the supervisor might respond, "That's not true. What I said was that many women decide to quit their jobs after having babies, and that I understood why they made that decision." In these situations, you'll have to decide which version of the facts makes the most sense—review the guidelines in Chapter 4 for help in sorting things out.

As you evaluate the evidence, remember that conduct may be improper even if it's not clearly illegal discrimination. In the example involving Manuel, above, a court may not find in Manuel's favor—at least, not without some other evidence that the supervisor's decisions may have been based on race or national origin (such as racist comments or a long history of denying Mexican-Americans' requests for time off). However, the supervisor's explanation is unsatisfactory and begs the question of why these other workers got to take time off when Manuel did not—which means that one of your company's supervisors is making decisions that are unpredictable and confusing to employees and have led at least one person to suspect that bias is at work. This is a situation you'll want to deal with as improper managerial conduct, whether or not it amounts to illegal discrimination.

Take Action

If you find that discrimination occurred—or that improper management decisions were made, even if you aren't convinced that they were intentionally discriminatory—then you should take corrective action. Your two goals in taking action are:

- to end the discrimination or other questionable management behavior, and
- to put the victim where he or she would have been had decisions been made appropriately.

Ending the Problematic Behavior

It can be very tough to decide what to do about a discrimination claim. If you face a really cut-and-dried case, in which a supervisor made bigoted comments or made employment decisions based on biased views, firing is clearly appropriate. However, cases like this are not that common. A more likely scenario is this: A supervisor makes employment decisions that aren't entirely consistent and objective but also aren't clearly discriminatory. What you decide to do in these situations will depend, in part, on the supervisor's explanation for the actions, your company's criteria for making the type of employment decision that's been challenged, and the supervisor's willingness to respond to the problem.

> **EXAMPLE:** Toby is a regional manager for a large company. In the last year, he has promoted three employees to be site supervisors, all of them men. One of the women who applied for this position complained of sex discrimination. Toby claims that he promoted the best-qualified candidates; however, the woman who complained had more experience and better performance evaluations than two of the men Toby chose. When you asked Toby about this, he says that the woman "looked fine on paper, but she didn't seem very assertive during the interview. She was very soft-spoken, and she didn't strike me as someone who could supervise a bunch of people on a hectic job site."
>
> What do you do now? Well, Toby had a reason for failing to promote the woman. The problem is, that reason is kind of subjective—and it could have some correlation to the gender-based stereotype that women are less assertive, less confident, and less comfortable holding positions of authority than men. Of course, it could also be true that this particular woman lacked the confidence necessary for the position. In this situation, you could look at
>
> - **The job description for the position.** Is a certain level of assertiveness necessary for this position? Is that explicitly stated or is it obvious from the nature of the job?

- **The qualities of the selected candidates.** If all three of the men are confident wielding authority, Toby's explanation makes sense. If, on the other hand, one or more of the men is known as shy and diffident, then it starts to look like Toby didn't apply the same standards to everyone.
- **The qualities of the rejected candidates.** If there were a number of female candidates whose qualifications were at least as good as any of the men who got the job, that raises some questions.
- **Toby's reaction.** If Toby reveals that bias played a role in his decisions ("very few women are going to have what it takes to supervise one of these sites"), there's clearly a big problem. If, however, Toby is willing to examine his decision-making process carefully, he'll be more likely to respond to training and advice about how to make these decisions more objectively in the future.

The action you take must stop the discrimination. However, if you are too severe in your response, you might be facing a lawsuit from the employee accused of discrimination. The only way to walk this fine line is to make the punishment fit the crime. Consider:

- the severity of the discrimination
- how many total incidents of discrimination took place
- the harm to the victim
- whether the law was violated
- whether workplace policies were violated
- whether the accused employee holds a position of authority in the company, such as officer, manager, or supervisor (discrimination by a higher-level employee is more serious and requires a heightened response)
- how the company has treated similar incidents in the past
- the accused employee's attitude towards the incident, and
- the accused employee's history at the company—does the employee have a record of similar problems, or is this a one-time lapse from an otherwise stellar worker?

Restoring the Victim

If you find that improper conduct occurred, you should take steps to right the wrong. If the complaining employee suffered some negative job action (as is often the case), it may be appropriate to undo the damage. Here are some actions you might consider:

- Remove negative performance evaluations or disciplinary warnings from an employee's file, if doubt has been cast on the fairness of those documents.
- If an employee was suspended without pay, make sure the employee is paid for that time.
- If an employee has been unfairly denied a transfer, promotion, raise, or other job benefit, grant the benefit retroactively.
- If an employee has been demoted or fired, reinstate the employee, with pay retroactive to the date of the decision.

Sometimes, you may have to work with an employee to figure out how to deal with a problem in the past. Remember Manuel, who was denied time off to attend his mother's funeral? There's no obvious way to undo this damage, but the company may be able to give Manuel a related benefit instead. For example, the company might give Manuel a week of paid leave to use whenever he wishes or make a donation to a charity in his mother's name.

In some situations, you may not know whether discrimination occurred, but you do know that the employment decision was not made properly. In these cases, it may not be appropriate to just give the complaining employee the denied benefit (such as a promotion or job transfer), because that wouldn't really be fair to others. At the same time, however, you should take some action to rectify the situation. The solution might be to make the decision again, this time using fair, job-related criteria that are consistently applied to everyone.

EXAMPLE: Jim has worked for a law firm for a couple of months as a file clerk. Jim has extensive experience and training as a paralegal, but the law firm had no paralegal positions open when he applied. When a paralegal position became vacant, Jim applied. Tom, who supervises the paralegals, hired someone from outside the firm. Jim alleges that this decision was based on his age (he is 62 years old, and the person Tom hired is 28). Tom responds that he assumed Jim didn't have the right experience for the position, because he was working as a file clerk. Tom admits that he didn't even look at Jim's application. The firm hires paralegals regularly—on average, a paralegal is hired every several months. Tom has hired dozens of paralegals for the firm in the past; many of them have been over the age of 40.

What do you do now? Clearly, Tom's decision was flawed. However, there's no clear indication that it was based on Jim's age. And, now, you've got someone else in the picture—the new employee who got the paralegal job. In this situation, your best move might be to promise that Jim will be considered for the next available position. (And, if Jim gets the position, you might also consider raising his pay to the paralegal level, retroactive to when his application should have been considered in the first place.) Because the firm hires so frequently, Jim won't have to wait long to be considered. And you won't have to displace a worker who has already been hired.

Document the Investigation

Document your discrimination investigation following the guidelines in Chapter 4. Remember, if an employee files a lawsuit based on the investigation (or the alleged discrimination you investigated), your documentation could well end up in the hands of a judge or jury. Make sure to write a report that's complete and professional and fully supports the conclusions you reached.

CAUTION

Don't create evidence that can be used against your company.
If you investigate a really egregious situation in which you believe rank discrimination took place, you might want to state this conclusion in your report. This is a temptation you should resist, however. Remember, if the affected employee decides to file a lawsuit, your company will generally be liable for discrimination by supervisors and managers. If you state, in your report, that discrimination occurred, you will be tying your company's hands in the courtroom. The employee's lawyer will tell the jury, "The company's own investigator admitted that my client was discriminated against"—and you can imagine how the argument goes from there. The better strategy is simply to state that company policies were violated and that the manager or supervisor acted inappropriately or unprofessionally, and leave it at that.

Follow Up

Once the investigation is complete, it's a good time to think about how the company can prevent future problems. For example, did your investigation reveal racial insensitivity, ignorance about the needs and contributions of disabled workers, or a general lack of understanding among different groups of employees? If so, some diversity training may be in order. You might also consider training for company managers, if you discover that they were making inconsistent or haphazard managerial decisions, or if they simply weren't clear about their obligations under the antidiscrimination laws.

This is also a good time to examine any company practices that the investigation has called into question. Do managers understand the company's criteria for promotions? For discipline and termination? Are these criteria fair, objective, and job related?

You should also follow up with the employees involved in the complaint. Retaliation can be a problem if the accused employee continues to work for the company—especially if you determined that the complaint was unfounded. An employee who was accused of discrimination and ultimately vindicated is likely to be angry, and may feel justified in taking out some of that anger on the complaining employee. To guard against this problem, meet with the complaining employee a few times after the investigation to make sure everything is going smoothly and no retaliation is taking place. You should also meet with the accused employee to make sure that things are getting back to normal.

If an employee raised any reasonable accommodation issues, you may need to follow up on that as well. If the employee and the company were able to come up with an accommodation, check in with everyone involved to make sure that the accommodation is working. If the employee's suggested accommodation ultimately created an undue burden on the company, you may need to spend some time with the employee (and perhaps the employee's manager), trying to come up with an alternative accommodation that will be effective. ●

Investigating Harassment

Y ou've probably heard about the multimillion dollar verdicts some employees have won in harassment lawsuits. Maybe you've even seen news reports about huge companies facing class action claims and government investigations for mistreating women, people of color, or disabled workers. These stories demonstrate that claims of workplace harassment can do serious damage to a business, in bad publicity and in dollars and cents. It's no wonder why most employers feel some anxiety when they get a complaint of harassment.

Harassment claims can also be uncomfortable to investigate. If you're looking into a complaint of sexual harassment, for example, you may need to pry into personal relationships, sexual misconduct, graphic language, and more. For other types of harassment claims—such as racial harassment or harassment based on disability—you may hear disturbing accounts of bigotry and insensitivity. And no matter what type of harassment you're investigating, you can be sure of one thing: The people involved will have very strong feelings about the situation and about how the company decides to handle it. This can put a lot of pressure on you to maintain your objectivity, stay focused on the facts, and make the right decision.

That's the bad news. The good news is that investigating these complaints properly can help your company avoid legal liability for harassment. And you'll have plenty of guidance on what you need to do to stay out of trouble: The Supreme Court has decided several cases explaining an employer's obligation to investigate harassment complaints. And the Equal Employment Opportunity Commission— the federal government agency that enforces laws prohibiting discrimination and harassment—has issued some written guidelines for employers on how to investigate harassment. Although harassment investigations can be challenging, the information in this chapter will help you do the job right and keep your company out of legal trouble.

This chapter explains the law of harassment: what it is, what it isn't, and what employers are obligated to do about it. It covers both sexual harassment and other types of workplace harassment. You'll also find information on how to apply the ten steps described in Part I to claims of harassment.

What Is Harassment?

Some workers are quick to cry "Harassment!" whenever they feel that a supervisor is being tough on them or they're being treated unfairly:

- "These deadlines are too tight. Forcing all of us to meet them is just harassment!"
- "Making us smoke outside the building when it's this cold out is ridiculous. I feel like we're being harassed."
- "Just because I forgot to call in sick, my supervisor called me to find out where I was. She shouldn't be calling me at home, regardless of the reason—this is harassment."

Complaints like these generally don't meet the legal definition of harassment. Harassment is an offshoot of the laws that prohibit discrimination—which means that harassment is illegal only if it is based on a person's race, gender, age, disability, or other protected characteristic. Such characteristics are determined by federal laws—such as Title VII, the Americans With Disabilities Act, and the Age Discrimination in Employment Act—and by state and local laws that prohibit discrimination. (For more on antidiscrimination laws, see Chapter 5.) General complaints about working conditions don't meet this standard unless the employee is being subjected to tougher supervision or more onerous rules because of, for example, race or gender.

EXAMPLE: Carla wants to leave work early two days a week to get a graduate degree. She works for a department store that does not offer flexible scheduling. Her supervisor tells her that she can't take the time off because company policy prohibits it and because it would be difficult to find someone to work her station for just a few hours a week. Her supervisor offers to let her take those days off entirely, but she would have to work on the weekend. Although this is unfortunate for Carla, it isn't harassment.

Now suppose Carla's supervisor has usually accommodated employees' requests to take time off for personal pursuits. In fact, Carla had spoken to her supervisor before she signed up for school, and her supervisor assured her that he would rearrange her schedule. However, when Carla told her supervisor that she would be attending divinity school to become a minister, his attitude changed. He was not as friendly towards her and seemed to avoid her at work. When she asked to meet with him to work out the scheduling details, he told her that he wasn't willing to lose an employee for several hours each week just so she could "go to Bible school." Carla may have a valid claim of religious harassment—she was subjected to different rules because of her religious beliefs.

The general rules that apply to all harassment cases are discussed in "Harassment: The Basics," below. There are a couple of additional issues that are more likely to come up in sexual harassment cases; these are covered in "Sexual Harassment," below.

Harassment: The Basics

Legally speaking, harassment is offensive, unwelcome conduct (whether words, actions, gestures, or visual displays) that is so severe or pervasive that it affects the terms and conditions of the victim's employment. Sometimes, harassment directly affects the victim's job opportunities— for example, when a supervisor tells an employee, "I'm not going to give you that promotion unless you agree to go on a date with me" or subjects an employee to harsher rules because of her protected status (like Carla in the example above). Other times, harassment doesn't result in discipline or lost opportunities but does make it difficult for the victim to do his or her job because of constant ridicule, belittling comments, teasing, or sexual come-ons. This second type of harassment is referred to as "hostile environment" harassment.

Harassing Conduct

As noted above, workplace mistreatment can be construed as harassment only if it is based on a protected characteristic. Under federal law, protected characteristics include race, color, national origin, sex, disability, age, and religion. Many states expand this list to include sexual orientation, marital status, and other categories. And some municipalities prohibit additional types of discrimination—on the basis of appearance, weight, or transgender status, for example. (See Chapter 5 for more information on protected categories; Appendix D provides information on state antidiscrimination laws.)

What kinds of conduct constitute harassment? Anything from derogatory jokes based on ethnicity or age to name-calling and slurs to threats and outright physical violence. Harassment may take the form of actual comments about an employee's protected characteristic or it may be more subtle—for example, an employer may treat workers of a certain ethnicity better than other workers. Here are some examples:

- A Jewish office worker is subjected to jokes about the Holocaust and is assigned to a bookkeeping position because "Jews know how to handle money."

- An African-American salesman works at a car dealership. His coworkers make racist comments about nonwhite customers; after he tells them that he finds their comments offensive, they start referring to themselves jokingly as "the KKK."

- A clerical worker with cerebral palsy is mimicked by her supervisor, who ridicules her speech and the way she walks, blames her for errors she did not commit, and tells her coworkers that she is incompetent "but we can't fire her because she's disabled."

Unwelcome Conduct

To constitute illegal harassment, conduct or statements must be unwelcome to the victim. In many harassment cases, this isn't really an issue. Someone who is referred to in offensive or derogatory terms, made fun of because of age or disability, or threatened with racial violence generally finds the conduct unwelcome. However, this sometimes is a disputed issue in sexual harassment cases, because some sexual advances, comments, or jokes might not offend their target. (See "Sexual Harassment," below, for more information.)

There may be a legitimate question of welcomeness in some cases that don't involve sexual harassment. For example, if an older worker frequently refers to himself as "gramps" or "the old-timer" and makes jokes about his "senior moments," other employees may feel that he doesn't mind being teased about his age. Similarly, workers who share a protected characteristic (such as the same ethnic background or sexual orientation) may feel comfortable exchanging jokes about it but quite uncomfortable hearing the same kinds of comments from someone else.

Severe or Pervasive

Harassment is illegal only if it is severe or pervasive. Generally, this means that there must be a pattern of harassment or a series of incidents over time. One teasing comment, request for a date, or even use of a bigoted epithet probably does not constitute harassment by itself. On the other hand, courts have found that a single act can be harassment if the act is truly extreme—such as rape or a racially motivated physical assault.

There's no clear line or "magic number" of incidents when name-calling, teasing, and such cross the line to become harassment. Courts will look at all of the circumstances in deciding whether harassment has occurred. This means that the court will consider all of the incidents in context. The more egregious each incident is, the fewer will be necessary for an employer to be held liable.

CAUTION

It may be inappropriate even if it isn't illegal. This section explains how the law defines harassment. However, you shouldn't base your decision to investigate solely on whether the conduct alleged meets these legal standards. For one thing, you can't predict with utter certainty how a judge or jury will decide a particular harassment claim. More important, behavior doesn't have to be illegal to violate your company's standards on proper workplace behavior. A few isolated sexual jokes or bigoted comments can quickly escalate into a full-blown harassment claim—and even if they don't, they will certainly create an uncomfortable atmosphere for at least some of your workers. If you investigate, you can put a stop to this type of unprofessional behavior right away, before legal trouble develops.

Terms and Conditions of Employment

In order for a court to determine that harassment occurred, the conduct must affect the terms and conditions of the victim's employment. There are several ways this might happen. If the harasser is a supervisor or someone else who has the right and authority to make job decisions, harassment might take the form of a negative job action, such as firing, failure to promote, demotion, discipline, a pay cut (or refusal to grant a pay raise), or an undesirable transfer, reassignment, or change in job duties or title.

However, harassment can occur even if the victim is not subjected to a negative job action like this. The victim can make a hostile environment claim if he or she reasonably finds the workplace to be abusive or hostile as a result of the harassment. The key word here is "reasonable." It is not enough that the victim believes the workplace is hostile; the circumstances must be such that a reasonable worker in the victim's position would also find the workplace hostile. This rule ensures that employers won't be liable to hypersensitive employees who see harassment behind every smile and gesture.

Who's a Reasonable Worker?

The "reasonable person" test for harassment can be tough to figure out. After all, reasonable people can differ on what constitutes harassment or whether a particular situation has crossed the line from sophomoric to abusive.

The law says that employers (and juries, if it comes to that) must consider the situation from the viewpoint of a reasonable worker in the victim's position. This means that the typical sexual harassment claim must be considered from the perspective of a reasonable woman, and a case of racial harassment against an African-American employee must be looked at from the vantage point of a reasonable African-American. This rule is an effort to acknowledge the fact that different groups in our society may react differently to particular actions, words, and comments.

Sexual Harassment

Sexual harassment is defined in essentially the same way as other types of harassment: It's offensive, unwelcome sexual conduct that is so severe or pervasive that it affects the terms and conditions of the victim's employment—either because the victim's submission or failure to submit to the behavior is the basis for job-related decisions (like firing or demotion) or because the victim reasonably finds the workplace abusive or hostile as a result of the harassment. However, sexual harassment cases tend to spend more time analyzing whether the behavior was welcome, due to the fact that not all sexual or romantic behavior in the workplace is offensive to the recipient.

It's safe to say that harassment based on race, disability, and so on is rarely a misguided effort to establish a closer relationship with the victim. Although such harassment is sometimes meant in fun, its victims tend not to find it very amusing. In contrast, behavior that could be construed as sexual harassment under certain circumstances might not bother the recipient at all. After all, some requests for dates are accepted happily—and lead to mutually satisfying relationships. While one person might find sexually explicit comments and jokes offensive, another might find them flattering and flirtatious. In an era when everyone spends so much time on the job—and, according to some surveys, a majority of us have had a relationship with someone we met at work—the law can't presume that every sexual advance or provocative comment is offensive.

At the same time, of course, it is very disturbing to be subjected to unwanted sexual attention, to be told that you have to submit to sexual advances in order to get ahead, or to work in an environment where X-rated jokes are the order of the day.

Unwelcome Harassment

Sexual harassment is unwelcome when the victim finds it offensive rather than flattering or innocent. Notice the focus on the victim—unlike the reasonableness standard discussed above, unwelcomeness is in the eye of the beholder. It's subjective—which means that when you are investigating a sexual harassment claim, you will want to ask the victim how he or she felt about the alleged harassment and what impact it had on him or her.

Who's Harassing Whom?

The majority of sexual harassment claims involve a male harasser and a female victim. However, courts have recognized harassment claims by male victims of female harassers, male victims of male harassers, and female victims of female harassers. And the Equal Employment Opportunity Commission, or EEOC (the federal government agency that enforces antidiscrimination and harassment laws) reports that harassment claims by men have been steadily increasing—for the last few years, such claims have made up almost 15% of all sexual harassment charges filed under federal law (these statistics don't indicate the gender of the harasser).

Regardless of the gender of the victim or harasser, the same standards apply: The victim must be subjected to offensive sexual conduct that is severe or pervasive, affects the terms and conditions of employment, and is unwelcome.

Keep in mind that what may be welcome to one employee could be unwelcome to others. For example, a group of men enjoy teasing and making sexual jokes with the office receptionist, an attractive young woman. The receptionist finds the jokes amusing and harmless, and sometimes tells one herself. This isn't illegal harassment of the receptionist, because she finds the conduct welcome. However, a female secretary who shares space with the receptionist finds these comments offensive and disruptive. Although none of the jokes are directed at her, she finds them unwelcome and must put up with them to do her job. She may be a victim of sexual harassment.

Claims of Sexual Favoritism

If a worker is required to submit to sexual advances in order to get some type of job benefit (such as a promotion or desired assignment), that worker has a pretty good sexual harassment claim. But what about the other workers, those who weren't put under sexual pressure but also didn't get the job benefit? According to the EEOC, these workers may also have a legal claim against the company for harassment. Even though they weren't directly subjected to harassment, their job opportunities suffered because of sexual harassment against another employee.

What if the favoritism is based not on harassment, but on a consensual relationship? Some courts have found that this type of favoritism cannot give rise to a harassment claim, but the California Supreme Court has held that other employees might have a harassment claim even if the employee(s) who received the benefits do not. While an isolated incident of sexual favoritism—such as giving a plum job assignment to a girlfriend—might not be actionable, the court found that the situation is different if favoritism is widespread. If, for example, a manager is having sexual relationships with several employees, all of whom receive job benefits that aren't provided to others, the manager is sending a message that the only way to get ahead at work is to have sex with the boss. This might be actionable harassment.

Whether the courts in your state decide to follow California's example or not, one thing is clear: Managers should not be favoring their paramours with job benefits that are not available to other employees. Basing employment decisions on personal relationships or other factors that are not directly related to the job is a poor management practice—and if it doesn't lead to a lawsuit, it will certainly lead to resentment, poor morale, and increased employee turnover. If you hear of sexual favoritism at your company, you should investigate and take action to stop it, even if it wouldn't provide sufficient fodder for a successful lawsuit.

Prior Relationships

Remember all of those consensual relationships that began at work? Well, common sense tell us that many of them are bound to end at some point—which means that all of the drama, hurt feelings, and denial that can accompany a relationship's demise might find their way into the workplace.

Unfortunately, it also means that sexual harassment claims might not be far behind. Some sexual harassment claims are brought by a victim who used to be in a consensual relationship with the harasser. This is a particular danger when one member of the former couple supervises the other or holds a position that provides an opportunity to make decisions about the other's future at the company. The subordinate employee might claim that she is being punished for ending the relationship or that she is being subjected to advances that are now unwanted. In extreme cases, one employee might even make a false claim of harassment against the other, out of spite or anger over the breakup.

If you learn, during the course of your investigation, that the alleged harasser and victim used to be romantically involved, you'll probably have to ask some questions about that relationship so you can figure out how it plays into the harassment allegations. This can be a sticky situation for investigators, as it requires you to get into some issues that the parties might think of as private. (You'll find tips below that will help you handle this type of problem.)

Sex-Based Harassment

Some courts have recognized claims of sex-based harassment—that is, harassment that is based on sex but is not sexual in nature. In these cases, the harasser is not interested in having a sexual relationship with the victim(s) or otherwise "sexualizing" the workplace with jokes and stories but instead wants to intentionally create a hostile environment for workers of a particular gender (almost always women). Often, these claims are made by women working in traditionally male professions.

Although women in these cases have clearly been subjected to a hostile work environment because of their sex, there are none of the traditional signs of sexual harassment—requests for dates, dirty jokes, sexualized comments about women's bodies, and so on. Instead, harassing conduct in these cases might include sabotaging the tools, vehicles, or work of women employees; soiling or defacing women's workspaces, lockers, or restroom facilities; subjecting women to dangerous work conditions; displaying cartoons or telling jokes that depict violence towards women; and making comments about women's inability to do the job.

Some states have not yet recognized these claims. Whether or not the courts in your state treat this kind of behavior as sexual harassment, you will obviously want to investigate and put a stop to it. When employees are spending part of their workdays engaging in, or being subjected to, cruel or dangerous conduct, productivity and morale are suffering. Your company also may be at risk for workers' compensation claims or personal injury lawsuits if an employee is harmed by this kind of behavior. And female employees won't stay at your company for long if they have to put up with daily abuse on the job.

Legal Liability for Harassment

In 1998, the Supreme Court decided two cases that spell out when an employer will be legally responsible for harassment. In these cases, the Court held that employers who have an antiharassment policy and investigate harassment complaints quickly and fairly can avoid liability in certain kinds of cases—even if the employee proves that he or she was harassed.

Generally, your company has a legal duty to take effective action to stop harassment as soon as management learns of it, whether the harasser is a supervisor or a coworker of the victim. But in some cases, your company will also be held responsible for harassment committed by a manager or supervisor, even if no one in human resources knew what was going on. The Supreme Court and the Equal Employment Opportunity Commission (EEOC), the government agency charged with handling complaints of discrimination and harassment, have come up with the following rules for employer responsibility for harassment.

An employer is generally responsible for harassment by a manager or supervisor if the harassment results in a "tangible employment action"—an action that significantly changes the harassed employee's job status, like getting fired, demoted, or reassigned—even if the employee never complained and the employer had no idea what was going on. The logic behind this liability is that when managers and supervisors make these types of decisions, they are acting for the company. Therefore, if their decisions are influenced by discrimination, the company is responsible.

Who's a Supervisor?

These rules—which make employers liable for harassment that results in a negative job action, even if the employer isn't aware of it—apply only to harassment by supervisors. So which employees qualify as supervisors? According to the EEOC, a supervisor is someone who either has the authority to make or recommend decisions affecting the employee or has the authority to direct the employee's daily work activities.

However, certain employees may occupy such a lofty position on the corporate ladder that they are something more than supervisors. These employees—which might include corporate officers, the president, the CEO, an owner, or a partner, depending on how the company is organized—generally have the authority to act on the company's behalf in all matters. Therefore, if they harass employees, the law will presume that the company knows about it, even if the harassment doesn't result in a negative job action. In these situations, employers can't rely on the defense described in this section: The company will always be liable for harassment by these high-ranking employees.

However, an employer is not necessarily responsible for harassment by a manager or supervisor that doesn't have any of these repercussions—for example, a manager who tells racist jokes or repeatedly asks an employee out on dates. In these cases, an employer can defend itself by showing that:

- the employer exercised reasonable care to prevent and promptly correct any harassment, and
- the employee unreasonably failed to take advantage of opportunities the employer offered to prevent or correct the harassment—for example, by failing to make a complaint.

The first step requires employers to make efforts to create a harassment-free work environment—for example, by training employees and managers to recognize and report harassment, by adopting a policy prohibiting harassment and a complaint procedure that encourages employees to come forward, and by investigating harassment complaints quickly and fairly. If the employer takes these precautions and a harassed worker delays in making a complaint or fails to complain at all, the employer will not be responsible for harassment that occurred prior to the complaint.

CROSS-REFERENCE

Need an antiharassment policy? A sample antiharassment policy, which you can modify to fit the needs of your workplace, is included in Appendix A and on the CD-ROM.

The policy behind this defense is pretty simple: If an employer has an antiharassment and investigation policy that it follows faithfully, the employee has to use it if he or she wants the problem to stop. If an employee fails to make a complaint, the employer has no notice of the problem and, therefore, no reason to investigate or take action. But in order to take advantage of this protection, the employer must make clear to employees that their complaints will be investigated fully and fairly. The only way to drive this point home is to investigate every harassment complaint. This way, no employee can argue that he or she didn't report harassment because the employer would not have done anything about it. Remember that once the employer learns of this second kind of harassment—through a complaint or in any other way—it is responsible for any harassment that continues after that point. This gives the employer an incentive to investigate and take action quickly.

EXAMPLE 1: Sheila's boss, Roger, has asked her out several times. She has turned him down each time, explaining that she has no romantic interest in him and would prefer to keep their relationship professional. Roger refuses to approve Sheila's scheduled raise, because she will not go out with him. Roger's employer will be legally responsible for Roger's harassment, even if Sheila never complains about it, because she has been subjected to a negative job action.

EXAMPLE 2: Katherine works on the production line in an auto plant. Her coworkers and supervisor, mostly men, constantly tell sexual jokes and refer to women in crude terms. The top executives in the company visit the plant. Although the men are on their best behavior during the official tour, several executives remain in the building afterwards to review paperwork and overhear the men's crude remarks. The company will be liable for any harassment Katherine suffers after the visit. Although she has not made a complaint or suffered a negative job action, the company now knows about the harassment and has a duty to take action.

EXAMPLE 3: Same as Example 2, except the executives never visit the plant. If Katherine wants to hold the company responsible for her harassment, she will have to make a complaint to put the company on notice of the problem. If Katherine fails to make a complaint, she can hold the company responsible only if she can show that (1) the company had no policy against harassment, or (2) the company did not take complaints seriously, failed to investigate, or failed to act on reported problems. For example, if Katherine can show that several women from her plant had complained in the past few years and nothing had been done about the problem, the employer will be liable despite her failure to complain.

For more information on employer liability for harassment by supervisors and managers, check out the EEOC's guidelines, "EEOC Enforcement Guidance: Vicarious Employer Liability for Unlawful Harassment by Supervisors" (June 1999), available from the EEOC's website at www.eeoc.gov/policy/docs/harassment.html.

> **CAUTION**
>
> **Check your state's laws.** Although many states have adopted the rules explained in this section and most others are likely to adopt them, there may be a few states that buck the trend. States that have stronger antiharassment laws—and therefore are more likely to hold employers responsible for harassment—might not follow the Supreme Court's lead. For example, a state that uses a strict liability standard will hold the employer liable for all harassment, whether management participated in it or not, and whether the company knew about it or not. In this situation, it's even more imperative that a company do all it can to prevent harassment in the first place. An employment lawyer can help you figure out how your company can protect itself.

Ten Steps to a Successful Harassment Investigation

This section explains how to apply the basic investigation steps covered in Part I of this book to a harassment investigation. If you haven't read Part I, you should do so before getting into this more specific material— the discussion that follows assumes that you are already familiar with basic investigation procedures.

Decide Whether to Investigate

When you're dealing with possible harassment, it's best to err on the side of investigating, even if the allegations don't seem that serious. As explained above, failing to investigate harassment claims can have serious consequences—not just for the claim you decide not to investigate, but for future claims of harassment that might be made against your company.

But this doesn't mean you have to jump into investigative high gear every time an employee utters the "h" word. First, figure out whether the employee is complaining about conduct based on a protected characteristic—race, gender, disability, and so on. If not, you may still want to look into the incident further, depending on the allegations, or refer them to an appropriate person in management for further consideration.

EXAMPLE: Roland complains to the human resources department about his supervisor, Marie. Marie was recently hired to improve the performance of the sales department. Roland complains that Marie has imposed deadlines on the department that are difficult to meet and has required everyone to attend sales training, even if they have years of experience. She has arranged a standing meeting with every employee once a week to review their sales figures and talk about ways they could improve their numbers. Roland claims this is harassment: "She's working all of us like dogs. She's always there, looking over someone's shoulder, telling them what they're doing is wrong. Our group is really demoralized—it feels like she doesn't respect our experience and opinions."

Even though Roland used the term "harassment," he isn't complaining about illegal harassment based on a protected characteristic. Although Marie's management style isn't winning her any friends, she is applying it equally to all, regardless of race, gender, and so on. This isn't a complaint that demands an investigation. However, it is a legitimate concern that should be communicated to Marie and her supervisors. The company may decide that Marie is doing exactly what it hired her to do and urge her to keep up the good work. Or it may decide to tell Marie to back off a bit and try using some management techniques that are a bit more successful at motivating her employees.

Even if the conduct appears to be based on a protected characteristic, the situation may not call for a full-blown investigation. There may be cases in which the alleged conduct is minor, everyone agrees on what happened, and a simple discussion with both parties (carefully documented, of course) will put the matter to rest.

EXAMPLE: Mark asks Georgia, his coworker, to have dinner with him one night after work. Georgia declines, telling Mark that she has a boyfriend. Mark says, "Well, he's a very lucky man." Nothing further happens between them, but Georgia tells her supervisor about the incident and confides that it made her a bit uncomfortable to know that Mark finds her attractive. You interview Georgia, who confirms what she told her supervisor and says that Mark has never asked her out again or acted inappropriately towards her. Mark tells you that Georgia's statement is accurate. He says that he won't approach her socially again—"I don't want to make her uncomfortable. In fact, I feel kind of bad for asking her out in the first place."

In this situation, you won't have to interview witnesses, comb through files, and carefully weigh the evidence. Once you've talked to the two employees involved, made sure that Mark understands that he shouldn't bother Georgia, (or retaliate against her for complaining), explained the outcome to Georgia, and documented your conversations, you're done. Of course, a few different facts could lead to a different conclusion. For example, if Mark's response was "I can't believe my bad luck—she's the third person in my department I asked out this month, and they all turned me down" or Georgia said, "I think Mark felt comfortable asking me out because our supervisor is always joking and making comments about the supposedly wild sex lives I and the other women in our department have," then you've got a more serious problem on your hands that will require a more extensive investigation.

> **CAUTION**
>
> **When there is no complaint.** Remember, your company has an obligation to investigate harassment, no matter how you find out about it. Although you may learn of harassment through an employee complaint, there are lots of other ways harassment might come to your attention. For example, a supervisor might notice racist graffiti on the walls of the employee locker room, overhear an X-rated joke, or see employees picking on a disabled coworker. An employee might make an anonymous complaint of harassment or raise the issue in an exit interview. Your duty to investigate kicks in as soon as you know of the allegations, regardless of how they surface.

Take Immediate Action, If Necessary

Before you begin your investigation, you will have to decide whether some immediate changes are necessary in the workplace to prevent further harm and to ensure that the investigation won't be disrupted. You should consider taking steps to separate the alleged harasser from the alleged victims when:

- Very serious allegations—for example, unwanted sexual touching, sexual assault, violence, threats, or extremely abusive verbal harassment (such as the use of offensive racist epithets)—have been made.
- Ongoing harassment is alleged.
- The alleged victim(s) and/or witnesses appear to be intimidated by the alleged harasser.

You must be very careful to avoid retaliation (or the appearance of retaliation) when you decide what to do. If you separate the employees by moving the worker who complained to another shift or a different work area, you could be accused of retaliating: "As soon as I complained, they moved me to the night shift, while the person who harassed me got to continue working his usual shift, just like nothing happened."

Time Off for the Complaining Employee

Sometimes, an employee who complains of harassment asks to take some time off. If you face a request like this, find out exactly why the employee wants out of the workplace. For example, if the employee has been threatened with retaliation or her coworkers are shunning her because she made a complaint, these are facts you'll need to know. Explain that retaliation is prohibited and that you will investigate as quickly as possible.

If an employee simply wants to take some time to catch her breath, you can arrange for a brief period of paid leave. However, make sure that the employee will be available to participate in the investigation.

The best way to avoid these types of charges is to move the harasser or suspend him with pay while you investigate. When you tell the alleged harasser about the change, emphasize that it's a temporary situation, that no conclusions have been made about the truth or falsity of the allegations, and that the transfer or suspension is not punitive. If you must take an immediate action like this, make extra efforts to complete the investigation quickly, to minimize workplace disruption.

> ## CAUTION
>
> **Don't suspend workers without pay.** From a legal standpoint, suspending exempt, salaried employees—those who are not entitled to earn overtime if they work extra hours—without pay while you investigate violates wage and hour laws. And even though you can suspend hourly, nonexempt workers without pay, it's not a good idea. A suspension without pay is punitive: It improperly signals that you have made up your mind about the allegations before you've even begun to investigate. A worker who is suspended without pay will probably be angry about it—and if the allegations against him or her are false, that anger may well provide the fuel for a lawsuit. And unpaid suspensions can be an administrative hassle, as they require your company to interrupt its usual payroll system.

If criminal allegations have been made—of sexual assault, physical violence, or serious threats—you might be wondering whether you should call the police. In this situation, you should talk to a lawyer right away. There are pros and cons to having the police involved: They can use a wide range of investigative methods and bring the force of the state to bear when trying to get to the truth, but they also have their own priorities, which may differ from those of your company. A lawyer can help you weigh the alternatives and decide what to do. Of course, the victim can always report the incident and, if this happens, you should cooperate with the authorities.

Choose the Investigator

Chapter 2 explains the qualities that make an investigator particularly effective—such as professionalism, experience, and impartiality. Those considerations always apply, no matter what type of problem you're investigating. However, there are a few special issues to consider when you're choosing an investigator for a harassment complaint.

Your Company's Chances in Court Depend on Its Investigator

Because the Supreme Court has held that a prompt, complete, and impartial investigation could shield you from liability for certain types of harassment, a company's ability to defend itself in a harassment case could well depend on the investigator. Will the investigator handle the job carefully and quickly, without letting personal feelings get in the way? Will the investigator be able to testify professionally and accurately in court, in a manner that a jury will believe?

CAUTION

Watch out for claims of bias. Some courts have disregarded a company's efforts to investigate—and the conclusions of the investigation—if any of the employees involved in a harassment claim perceived the investigator as biased. This means you must be especially careful to choose an investigator who is beyond reproach, and to confirm with the complaining employee and the accused employee that they are comfortable with the investigator. The investigator should not be someone who directly supervises or has a personal relationship (or a history of negative encounters) with either worker. For more on choosing an unbiased investigator, see Chapter 2.

Of course, these are important questions to ask yourself when choosing an investigator for *any* type of workplace problem. But they are particularly important in cases of harassment, because the Supreme Court's decisions have virtually guaranteed that the quality of the investigation will be on trial, if your company is faced with a lawsuit.

Sensitivity

Harassment claims can be particularly uncomfortable, for alleged harassers and alleged victims alike. In a sexual harassment case, for example, the investigator may have to ask about prior relationships, sexual comments, flirtations, and more. To investigate a case of racial harassment, the investigator might have to ask the victim to repeat racial slurs and offensive statements that are deeply disturbing. Many of us are reluctant to reveal or talk in detail about these kinds of incidents, which means the investigator must be especially skilled at drawing people out and encouraging them to speak openly.

Some experts recommend choosing an investigator who shares the victim's protected characteristics (to the extent possible), to encourage the victim to open up. And this is often sound advice—for example, many women would feel more comfortable (and less embarrassed) discussing sexual harassment with another woman. And a victim of racial harassment might feel that an investigator of the same race is more likely to understand how offensive certain statements or actions were.

However, you won't always be able to follow this advice, particularly if your company is a small business. No company will have the wherewithal to come up with a "demographically correct" investigator for every claim—and that's okay. Your main concern is to find an investigator who can listen attentively and carefully to everyone and who won't come to the investigation with preconceived notions about what happened.

When to Use an Outside Investigator

As explained in Chapter 2, it makes sense to consider hiring an outside investigator in certain circumstances. You may want to bring in a professional investigator for a harassment claim if:

- An employee has raised allegations of sexual assault, rape, or violence motivated by bias.
- Several employees have complained about the same problem—for example, a group of African-American employees complain of widespread racial harassment.
- The accused harasser is a high-ranking company official (in this situation, employees might not believe that an investigator who works for the company can be impartial).
- An employee has filed a lawsuit or an administrative charge (with the Equal Employment Opportunity Commission or a state antidiscrimination agency) based on the harassment.
- An employee has hired a lawyer because of the harassment.
- The allegations have been publicized in the media.

Plan the Investigation

Although you might become aware of harassment in any number of ways (see Chapter 2), you will often be dealing with an employee complaint of inappropriate behavior. This gives you a leg up on the investigation—you'll have some basic information before you begin your interviews, and you'll be able to plan your investigation accordingly.

You won't always have a complaint to work from, however. If a manager happens to notice X-rated cartoons or racist graffiti on the walls, for example, or if you receive an anonymous complaint of harassment, you'll have to begin your investigation without knowing who may have committed wrongdoing or who may have been harmed by it.

When Someone Has Complained

If an employee has complained of harassment, that complaint is your natural starting point for planning the investigation. Using the complaint as your guide, these questions will help you define the scope of your inquiries:

- Who complained? Is there more than one complaining employee? If not, does the complaining employee allege that other employees were also harassed?
- What misconduct is alleged? Is the victim alleging harassment based on a protected characteristic? Is the victim alleging that he or she suffered a tangible job action—such as demotion, failure to get a raise or promotion, or a change in job duties—or a hostile work environment?
- Who is the alleged wrongdoer? Are there more than one alleged harassers? What position does the alleged harasser hold?
- How many incidents of harassment does the victim allege?
- Has the victim named any potential witnesses?
- Where did the alleged incidents take place? Is the alleged misconduct limited to one work group, one shift, or one area of the workplace, or is it more widespread? If the incidents took place as the victim says they did, are there any employees who may have witnessed them?

The answers to these questions will help you decide whom to interview, what documents or other evidence may be available to shed some light on the allegations, and what kinds of questions you'll need to ask. Of course, you may not know the answers to all of these questions right now—if the victim made a barebones complaint, for example, you might not find out any details until you actually begin to investigate. In this situation, simply keep these questions in mind as you conduct your initial interview with the complaining employee.

When There's No Complaint

Where should you start when there's no complaining employee? As always, start with what you know. How did the alleged harassment come to your attention? Did a manager or another employee report it? If so, what did that person notice? If you received a report of interpersonal harassment—that is, one employee harassing another—consider starting with the alleged victim. Even though that person hasn't come forward, he or she is probably in the best position to tell you exactly what happened.

You might learn of possible harassment that isn't focused on a particular victim (for example, that particular employees frequently use foul language or refer to others in racist or ageist terms, that sexually explicit images or jokes have been posted on an employee bulletin board or electronic mail message board, or that disabled employees have been the victims of anonymous practical jokes). In cases like these, you may wish to start by talking to someone who manages the work group where the problem arose to find out which employees may be involved, what schedules they work, how the employees seem to get along, and so forth.

If the information you begin with isn't sufficient to identify the alleged harasser(s), remember that anyone you interview to gather background information could be involved in the wrongdoing—and plan your questions accordingly.

Documents and Other Physical Evidence

No matter how you learn of the harassment, part of your investigation planning should include gathering relevant documents. For example, these types of documents may help you figure out who to interview and what questions to ask:

- the company's harassment policy
- the personnel files of the alleged harasser and the complaining employee or victim (if there is one)
- any allegedly harassing documents, including emails, correspondence, cartoons, postings on company property, or notes
- performance evaluations and other documents reflecting personnel decisions, if the complaining employee claims to have suffered a negative job action as a result of the harassment, and
- attendance records for any company trainings on harassment.

You should also consider whether any physical evidence other than documents might exist. If someone has reported sexist graffiti in the locker room, for example, you will want to photograph the graffiti and record exactly what it says. Other types of evidence that may be relevant in a harassment investigation include:

- objects given to or left for the victim—including gifts, suggestive clothing, sexual toys, offensive items (like a noose or Ku Klux Klan imagery), or pictures
- photographs from company events where harassment allegedly took place (such as a company holiday party or other social event), and
- work-related items connected with the alleged harassment. For example, if the victim alleges that her toolbox was tampered with, his briefcase or computer was defaced, or his equipment was sabotaged, you will want to collect those items (or at least photograph them and take careful notes of the apparent damage).

Interviews

Once you've finished your investigation planning, you'll have some ideas about which employees you should interview. If an employee has made a complaint, you should generally start by interviewing that person. If no employee has complained, you can start by interviewing whomever noticed the problem, a manager in the work group where the problem exists, or any known victims.

No matter who you're interviewing, you should start the interview with some opening remarks to set the employee at ease and explain the process. You should also give the witness a written notice regarding retaliation, confidentiality, and so on (Appendix B contains a form you can use for this purpose). Next, proceed to your specific questions, remembering to follow up on any new information raised by the witness's responses. Close the interview by letting the witness know what will happen next and inviting him or her to come to you with any concerns or additional information. And conduct follow-up interviews if any new information comes to light.

Getting Started

Some of your opening comments will be the same, no matter whom you're interviewing. Some of them will be geared more specifically towards a complaining employee, an accused employee, or a witness. The opening statement you make to every person you interview should cover these points:

- **The purpose of the meeting.** The information you give here will depend on whom you're interviewing. You can tell the complaining employee that the company will be investigating the complaint and that the purpose of the meeting is to gather as much information as possible. The accused employee will need to be told that a complaint has been made, that you're investigating, and that your role is to gather as much information as possible. A witness can simply be told that you're investigating a workplace problem and you believe the witness might have some relevant information.

- **The investigation process.** Explain that the company will be investigating the problem and interviewing other employees and will take appropriate steps if it finds that misconduct occurred.

- **Confidentiality.** Emphasize that you expect the employee to keep the investigation confidential and that talking about the investigation to other employees could be grounds for discipline. Explain that you will maintain confidentiality to the extent possible, although it will be necessary to reveal certain details in order to conduct thorough interviews and reach a decision.

- **Retaliation.** Explain that retaliation is prohibited and that the company will take immediate steps to discipline anyone who retaliates based on the complaint or investigation. Ask the employee to come to you with any concerns about retaliation.

- **Questions or concerns.** Ask whether the employee has any questions or concerns about the process.

When you interview the accused employee, emphasize that the company has not reached any decisions about what happened. Explain that you are interested in hearing what everyone involved has to say before making a decision or taking any action. Because you will probably have to reveal the name of the complaining employee (as explained below), spend some extra time discussing retaliation: what it is, that the company prohibits it, and that employees who engage in retaliation will be subject to discipline. Although the accused employee will probably want to know the allegations right away, you are better off postponing this discussion until later in the interview, after you have had a chance to gather some important background information. Assure the accused employee that he or she will have the opportunity to hear and respond to the allegations before the interview is over.

For witnesses, your opening remarks can be brief. The witness doesn't need to know who complained, who is accused, or what the specific allegations are. Once you have explained that you are investigating a workplace problem and talked about confidentiality and retaliation, you can begin asking your questions.

Questions for the Complaining Employee or Victim

Harassment is usually a pattern of incidents rather than one single event. Because the complaining employee will probably be describing several separate occurrences, you need to be especially careful to ask precise questions and take clear notes—otherwise, you could easily get confused about the details. Experienced investigators advise discussing each incident separately. First, ask the complaining employee to tell you briefly about every incident. Then, go through the list and ask for the details of each, starting with the most recent problem and working backwards. Here are some sample questions you can tailor to the facts of your investigation:

> **TIP**
>
> **Act like a reporter.** When interviewing the complaining employee, follow the universal rule of journalists everywhere: Ask who, what, where, when, and how (and sometimes why). By sticking to these open-ended questions, you'll elicit as much information as possible while keeping the witness focused on the facts.

SAMPLE QUESTIONS

- What happened? How many incidents have there been?

- Who was involved? What did that person say or do?

- How did you react? Did you say anything to [the accused employee]? What did you say? Did you react physically [for example, by leaving the room, slamming a door, crying, or blushing]?

- Prior to these incidents, what was your relationship like with [the accused employee]? Did you work together frequently? Did you have any problems working together? Did you socialize outside of work?

- When did each incident take place? How often did they occur? When did they begin?

- Where did each incident take place?

- Was anyone else present? Could anyone else have witnessed the incident(s)?

- Did you tell anyone about the incidents? Who did you tell? What did you tell them?

- Do you know of any similar incidents involving other people?

- Have you been affected by the incidents? How? Did you take any time off as a result of the incidents? Did you seek medical treatment or counseling?

- Are there any documents or other kinds of evidence relating to the incidents? Did you take notes or keep a journal recording these incidents?

- When did you first complain about these incidents [if the employee says she complained earlier and nothing was done]? Whom did you complain to? What did you say? What did the person you complained to say? [If the employee only complained after a delay:] Why did you decide to come forward now?

- How would you like to see this problem resolved?

- Is there anyone who might have information about these incidents that you'd like me to interview?

- Is there anything else you'd like to tell me?

Asking About a Prior Relationship in a Sexual Harassment Investigation

If the complaining employee and the alleged harasser used to be romantically involved with each other, you will have to ask some questions about that relationship. What each party says about the relationship, why it ended, and how it affected their dealings with each other at work will help you figure out whose story is more credible—and help you get to the bottom of the complaint.

But proceed with caution: Once you start asking about personal matters—and we can all agree that our romantic relationships fall into this category—you risk invading an employee's privacy. The best way to avoid this problem is to limit your questions to issues related to work and the complaint. In most cases, you could safely ask about when the relationship started, when it ended, who ended it and why, how the parties have gotten along at work since the breakup, and what relevance each party thinks the prior relationship has on the current situation. (For example, does the complaining employee think that she's being harassed because she ended the relationship, or does the accused harasser think his former paramour has made a false complaint out of jealousy or anger?)

In some situations, you might find yourself asking more intimate questions, based on the information that comes out in your interviews.

EXAMPLE: Rosalie complains that Xavier, her coworker and former boyfriend, is harassing her. She says that he hangs around her desk all of the time, and asks her a lot of questions about her personal life. She says she has told him to stop, but he persists in asking her out and asking whether she's dating anyone else. She decided to complain when she found a sexual toy on her desk. She says, with some embarrassment, that she and Xavier had used a similar toy when having sex, and that finding it on her desk convinced her that Xavier was not going to stop bothering her.

When you interview Xavier, are you going to ask him about the sexual toy? Ordinarily, you should stay very far away from any questions about sexual practices. In this case, however, you need to find out who left the item on Rosalie's desk—and the evidence so far points to Xavier. Because this particular sexual toy is relevant to the complaint, you will have to ask about it. Just make sure to limit your questions to what you need to know to resolve the complaint. (In other words, you can ask whether Xavier put the item on her desk, but not why the couple used it or "How the heck does this thing work?")

Questions for the Accused Employee

Your interview with the accused employee is likely to be a tense affair. An employee who committed misconduct may try to evade your questions or lie about what happened. An employee who has been wrongly accused is likely to be upset—at both the complaining employee and the company, for taking the allegations seriously. Either way, you may be facing a defensive and combative interview.

One way to defuse the tension is to emphasize that the company has a legal obligation to investigate the allegations and that you haven't reached any conclusions yet. Explain that the purpose of the investigation is to figure out what really happened. Assure the employee that you are eager to hear what he or she has to say and that you will be interviewing witnesses and examining documents to help you get to the truth.

TIP

You work for the company. It can be tough to interview an angry witness, particularly one who blames the company—or even you, personally—for the investigation. You may hear things like "I can't believe you think I did this," "I won't sit here and be accused of this nonsense," or "I'm outraged that anyone would take these allegations seriously." To avoid taking these kinds of statements personally, just remember that you are playing a very important role for the company. Your job is to find out what happened and resolve the situation—and you should explain this to the accused employee.

Because the accused employee is likely to be defensive—and may have something to hide—you'll have to plan the order of your questions carefully. Start with easy, basic questions about the employee's work. This will allow both of you to ease into the interview and will give you the opportunity to gather potentially important facts while the employee's guard is down.

EXAMPLE: Ricardo, a Mexican-American supervisor at a company that manufactures food products, complains that another supervisor, Jessica, has harassed him based on his national origin. He says that Jessica constantly teases him about his accent and the foods he likes to eat and tells jokes about Ricardo being an illegal alien. Ricardo is responsible for giving biweekly safety presentations to the line workers. As a fellow supervisor, Jessica is neither required nor expected to attend these meetings, but Ricardo says she has attended the last five meetings and made comments about his accent.

If you start your interview with Jessica by saying, "Ricardo claims that you've been attending his safety meetings and making inappropriate comments about his accent. Is this true?," Jessica now thinks to herself, "Aha! They're saying I did something wrong at these safety meetings." This could give her a reason to lie or make up an innocent explanation for her attendance.

If you start your interview instead by asking, "Tell me about your job responsibilities," then following up with questions about who she supervises, what she does in a typical workday and workweek, and whether she is required to attend or run any regular meetings with other workers, Jessica may not know what you're fishing for, and won't have a chance to shape her answers to put herself in the best possible light. This means you'll have a better chance of getting an honest answer.

(!) **CAUTION**

You must allow the accused employee to respond to the allegations. Some investigators are so eager to keep the interview civil—or to protect the complaining employee's privacy—that they never actually get around to confronting the accuser with the allegations. This is a big mistake, one that could undermine the legitimacy of the entire investigation. Courts have held that accused employees who never learn precisely what they are accused of haven't had a fair opportunity to tell respond, to offer the names of relevant witnesses, or to explain why the complaining employee might have made the accusation. You don't necessarily have to say who complained, but you should say whom the employee is accused of harassing. And don't worry about privacy concerns—you have a very compelling business reason for revealing this information.

Once you are done with the background questions, tell the accused employee what the allegations are and ask for a response. As you did with the complaining employee, go through each allegation chronologically, asking whether the accused employee was present at the time and place alleged, who else was present, what happened, and how everyone reacted. Give the accused employee the opportunity to offer any explanations, denials, alibis, and witnesses for each alleged incident. Here are some sample questions to consider:

SAMPLE QUESTIONS

- What is your typical workday or workweek like? What time do you arrive? What time do you leave? What are your job responsibilities?

- Do you supervise any employees? What are their names and positions?

- How would you characterize your working relationship with your direct reports? Your coworkers?

- [Tell the accused employee what misconduct is alleged or suspected.] What is your response to these allegations?

- Did these things happen? [If the accused employee does not completely deny the allegations:] What did happen? When and where?

- How did [the alleged victim] respond? Did [the alleged victim] indicate that your statements or actions were offensive?

- Did anyone witness these incidents?

- Have you told anyone about these incidents?

- Have you kept any notes or a journal about these incidents?

- What is your work relationship like with [the alleged victim]?

- [If the accused employee denies the allegations:] Could another person have misunderstood your actions or statements? Do you think someone made up these incidents? Why?

- Have you ever used foul language in the workplace?

- Have you ever used racial epithets in the workplace? [Ask about other biases as appropriate, based on the allegations.]

- [For sexual harassment complaints:] Have you ever seen [the alleged victim] outside of work? Have you ever had a social relationship with each other? A romantic relationship? Have you ever asked [the alleged victim] out on a date? What was [the alleged victim]'s response?

- Have you ever been accused of harassment? How was the issue resolved?

- Have you had any training on workplace harassment issues?

SAMPLE QUESTIONS (cont'd.)

- Are you aware of the company's antiharassment policy?

- Do you know of anyone who might have information about these incidents?

- Do you know of any documents or other evidence relating to these allegations?

- Is there anything else you'd like to tell me?

Questions for Witnesses

When questioning witnesses, your goal is to gather information without giving too much away. To plan your questions, consider who suggested the witness and why. Did the witness see or hear the misconduct? Was the witness told of the misconduct? Is the witness privy to some details of the relationship between the complaining employee and the accused?

Start by explaining, in very general terms, why the witness is being interviewed—that you are investigating a workplace problem and you believe the witness might have information that will help you figure out what happened. Then, move into questions that will help you figure out if the witness could have seen or heard the alleged incidents. Finally, find out what the witness knows. Here are some sample questions to consider:

SAMPLE QUESTIONS

- Describe your typical workday or workweek. Who is your supervisor? Where is your workstation? What time do you typically arrive at work each day? What time do you leave?

- Do you work with [the alleged victim] or [the accused employee]? How would you describe their work relationship?

- Has [the alleged victim] ever spoken to you about [the accused employee]? Has [the accused employee] ever spoken to you about [the alleged victim]?

- Have you seen any interactions between [the alleged victim] and [the accused employee] that made you uncomfortable? Describe them to me.

- [If the witness may have seen or heard the incident, ask questions to figure out whether the witness was there and what happened.]

- Have you heard these issues discussed in the workplace? When, where, and by whom?

- Have you ever had any problems working with [the alleged victim] or [the accused employee]?

- Do you know of anyone else who might have information about these incidents? Are there any documents or other evidence that you know of relating to these incidents?

EXAMPLE: If the complaining employee says that the witness was present when her supervisor told a racist joke, you might ask: Did you attend a meeting to discuss sales techniques last Monday? What time was the meeting? Were you present for the whole meeting, or did you leave the room at any time? Who else was at the meeting? Do you remember any comments Tom made at the meeting?

If these questions don't get you the information you need, you'll have to ask more specific questions, like: Did Tom tell any jokes at the meeting? Do you remember him making any comments about Native Americans? What did he say?

Closing the Interview

Once you have finished your questions, review your notes with the person you interviewed. Make sure that your notes include all of the important details. Ask the employee not to discuss the complaint or the investigation with any coworkers. Remind the employee about retaliation, especially the accused employee. And ask the employee to come to you immediately with any new information.

This is all you have to tell witnesses. When you close an interview with the complaining or accused employee, let them know what will happen next. Tell them that you'll interview them again if any important new information comes up.

Follow-Up Interviews

If any new information comes up during your investigation, you should conduct follow-up interviews with the complaining and accused employee. Both employees should have the opportunity to respond to new allegations or defenses, to make sure that you have a complete understanding of the facts when you make your decision and to give you the opportunity to gauge credibility. It is especially important to let the accused employee know of any additional allegations that come up during the investigation. If you don't, you may be accused of unfairness for refusing to give him or her an opportunity to give his or her side of the story.

EXAMPLE 1: Siri complains that her supervisor, Jeff, is sexually harassing her. She says that he has persistently asked her out and has recently told her that he will not recommend her for promotion unless she agrees to go on a weekend trip with him. When you interview Jeff, he says that he has never asked Siri out or invited her away for the weekend, but that he has told her that he cannot recommend her for promotion because her performance has been slipping in recent months. He also says that Siri responded that she would get the promotion, regardless of his recommendation. In this case, you should definitely reinterview Siri and find out how she responds to Jeff's comments.

EXAMPLE 2: Emily complains that a coworker, Gabe, has harassed her because she is a member of Jews for Jesus. She says that Gabe frequently taunts her because of her religion, making comments like "If the Jews really liked Jesus, they wouldn't have killed him." You interview Gretchen, who works with both Emily and Gabe. Gretchen tells you that Gabe has made offensive anti-Semitic comments to her on several occasions, including calling Emily a "kike" and saying that Hitler had the right idea. Before you wrap up the investigation, you should go back to Gabe and confront him with these new allegations.

Gather Documents and Other Evidence

Unless harassment has escalated to physical touching or violence, it is primarily accomplished through communication. Racist epithets, pornographic images, demeaning jokes, slurs, or cartoons become harassment only when they are conveyed to another person who finds them offensive. Sometimes this communication is carried out in writing, at least in part. In a harassment investigation, part of your job is to gather any written communications relating to the problem—which could include email messages, letter, notes, and items posted in cubicles, on company bulletin boards, or in shared company spaces (such as locker rooms, restrooms, or the mail room).

If the victim alleges that harassment resulted in a negative job action—for example, denial of a promotion, raise, or desired transfer—there should be a paper trail. Consider whether performance evaluations, payroll records, or other personnel documents will shed some light on what happened.

Official company documents might also corroborate or raise doubts about one person's story. For example, an employee complains that his supervisor harassed him by making fun of his disability during a meeting with a client. The supervisor denies the harassment and contends that he wasn't even in the office on the date of the alleged incident—he was on a long-planned vacation with his family. In this situation, you could take a look at schedules and attendance records to find out the truth.

Finally, physical evidence (other than documents) may play an important role in the investigation. If the complaining employee claims that the alleged harasser left gifts or offensive objects (such as some racy lingerie or a photo of a mass murderer), try to track down those items. Ask about photographs of offensive items, if they aren't still available. For example, several female employees complain that a cake baked in the shape of a naked woman was served at an office function. Obviously, the cake is long gone—but someone may have taken a picture of it (or you might be able to find out which bakery supplied the creation).

Evaluate the Evidence

Sometimes, there are many witnesses to harassment. For example, an entire work group may hear a supervisor's racist jokes or sexual come-ons. If the victim is complaining of a hostile work environment, other workers may have seen or heard something. Often, however, harassment occurs behind closed doors, and only the harasser and harassee really know what happened. If you're facing this type of investigation and you've received conflicting stories, your credibility determinations will be especially important.

Review the factors listed in Chapter 4 as you try to figure out where the truth lies. Two factors can be especially relevant in harassment cases: corroboration and motive.

- **Corroboration.** Even if no one else was in the room when the alleged harassment took place, you can still try to corroborate other details of each person's story. For example, a secretary complains that her boss called her into his office several times a week to tell her racist jokes a friend sends him by email. Although no one else was in the room, you might find other corroborating evidence. Did anyone see her entering or leaving his office? If so, did she appear to be upset? Did she tell anyone about the incidents? Has he told similar jokes to other employees? Can his email messages be retrieved?

- **Motive.** Does either party have a motive to lie? Has either party told any other employees that he or she might make a false claim or false denial? Does the alleged harasser have any reason to act—or not to act—as the victim has claimed? Especially in sexual harassment cases where the parties have a prior relationship, it's important to consider any reasons they might have for their actions and statements.

If the Harassment Stops, You Made the Right Call

When courts have to decide whether an employer took appropriate corrective action, they focus on whether the harassment stopped. The ultimate test of whether an action was appropriate is effectiveness: Actions short of serious disciplinary measures can pass this test if they work.

EXAMPLE: Hattie, a housekeeper at a veterans medical center, complained that her coworker, Oliver, had grabbed her and put his arms around her twice during a work shift in September of 1996. Hattie reported the incidents to her supervisor, who investigated, confronted Oliver and told him the allegations were serious, and warned him to stay away from Hattie. Hattie told her supervisor that she was afraid of Oliver, although he hadn't done anything else to her since the incidents. A month later, Hattie filed a charge of sexual harassment; in response, Oliver was switched to a different shift, which overlapped Hattie's shift by an hour and a half.

Hattie sued for sexual harassment, complaining that her employer was required to "discipline" Oliver and that telling him to stay away from her and changing his shift didn't constitute discipline. The court disagreed. Because the employer took action that was effective in ending the harassment, the court found that it had met its obligation to take prompt remedial action. (*Star v. West*, 237 F.3d 1036 (9th Cir. 2001).)

If the harassment continues, however, the same corrective action might be insufficient. In the case of *Grego v. Meijer* (239 F.Supp.2d 676, W.D. Ky, 2002), an employer told the harasser that his comments were inappropriate and told him to leave the plaintiff alone. However, the court found these actions insufficient, because the victim had twice reported the harassment, the employer was aware that other women were being harassed by the same man, and the harassment continued after the reports.

Take Action

If you find that some form of harassment occurred, your company has a legal obligation to take prompt corrective action, reasonably calculated to end the harassment. The right corrective action is one that:

- stops the harassment,
- prevents harassment from recurring, and
- restores the victim to the position he or she would have held absent the harassment.

Employers face some tough decisions when considering how to deal with harassment. On the one hand, an employer will be legally liable for any harassment that occurs following a complaint. In other words, the action you take must be effective at stopping the harassment—if it isn't, your company will be on the hook for any further incidents. On the other hand, an employee who is punished too severely might have a separate legal claim against your company for breach of contract, discrimination, or defamation, depending on the circumstances. The only way to walk this fine line is to make the punishment fit the crime. Consider:

- the severity of the incidents
- how often they occurred
- how many total incidents took place
- the harm to the victim
- whether the law was violated
- whether workplace policies were violated
- whether the harasser holds a position of authority in the company, such as officer, manager, or supervisor (harassment by a higher-level employee is more serious and requires a heightened response)
- how the company has treated similar incidents in the past, and
- the harasser's history at the company—does the employee have a record of similar problems, or is this a one-time lapse from an otherwise stellar worker?

(For more information on choosing an appropriate response to wrongdoing—and on what to do if your investigation is inconclusive or reveals that no wrongdoing took place—see Chapter 4.)

Finally, don't forget the victim. Your company has a legal obligation to undo any harm the victim suffered as a result of the harassment. This could include:

- reinstating a victim who was fired for refusing to acquiesce to harassment

- restoring any job benefits or promotions a victim lost as a result of the harassment

- removing negative evaluations or critical comments in the victim's personnel file, if they arose from the harassment, and

- crediting the victim with any paid leave taken as a result of the harassment.

Document the Investigation

Document your harassment investigation just as you would any other workplace investigation. (See Chapter 4 for details.) Because of the Supreme Court's decisions creating a potential defense for employers who promptly investigate claims and take other steps to prevent harassment, you can expect that your report will end up in the hands of a jury if an employee files a lawsuit based on the underlying incidents. Make sure to write a report that's complete and professional and fully supports the conclusions you reached. (Appendix C includes a sample report of a harassment investigation.)

Follow Up

Once the investigation is over, take some time to consider what you discovered. If you concluded that harassment—or even inappropriate behavior short of harassment—occurred, think about whether your company's policies against harassment and misconduct could use some revamping. Do employees understand what types of conduct violate company policy? Is there some confusion over whether particular types of behavior—joking around, teasing, flirtatious comments, or references to an employee's race or religion—are appropriate in the workplace? You may need to update company policies against harassment to ensure that everyone understands what's allowed and what's prohibited.

This is also a good time to consider harassment training. Many companies and workplace consultants offer harassment training, often in separate sessions for managers and employees. If your employees don't seem to get the difference between an innocent compliment and an offensive come-on, training can help make these distinctions clear.

You should also follow up directly with the employees involved in the incident, particularly if an employee complained of harassment. Retaliation can be a problem if the alleged harasser remains in the workplace—and it may be more likely if the accused employee was cleared of wrongdoing. That employee probably feels pretty upset about the allegations and the investigation, and that anger may naturally focus on the employee who complained. The accused employee may feel entitled to take this frustration out on the complaining employee, because the company found that the allegations weren't supported by evidence.

To guard against this risk, meet with the complaining employee regularly after the investigation ends. You might hold these meetings every couple of weeks for a month or so, then check in once a month for a few months to make sure that no retaliation is taking place. You should also meet with the accused employee a few times to make sure that things are getting back to normal and that there have been no repercussions as a result of the investigation.

Investigating Workplace Theft

S ome readers might be tempted to skip this chapter, thinking to themselves, "Our company couldn't have a theft problem—our employees wouldn't steal from us." Well, guess again. Businesses lose billions of dollars a year to employee theft. In fact, retailers lose more to their own employees than to shoplifters, according to a 2002 survey by Ernst & Young. And experts estimate that up to one-third of small business closures and bankruptcies are due to employee theft.

Perhaps the most surprising statistics are not about the dollars lost to employee theft, but about employees' willingness to steal. According to a 1998 survey by The Security Group of Cahner's Business Information, 66% of employees would steal if they saw others getting away with it— and that's on top of the 13% who will steal regardless. These statistics show that an employer's response to theft can make a huge impact. A company that investigates and punishes thieves shows other employees that they shouldn't expect to get away with anything. Given these facts, it's imperative for companies to investigate every internal theft, no matter how large or small.

Theft investigations differ from investigation of workplace violence, harassment, or discrimination in several ways:

- **The company is usually the victim.** This means that you probably won't have to anticipate a potential lawsuit from an employee who was harmed by theft, so proving that your company took appropriate action to stop the misconduct won't be your foremost concern (as it often is in other types of investigations). It also means that you won't have a complaint or an interview to fill in the basic facts, which is why documents are the backbone of many theft investigations.

- **Theft is unlikely to be reported.** Most employees are not highly motivated to rat out their coworkers, especially if they are stealing from the company rather than from a particular individual. So, unlike other investigations, the real trick in a theft investigation is learning about the problem in the first place. This chapter describes some of the warning signs of various types of theft, so you'll know what types of situations warrant a closer look.

- **Theft investigations are whodunits.** Unlike a harassment or discrimination investigation, in which you sort out conflicting stories to determine whether something improper occurred, a theft investigation is usually about one thing: catching a thief. This means that you'll want to gather all of your evidence—and, usually, conduct all of your other interviews—before you confront your suspect.

- **Employers want payback.** In addition to stopping the flow of stolen money or property, you'll also want to get your cash or goods back, if possible.

Because theft investigations are unique, this chapter differs slightly from others in this book. First, it describes some common types of scams, rip-offs, and embezzlement that can occur in the workplace. This information will help you figure out if your company has a theft problem that requires investigation.

As in the other chapters in Part II, the second part of this chapter explains how the ten steps to an effective investigation work when you're faced with employee theft. But you will notice that the order of the steps is slightly different—here, you'll look at documents before you conduct your interviews. You can't confront or interview a workplace suspect until you have examined all of the evidence that supports your position; this will help you elicit a confession, if possible. This chapter also addresses other unique features of a theft investigation, including tips for minimizing theft and dealing with insurers.

How Employees Steal

Most employee theft is never discovered. In most cases, employees get away with theft—the money is never returned and the employers never figure out that profits are trickling out through the back door. That's why the real trick in a theft investigation is figuring out that theft has occurred in the first place.

The bad news is that the methods and means of employee thieves are unlimited—thieves invent new ways to rip off their employers every day. The good news is that a handful of schemes and patterns come up again and again and account for much of the theft most employers are likely to face. By familiarizing yourself with these methods—and the telltale signs of workplace thievery—you'll know when your company might have an employee theft problem on its hands, which in turn will help you figure out when you need to investigate.

Follow the Money

No matter how an employee steals from an employer, the net result is the same: The employee has more money, while the company has less. The employee's found money is one key to discovering employee fraud. An employee who suddenly has fancy cars, a new summer home, and expensive clothing and jewelry (and no good explanation of how it all came about) is someone you'll want to talk to if you uncover a theft problem. Tread carefully when making inquiries, however, because snooping into an employee's personal finances can leave you open to an invasion of privacy claim. (See "Plan the Investigation," below, for more information).

Employee theft can be broken down into four basic categories:

- schemes for stealing money
- schemes for stealing property
- false disbursements—schemes that trick the company into paying money to the employee, and
- conflicts of interest, in which the employee uses his or her position in the company to favor particular vendors, suppliers, or other third parties.

Why Do Employees Steal?

The most basic reason employees steal is because they can. In other words, the opportunity is there, and the employees believe they won't get caught or suffer any consequences. (Your company can nip this kind of theft in the bud by making it difficult to steal and by disciplining those who do steal.)

In addition to plain old opportunism, some other common reasons for workplace theft are:

- financial need (sometimes caused by problems like gambling or substance abuse)
- revenge for perceived mistreatment by the employer, and
- excitement—some employees report stealing to see if they can get away with it or because they are bored.

Stealing Money

Employees can steal money in a variety of ways, from simply pocketing cash rather than putting it in the register to developing elaborate schemes for diverting funds (and covering their tracks). Here are some common ways employees steal money—and a few of the warning signs of a money theft problem.

Skimming

In a skimming scheme, an employee steals money before it is entered into the company's records. Any employee who is responsible for receiving payments to the company can skim—this includes an employee who runs a register, records customer payments, does the company's books, or otherwise acts as an intake point for money coming into the company. Skimming can be tough to detect because it doesn't "unbalance" the company's books. Because the money is taken before it is entered into the records, the thief doesn't have to make up a reason why the money disappeared or make false entries in the company's accounting system.

EXAMPLES OF SKIMMING:

- **Failing to ring up or record sales.** The employee charges the customer and pockets the money, and the company never knows the sale was made. The skim can be accomplished at a cash register or anywhere else money comes in—for example, at customers' homes for an outside salesperson.
- **Diverting checks.** The employee endorses the incoming check on behalf of the company, then on his or her own behalf. The employee then cashes the check or deposits it in a personal account.
- **Under-ringing sales.** The employee records the sale for a particular amount, charges the customer more, and then pockets the difference.

WARNING SIGNS: Skimming

Most types of skimming work by the following equation: The customer is receiving goods or services, but the employee—rather than the company—is getting paid for them. Therefore, most of the warning signs of skimming involve discrepancies between how much work your company is doing (or how much product it is moving) and how much money it is taking in.

Red flags for skimming include:

- lower revenues than expected,
- increased inventory shrinkage (that is, goods are disappearing in numbers that are not accounted for in sales),
- declining cash sales as a percentage of total sales (because most employees want to pocket cash, these are the sales that don't get recorded), and
- customer complaints (a customer who notices an overcharge is likely to complain, but some customers will also tell you if they notice an employee who fails to ring up a sale, or if they receive a cancelled check endorsed to someone other than the company).

Lapping

Lapping is a more complex method of theft that resembles a pyramid scheme. The employee steals some money as it comes into the company, then uses subsequent incoming payments to make up the difference. As long as the employee keeps up the scheme, the shortfall won't be noticed.

EXAMPLE: Sam is the bookkeeper at a small company that supplies uniforms to institutional customers. All of the payments from customers go through Sam, who enters them in the company's books and deposits them into the company's bank account. Sam receives a payment for $100 from one customer, which he diverts to his own bank account and does not enter into the company's records. The next day, Sam receives a payment for $300 from a second customer. He credits $100 to the first customer's account, then waits for another payment to make up the shortfall to the second customer—and so on, and so on.

Many lapping schemes eventually collapse under their own weight. The employee won't be able to resist the temptation to take more and more money, which creates a larger and larger discrepancy to be hidden. At some point, there won't be enough money coming in to make up the shortfall. By the time this happens, however, your company might be out many thousands of dollars.

WARNING SIGNS: Lapping

Lapping is a pretty complicated affair, which requires the employee to keep careful track of precisely which Peter was robbed to pay which Paul, and by how much. Here are some of the red flags of lapping:

- a money-handling employee who never takes a day off work. If the lapper isn't in the office to apply incoming payments to shortchanged accounts (and to handle any queries about whether and when certain payments were made), the whole system will fall apart
- delays in posting customer payments
- a slowdown in incoming payments and/or an increase in late accounts, and
- customer complaints

Void/Refund Schemes

Anyone who has ever worked a register knows about the void function—it zeroes out a sale that has already been entered. Voiding is legitimately used when the cashier enters an incorrect amount or a customer decides not to buy an item after all. However, it can also be used to back money out of the system, which the employee can then steal.

Refund schemes are similar: The employee enters a false refund, then pockets the "refunded" money. Employees can also use an employer's promotional refunds or discounts to steal money. For example, an employee who can lay hands on a stack of cards offering "$10 off any purchase of $50 or more" can apply the cards to sales (unbeknownst to the customer), then pocket the $10 discount on each transaction. Similarly, a waiter can use "buy one entrée, get one free" promotional ads to get some quick cash by applying the discount to tables that paid in full.

Either method can be used at cash registers or at any other point where money comes into the company.

EXAMPLE: Joanna is a cashier in a drug store. The store offers customer refunds on items that have not been used and are returned in their original packaging within 30 days of purchase. The cashiers are responsible for checking the condition of the item and making sure the customer shows a receipt; the cashier is supposed to cross the returned item off of the receipt, return it to the customer, then tender the refund, using the "refund" key on the register to record the money paid out. Joanna gets a lot of use out of that refund key—she records at least a refund a day, to the tune of several hundred dollars a week, then pockets the money at the end of her shift.

WARNING SIGNS: Void/Refund Schemes

In void and refund schemes, the company pays out money (to the employee) for returned or "unsold" items, but those items never find their way back to the shelves. Therefore, as in a skimming scenario, these schemes result in depleted inventory and shrinking cash. Here are some of the red flags of void and refund frauds:

- increased refund and void transactions
- cash sales declining as a percentage of total sales (again, because the employee wants to be "paid" in cash)
- irregularities in refund paperwork (missing documents, illegible customer names, duplicates)
- one employee getting particularly high numbers of voids, refunds, or customers taking advantage of a promotional offer, and
- voids or refunds issued at the end of a shift.

Ripping Off Customers

Schemes to steal from customers (rather than from the company) are very troubling for business owners. Although the company isn't losing money directly off its bottom line, its employees are ripping off the very people it most wants to please. Because this kind of theft depends on customer ignorance, it doesn't always work. All it takes is a customer complaint or two, and you'll uncover the whole scheme—as long as you are vigilant.

Stealing From Other Employees

Some workplace thieves target their coworkers. For example, you may face a rash of missing wallets or personal items stolen from employee offices. This type of theft is less common than stealing from an employer, for two reasons: (1) While employees may perceive stealing from the company as a "victimless crime," stealing from a coworker directly harms a particular person, which makes it harder for the thief to justify; and (2) very few employees would hesitate to turn in a thief who was stealing from them, while many employees would be reluctant to turn in a coworker who was ripping off the company.

The warning signs of a thief who is ripping off coworkers are pretty straightforward: Employees will notice money or items missing. In addition, watch out for employees who spend time in another employee's workspace when that employee isn't there—or in a common area, such as a locker room or changing room, without a good reason. Some employees try to avoid detection by committing theft when they know other employees won't be in their usual places—before work hours, after work hours, during lunch, or during times when all employees are supposed to be elsewhere, such as during a fire drill, companywide event, or mandatory training.

The most common way employees steal from customers is simple overcharging. For example, a waiter might charge a diner for something the diner didn't order or receive, or a cashier might ring up an item twice or charge more than the store does for an item. If the customer doesn't notice, then the employee takes the money attributable to the overcharge. These schemes can get more elaborate—and more costly as well. An employee might steal customer credit card numbers to use for personal purchases, for example.

WARNING SIGNS: Stealing From Customers

When employees steal from customers, the customers themselves are your early warning system. Here are some red flags of this type of theft:

- customer complaints, especially when most of them point to the same employee
- frequent "errors" and voids attributable to the same employee. These are the signs that the customer caught on to the overcharge, and the employee had to correct the bill, and
- increased contacts from credit card issuers. Customers have the option of protesting an overcharge or unauthorized use of their credit card to their credit card issuer, which must then investigate the situation. If you start hearing about a number of questionable charges by your company, you know you have a problem on your hands.

Larceny

An employee commits larceny by taking money after it has been entered into the company's records. These are the least imaginative—and easiest to detect—theft schemes, because the losses will show up in your company's books eventually.

EXAMPLES OF LARCENY:

- A cashier takes $20 or $30 from the register during each shift.
- An employee responsible for making bank deposits takes cash out of the deposit bag, then alters the deposit slip to show the lower amount.
- An employee steals money from the petty cash drawer.
- An employee writes company checks payable to "cash" or to him- or herself.

> **WARNING SIGNS: Larceny**
>
> An employee who commits larceny makes either no efforts or halfhearted efforts to cover up the crime. Therefore, the red flags of larceny are all about discrepancies between how much money your company should have and how much money it actually has, including:
>
> - cash register drawers that are always short
> - bank deposits that don't match total sales, as shown by receipts, register tapes, and so on
> - cash missing from anywhere the company keeps it (the petty cash account, a safe, the area where the company keeps change for registers)
> - company checks that are missing or out of sequence, and
> - company checks made out to "cash" or to an employee, or excessive numbers of checks that are recorded as void.

Stealing Property

Although most workplace thieves are after money, some will go after other things, too—merchandise, raw materials, equipment, trade secrets, and so on. It's easy to understand why employees steal money: They can use it immediately, to purchase whatever they want. But stealing property is different. Unless the employee wants the item for personal use (as might be the case with a computer or jewelry), the employee will have to convert the item into cash or some other compensation. This means that those who steal goods may be working with an outsider, such as a fence or a competitor, who wants to buy.

Theft of Goods

If you take a look around your company, you'll probably find lots of things an enterprising thief could take. If your company is in the manufacturing industry, its raw materials and finished product could be stolen. If your company is in retail, its merchandise is up for grabs. And virtually every business uses some equipment, from computers and adding machines to tools, building supplies, and heavy machinery.

Common shipping and receiving theft schemes include undercounting goods received—or shorting customers on goods shipped—and keeping the extra stuff; categorizing received items as damaged; or fudging paperwork to make it look like more goods are legitimately leaving the warehouse than are actually being ordered by customers.

EXAMPLE: Roger works in the warehouse of a computer store. When he receives shipments from suppliers, he sometimes sets aside equipment like modems or speakers, which he steals at the end of his shift. To keep his theft from showing up when inventory is taken, Roger sets aside the invoice, alters the numbers, and submits a color photocopy of the doctored document.

Employees who steal merchandise often act just like shoplifters—they take your products and slip them into purses or bags, stuff them into coat pockets, or spirit them off to their cars during a break or after work hours.

Equipment thieves sometimes concoct stories to explain away the missing property. For example, an employee who has a company-issued laptop computer might falsely claim that it was stolen from the employee's car or home.

WARNING SIGNS: Theft of Goods

An employee who steals goods needs some way to get them out of your company and sometimes needs a third party to sell them to. Here are a few red flags:

- employees who are in the wrong place at the wrong time, take frequent breaks, or carry bags or wear bulky clothing
- employees who meet with outsiders on or near company property
- employees who leave work with large packages
- shipping and receiving paperwork that has been altered or is missing, and
- inventory numbers that don't add up.

Intellectual Property Theft

The real value of many businesses lies not in their equipment or their merchandise, but in their intellectual property (IP)—the trade secrets, customer lists, formulae, recipes, business methods, and other intangible information that make the company a success. An employee who steals these assets can wreak enormous damage on a company—usually because these assets are what give the company an edge over competitors. Once the information is out, the competitive edge is gone.

Some IP thieves sell business secrets to competing companies, while others use the secrets to start their own competitive businesses, publicize the information as acts of revenge, or give the secrets to subsequent employers.

EXAMPLE: Harold works for a sports food company that manufactures energy bars, drinks, and gels. The company recently developed a new line of energy bars that are salty rather than sweet—the end result is a bar that tastes like potato chips or pretzels rather than cookies or candy. The bars have proven enormously popular with athletes, and competitors are trying desperately to reverse engineer the product. Harold downloads the company's recipes on to a floppy disk and sells them to a competitor, who then claims to have successfully cracked the code.

WARNING SIGNS: IP Theft

Unfortunately, employers often learn of IP theft only after the horses have left the barn. Here are some red flags:

- An employee leaves to start a competing business.
- Competitors suddenly develop products that are similar to your company's or start calling on your company's customers.
- Unusual attempts are made to access physical areas of your company or portions of its computer system where trade secrets are kept. Employees who are in the wrong place at the wrong time—in the workplace or in cyberspace—bear a closer look.
- The number of computer password violations increases, indicating that someone is trying to get into sensitive files.

> ⚠ **CAUTION**
>
> **Watch out for identity theft.** Sometimes, a workplace thief steals a customer list not to do business with them, but to misuse their identities for financial fraud. Whenever personal information is stolen from your company, whether from customers or from other employees, identity theft may not be far behind. In these situations, your company might have an obligation to notify those whose identifying information has been stolen, so they can take steps to prevent fraud by, for example, putting a security freeze on their credit report.

Fake Disbursements

In a fake disbursement scheme, an employee gets the company to pay money to the employee on false pretenses. Rather than simply stealing the money, the employee submits phony invoices, expense reimbursements, or other paperwork so that the company will disburse money to the employee. In effect, the employee submits illegitimate requests through legitimate company channels to commit the crime. Here are a few of the most common types of fake disbursements.

Phony Vendor/Supplier and Other Billing Schemes

Many an employer has paid money to a nonexistent vendor—a company or account set up by an employee, who then submits fake invoices or other requests for payment to the company. An employee might also set up a false vendor in order to overcharge the company for goods. For example, an employee might establish a company to purchase raw materials the employer uses to make its products, then sell the materials to the employer at a steep mark-up.

EXAMPLE 1: George is in charge of buying materials for a clothing manufacturer. The company buys buttons in huge quantities from a variety of suppliers. George sets up his own company and purchases buttons from some of his employer's biggest suppliers. Then, in his role as buyer for the clothing company, he purchases buttons from his own company, at a sweet 100% mark-up.

EXAMPLE 2: Hannah is a bookkeeper for a company that provides human resources training to businesses across the nation. The company has some on-staff trainers, but it also uses consultants to provide training in distant locations. These consultants submit invoices for payment. Hannah starts drafting her own invoices and slipping them in with the consultants' requests for payment. The invoices are submitted in the name of "HHH Training," a name she also uses to open a bank account. When the checks are cut, she simply deposits the HHH Training check in her new bank account.

An employee can also set up a phony billing scheme using the company's existing vendors. For example, an employee might copy a legitimate invoice and submit it twice: The first check goes to the vendor, and the second goes to the employee. A more elaborate version of this scheme involves refunds. The employee submits the invoice twice and actually pays the vendor twice. When the vendor realizes the error and refunds the second payment, the employee keeps the money.

WARNING SIGNS: Phony Vendor Schemes

In a phony vendor scheme—as in other fake disbursement scenarios—an employee covers the theft with false paperwork. This means that your first clue to the problem will often be a document that doesn't look quite right.

Here are some red flags to phony vendor schemes:

- new vendors who are unknown to the company
- invoices that lack the usual information, such as a taxpayer ID number, address, or phone number, or are not printed on letterhead
- duplicate invoices or invoices that appear to have been altered
- invoices that don't contain the usual billing detail, or that request nice round numbers. For example, if most of your consulting invoices list hours expended on various types of tasks and an hourly rate, you should question an invoice that requests a flat $5,000 without explanation
- vendors who have the same name (or initials), address, or telephone number as one of your employees
- cancelled vendor or supplier checks that have been endorsed by one of your employees, and
- increased costs for vendors, suppliers, or materials.

Expense Schemes

If employees are entitled to claim expense reimbursements, your company is at risk of paying out money for expenses that were never incurred. For example, an employee might claim false expenses, claim that personal expenses were incurred for business purposes, or make unauthorized charges on a company credit card.

EXAMPLE: Marvin takes a three-day business trip for his employer. He submits an expense reimbursement form claiming that he spent $150 a night on a hotel room, about $50 each day on food, $50 on cab fare to get from the hotel to customer locations, and $300 taking a client and her husband to a fancy restaurant for dinner. In fact, Marvin stayed with his brother-in-law, ate fast food, took public transportation, and had dinner at the client's home. Less money spent on bus fare and hamburgers, Marvin can clear almost $1,000 in phony reimbursements from a single trip.

WARNING SIGNS: Phony Expenses
The documents an employee submits in order to be reimbursed are often the key to unraveling expense fraud. Here are some red flags:

- failure to submit receipts for claimed expenses
- receipts that have been doctored or photocopied, do not clearly show the merchant and amount of sale, are not dated, or appear to claim duplicate expenses (for example, two receipts for dinner on the same day)
- expense claims for personal items
- expense claims that are higher than they should be (for example, an especially high rate for a hotel room or meal), and
- expense claims that are just below the limit for an internal audit. Some companies routinely approve expense claims up to a certain amount but will look more closely at a claim that exceeds the limit. An employee whose expenses always approach the audit limit without crossing the line might be gaming the system.

Conflicts of Interest

In a conflict of interest scheme, an employee uses company resources or a company position to create illegitimate moneymaking opportunities. These schemes often involve hiring preferred vendors or suppliers, either in exchange for a bribe or kickback or because the vendor has some financial connection to the employee.

Bribes and Kickbacks

An employee who takes money to help an outsider get business with the company is participating in a bribe or kickback scheme. A bribe is a simple payment up front for the privilege of getting work; a kickback is a payment of a percentage or portion of the money the outsider makes from the company.

> **EXAMPLE:** Ron is the office manager for a large medical practice. His responsibilities include making sure that the vending machines are stocked and that coffee, snacks, and other amenities are available to the staff. A new vendor who is trying to break into the field offers Ron a 5% kickback to get the contract for coffee service at his company. Ron agrees and soon begins collecting a monthly payment from the vendor.

WARNING SIGNS: Bribes and Kickbacks

Bribe and kickback schemes involve third parties: not only the company that is paying the employee, but also the companies that are left out in the cold because they are not paying the employee. Here are some red flags:

- vendor complaints. If your company's usual vendors suddenly find themselves out of a contract, they might complain. And if an employee tries to hit up an unwilling company for a bribe, you might hear about it.
- new and unknown vendors
- increased costs—a vendor who has to pay a bribe or kickback is going to have to charge more to cover that cost. And an employee who is receiving a kickback wants the vendor to earn as much as possible from your company.

- increasing inventory or services (because the employee wants your company to buy as much as possible from the crooked vendor), and
- a high percentage of business going to one vendor or supplier (the one who's paying off the employee).

Self-Dealing

In a self-dealing scenario, an employee uses his or her position in the company to improperly favor outsiders who are connected with the employee—family members, friends, or the employee's own side business, for example. For example, an employee might hire her husband's law firm to provide legal services, contract to purchase computer training from a friend, or arrange to sell your company's products—at a discount—to her own company, for quick markup and resale.

> EXAMPLE: Shawna runs her own crafts business making scented candles and bath salts. Her boyfriend, Tom, works for a chain of gift shops that lease space in upscale hotels. Tom arranges for the company to purchase Shawna's products at a hefty markup, even though it already sells several similar items.

WARNING SIGNS: Self-Dealing

The whole point of self-dealing is to favor certain vendors and suppliers over others. This favoritism sometimes leads to discovery. Here are some red flags:

- new or unknown vendors
- vendors who have the same name, address, or telephone number as an employee
- complaints from vendors who are not receiving special treatment or who were frozen out so the employee could favor a relative or friend
- higher than usual costs for products or services, and
- a high percentage of business going to one vendor.

Ten Steps to a Successful Theft Investigation

This section explains how to apply the basic investigation steps covered in Part I of this book to an investigation of employee theft. If you haven't read Part I, you should do so before getting into this more specific material—the discussion that follows assumes that you are already familiar with basic investigation procedures and will not repeat all of the information covered in Part I.

How Employers Learn of Theft

According to the Association of Certified Fraud Examiners, employers find out about workplace fraud—including theft by employees and managers—in a variety of ways. The most common way is a tip from another employee. Somewhat less encouraging is the second most common method employers learn of workplace fraud: by accident. Here are some others:

- internal audits or internal controls
- external audits
- tips from vendors or customers
- anonymous tips, and
- notification by law enforcement personnel.

Decide Whether to Investigate

Once you learn about employee theft, you should always investigate, regardless of how much is missing. Studies have shown that workplace thieves tend to start small, then expand their operations. They take small amounts of money or items that aren't very valuable, then wait to see what happens. If nobody catches on, pretty soon the sky's the limit. Investigating a $50 register shortage or slight increase in inventory shrinkage today could save your company from a much more expensive theft scheme tomorrow.

Your investigation will also serve as a deterrent to others. If other employees see a coworker getting away with stealing from the company, they are more likely to start taking a five-finger discount as well.

Investigating will also shield your company from legal hassles down the road. If you want to take action against an employee whom you believe is stealing from the company, you will want some solid evidence to back up your decision. Otherwise, the employee might sue for defamation.

EXAMPLE: Maurice is a sales clerk at a clothing store. Another clerk, Rhonda, tells you that she saw Maurice putting several expensive leather jackets into a bag and taking it out to his car. You immediately fire Maurice. If Maurice actually stole the jackets, then there's nothing to worry about—because truth is a defense to a defamation claim, treating Maurice as a thief doesn't constitute defamation if he actually is a thief. But if Maurice didn't steal the jackets—if Rhonda made the whole story up to cover her own theft, for example—then you have a major problem. Not only did you falsely treat Maurice as a thief, but you also didn't even bother to look into the allegations. Now you're facing a potential lawsuit and you still have a thief on the payroll.

Also, if the thief stole from someone outside of the company—for example, a customer, client, or vendor—then your company could be liable for any future losses that person suffers if it fails to take reasonable precautions to stop the theft. And reasonable precautions include investigating to find and stop the culprit.

Employee Theft and the Sarbanes-Oxley Act

In the wake of Enron and other corporate accounting scandals, Congress passed the Sarbanes-Oxley Act of 2002. This law is intended to increase the accountability of publicly traded companies for their reported financial results, thereby making sure that investors have accurate information on which to base their decisions. Among the law's many requirements is a mandate that all publicly traded companies must establish procedures by which employees can anonymously and confidentially submit concerns about questionable accounting and auditing matters. Certain kinds of employee theft might fall within this category, particularly if they result in doctored financial records. The Act also imposes obligations on public companies that discover errors or falsifications in their financial reports.

Take Immediate Action, If Necessary

If you suspect employee theft (or you know that someone is stealing, but you don't know who), there are a few actions you can take right away, before you start investigating. Of course, the options available to you will depend on what you know, what type of theft you suspect, and who might be responsible.

Enhance Security and Safeguards

If you can isolate the theft to one area of operations, you can take some steps to make stealing more difficult. An effective way to do this is to simply add more people to any process where money might be disappearing. Because most workplace theft is committed by employees acting alone, increasing the number of people who have to be involved in any transaction will foil opportunities for theft. Fraud experts call this "segregation" of job duties—if you make sure that no one employee is responsible for every step of a transaction, you will make it much more difficult for any employee to use the transaction as a vehicle for theft.

For example, if you know that there is something amiss in the bookkeeping department, your company could require a second signature (of the company president or other high-ranking official) on all outgoing checks, or have someone outside the department open all incoming mail and log any payments received. If there's a problem in the receiving department, the company could require two employees to check the items received against the purchase order, invoice, and/or packing slip.

There are other ways to increase workplace controls against theft. Requiring additional paperwork—particularly paperwork that involves other people—is another good way to cut down on theft. For example, if you suspect that a cashier is giving false refunds, your company could require all cashiers to fill in a form with the name, address, and phone number of every customer who received a refund. Let employees know that you will follow up with the customers—then do it. Or, if you are concerned about inflated expense reports, require employees to submit a dated, itemized receipt for all claimed expenses.

 TIP

Make safeguards permanent once the investigation is over. The same procedures that will help you draw the brakes on theft while you conduct your investigation will help your company prevent theft in the future. See "Follow Up," below, for more information on preventing theft.

Another way to deter employee theft (at least temporarily) is to tell employees that the company will be conducting a routine audit for the next couple of weeks. (This will also give you a good cover for your investigation.) Of course, you can't do this forever, but most workplace thieves will put their schemes on hold if they know that scrutiny will be especially high.

Suspend the Suspected Wrongdoer

If you have a pretty good idea who is behind a theft problem, you might consider suspending that employee while you conduct the investigation. One benefit of this approach—other than immediately stopping the theft—is that the employee won't have time to destroy workplace evidence. On the other hand, by tipping your hand at the outset, you lose any chance you might have to catch the employee in the act. You'll have to weigh the company's risk of further losses against your need for this kind of evidence of the theft.

> **EXAMPLE:** Rick is the night manager of a department store's warehouse. In the past several months, the warehouse has had some serious "shrinkage" problems, particularly in big screen televisions. The store owner suspects Rick because the thefts are taking place at night and Rick is the only worker who has a key to the loading dock area—the only place where the televisions could be removed without attracting suspicion. If he suspended Rick right away, the owner could stop the theft problem, but he might never get proof that Rick is behind the robberies. Instead, the owner decides to hang around outside the loading dock for a few nights after the store receives a large shipment of television sets. When he sees Rick and a couple of his friends making off with a few TVs, the owner has all the proof he needs.

Suspending an employee before you conduct an investigation also poses some legal risks. If your hunch proves wrong, the company could be liable for damaging the suspended employee's reputation. For this reason, you should only suspend an employee if you have strong, objective evidence of wrongdoing—and you should not publicize the suspension in the workplace. You should also make special efforts to wrap up your investigation quickly.

CAUTION

Don't suspend workers without pay. From a legal standpoint, suspending exempt, salaried employees—those who are not entitled to overtime pay for working extra hours—without pay while you investigate violates wage and hour laws. And even though you can suspend hourly, nonexempt workers without pay, it's not a good idea. A suspension without pay is punitive: It improperly signals that you have made up your mind about the allegations before you've even begun to investigate. A worker who is suspended without pay will probably be angry about it—and if the allegations are false, that anger may well provide the fuel for a lawsuit. And unpaid suspensions can be an administrative hassle, as they require you to interrupt your usual payroll system. The wages you shell out to a temporarily suspended employee will be a small price to pay to avoid these problems.

Contact Your Company's Insurance Carrier

Most businesses carry insurance for a variety of potential mishaps. Believe it or not, a company can insure itself against employee theft—and it's possible your business already has such coverage. If your company has a fidelity bond or a crime loss or employee dishonesty policy, contact the insurance agent right away to find out how to file a claim. If an employee theft is covered under one of these policies, you will ordinarily have a short period of time after you discover the loss to notify the insurance company. Your agent or a business lawyer can tell you what documents and information you need to file a claim.

> **! CAUTION**
>
> **If theft may be covered by insurance, contact a lawyer before you investigate—and before you report the loss.** When your company buys an insurance policy, it gives the insurance company the right of "subrogation." This means that the insurance company has the legal authority to proceed against anyone who causes a covered loss in order to get back the money it had to pay out on the policy. If you take any action that compromises the insurance company's subrogation right, your company may not be entitled to collect on its policy. If your company's insurance covers employee theft, talk to a lawyer right away to get some advice on conducting an investigation that won't run afoul of the insurance company's rights. Otherwise, the insurance company may refuse to make good on your company's claim.

Choose the Investigator

You'll find general information on choosing an investigator—including the importance of impartiality, experience, and professionalism—in Chapter 2. While those qualities are important when investigating any kind of workplace problem, investigating employee theft often requires some additional qualifications, including subject matter expertise and interview skills.

Subject Matter Expertise

As you can see from the discussion above, unraveling an employee theft scheme sometimes requires a good deal of technical knowledge. Depending on the type of theft you are facing, you may need some special expertise to complete the investigation. For example, investigating the theft of intellectual property might require a background in computer technology or science. Investigating a complex vendor fraud or lapping scheme might require accounting or auditing skills.

If you're facing a large-scale or highly sophisticated theft problem, you should consider using an outside investigator who has the necessary expertise. Another option is to team up an in-house investigator with an expert who can provide the necessary information. You can use an internal expert (for example, the head of your company's technology services division or its chief financial officer) or bring in an expert from the outside. If you decide to bring in an outside expert to assist with the investigation, remember that your company will ultimately be responsible for any actions the expert takes. This means that someone on your company's payroll should be overseeing the expert's work. In addition, if the theft is related to confidential company information, you should have the expert sign a nondisclosure agreement.

> **CAUTION**
>
> **Don't use an internal expert unless you're sure that person isn't involved in the theft.** If you need a particular type of expertise to ferret out a theft, chances are good that your thief also has some experience in that area. This means that your in-house expert could also be your prime suspect—and ultimately, your thief. To avoid this "fox guarding the henhouse" problem, make certain that any internal expert you use could not have committed the theft. If you aren't sure, bring in an outsider.

Here are some examples of experts who might be valuable in an employee theft investigation:

- **Forensic accountants.** These experts review a company's financial documents for signs of fraud. They comb through the books looking for missing paperwork, financial improprieties, unexplained transactions, and other red flags of theft. (Although their title makes them sound like crime scene specialists, "forensic" refers to work that is done in possible preparation for legal proceedings.)

- **Certified fraud examiners.** These specialists—who come from many different professional backgrounds, including criminology, accounting, and law—are trained in the prevention and detection of fraud. Like forensic accountants, they can help uncover signs of fraud in your company's books.

- **Document examiners.** These experts examine disputed or suspect documents and determine how old they are, whether they are copies or originals, whether they have been altered or supplemented, and whether handwriting and signatures are genuine, among other things. If you are facing a document-intensive investigation—particularly if there is a question about whether documents have been altered—these experts may be useful.

- **Computer specialists.** Sometimes, you just need a techie to help you sort things out. A computer specialist can help you figure out whether certain files or documents were accessed, altered, deleted, or copied. They can also track who has been where in your company's computer system—valuable information for uncovering bookkeeping fraud or intellectual property theft.

- **Experts in your company's field.** If you are trying to figure out whether your company's intellectual property has been copied, taken, or handed off to others, an expert who is familiar with the type of work your company does can help.

Interviewing Skills

An investigation of employee theft has a slightly different focus than other investigations. Unlike a harassment or discrimination case, in which your ultimate goal is to find out what happened, your goal in a theft investigation is to gather the proof you need and then get a particular employee to admit committing the theft.

This means your investigator will have to be skilled not only at gathering information, but also at eliciting confessions. Some techniques for interviewing a suspected employee are described in "Interviews," below. However, if you don't have anyone on your staff who has some experience in these types of interviews—including how to press for admissions without crossing any legal lines—it might be a good idea to hire an outside investigator or certified fraud examiner to help out.

Bringing in the Police

Should you call the police to investigate your workplace theft? It depends on the situation. Once you bring in the police, the investigation will be out of your hands—and you'll have the law in your workplace. This can lead to all kinds of problems, from discovery of things that you wish they hadn't found to serious morale problems in your workforce. On the other hand, the police can use investigative tools that are pretty much off limits to private employers—and they are very experienced at conducting interrogations and getting suspects to confess.

Ultimately, it probably isn't worth bringing in the police unless your company has a very serious problem that it can't handle alone—such as an employee who has stolen controlled substances or weapons. Investigating these types of situations yourself could lead to greater problems, such as liability for personal injuries that result from use of the dangerous items or from your investigation. In situations that are less urgent, your company might lose more than it gains by calling the police. And unless the problem is fairly sizable, the police may not be willing to spend many resources going after your workplace thief.

If you do bring in the police, make sure that the information you give them is accurate and fair. Employees who are ultimately exonerated can sue for malicious prosecution if there was no good cause for the prosecution and your company maliciously gave the police false or misleading information. The likelihood of being sued for malicious prosecution is quite low, but you should still consult with an attorney if you are considering going to the police.

Plan the Investigation

In a theft investigation, you have several goals. First and foremost, you have to figure out whether theft occurred or there's some other explanation for the problem. If you conclude that you are dealing with theft, you will want to find the thief, extract a confession if you can, and get back as much of the stolen property as possible. This means that you'll want to gather as much information as you can up front, before you interview the suspect, so you'll have lots of ammunition and evidence to encourage a confession. The point of your investigation planning is either to come up with a suspect or list of suspects or to figure out what evidence of theft might exist that exonerates or implicates your suspect. So your planning will depend on whether or not you have a suspect at the outset.

If you learned of the theft through a complaint, anonymous or otherwise, you can begin with those allegations. If theft is suspected because of anomalies in paperwork, problems in bank balances, or inventory shortages, you can start there.

Starting Without a Suspect

If there is no immediate suspect, start by figuring out what you know. Did someone make a complaint about theft? If so, review the allegations. What was stolen? When and where? Some complaints are quite detailed; others are more enigmatic ("Your employees are robbing you blind!"). In either situation, catalogue the information carefully.

EXAMPLE: The XYZ Corporation supplies canned food products to hospitals, schools, and other institutions. The food is shipped to XYZ's warehouses, where it is stored until it is packaged and loaded in response to customer orders. XYZ receives an anonymous complaint, dropped in a company suggestion box, that says this: "Wonder why the Seattle warehouse is missing so much inventory? You might want to check out what the night shift is up to."

Pretty sparse complaint, right? Well, yes and no. The complaint doesn't indicate exactly what is happening and who is responsible. But it does indicate that there is some kind of inventory theft going on during the night shift at the Seattle warehouse. Based on this complaint, you might immediately pull inventory records for all of the company's warehouses, get an employee roster of the night shift workers in Seattle, and plan to visit the Seattle warehouse at night, unannounced, to see what's going on.

Whether you start from a complaint or simply some management suspicions or "funny numbers," you'll want to figure out two things: what's missing and who had access to it. Often, this will require you to review financial records and other documents. (See "Gather Documents and Other Evidence," below, for information on documents that might be helpful to a theft investigation.) Before you actually begin interviewing anyone, you'll want to have the best possible handle on what has been stolen, how, when, and where. This information will help you narrow down your list of suspects.

As you review what you know, start piecing together the information you need to figure out who's behind the theft. Depending on the circumstances, you may need to find out who makes bank deposits; who works each cash register and when; what the inventory, sales, and bookkeeping records show; or who has access to altered records or missing cash. Gather any information you can behind the scenes, before you start your interviews.

Starting With a Suspect

If you are beginning your investigation with a suspect in mind, your first steps will depend on why this person has come under suspicion. Do you know what the alleged theft is? If so, consider what documents, witnesses, or other evidence will help you figure out what (if anything) is missing and how it was taken.

If you have only a name and little other information to go on (as might be the case if you receive a vague, anonymous complaint, such as "John is crooked" or "Kathy is a thief"), consider what types of assets the suspect has access to. Then, think about documents, witnesses, or other evidence that might help you figure out whether anything was taken, and how.

CAUTION

The theft you know about may be just the tip of the iceberg.
Some thieves aren't satisfied with one type of scam. Like the murderer who is discovered by police after being pulled over for a traffic violation, a workplace thief may be caught for a relatively small offense but be guilty of much more. For example, you might catch a manager submitting reimbursement forms for expenses he never incurred but never discover that he is also accepting bribes from clients. Once you have evidence of a theft, don't stop there. Examine everything the employee had access to and every transaction the employee was involved in to make sure you know all of the bad news.

Privacy Issues

This section offers some basic tips that will help you plan an investigation that won't violate employees' privacy rights. Generally, however, the best strategy to avoid privacy problems is to gather only the information you need to know, through the least intrusive means possible—usually through interviewing employees and reviewing company documents, rather than through searches, surveillance, or lie detector tests.

For an overview of privacy issues, see Chapter 1. This section focuses on a couple of issues that are of particular concern in a theft investigation: workplace searches and polygraph testing.

Workplace Searches

Workplace thieves have to put the money and property they steal somewhere. And an employee who is running a complicated bookkeeping scam (such as a lapping scheme) probably keeps an extra set of books nearby, to help keep track of things. To uncover this kind of evidence, you may need to search an employee's desk, locker, or other workspace, or to look inside an employee's personal belongings, such as a purse or knapsack. But whenever you conduct a workplace search, you risk violating your employees' privacy rights, particularly if your company doesn't have the right policies in place.

When judges evaluate whether a particular workplace search is legal, they usually try to balance two competing concerns. First, the law considers the employer's justification for performing the search: An employer with a strong, work-related reason for searching has the best chance of prevailing. The court balances the employer's reason for searching against the worker's reasonable expectations of privacy. An employee who reasonably expects—based on the employer's policies, past practices, and common sense—that the employer will not search certain areas has the strongest argument here.

The court considers the relative strengths of these two competing interests to decide whether a particular search passes legal muster. The more steps employers take to lessen their workers' expectations of privacy and the stronger the employer's reason to search, the more likely a court is to find the search legal.

EXAMPLE 1: The owner of a large jewelry store notices that several expensive rings are missing from the display case. He immediately cuts the locks on every employee's locker and rifles through the employees' personal belongings. The store has no search policies, employee lockers have never been searched before, and the store has made no efforts to warn employees that their lockers might be searched. This search might violate employees' privacy rights.

EXAMPLE 2: Now assume that the jewelry store has a search policy warning employees that all company property, including lockers, is subject to search. The store also requires employees to give the store owner a copy of their locker combination or a duplicate key to their locker. In this situation, the store has a much better argument that the search is legal. By warning employees that their lockers might be searched and by driving this point home by insisting that employees provide the store with a means of entering their lockers, the store has done all it can to diminish the employees' expectations of privacy.

> ⚠ **CAUTION**
>
> **Privacy is a highly volatile legal issue.** Each year, workers bring lawsuits claiming that employers have invaded their privacy by conducting improper searches. The outcome of each of these cases depends on the judge's view of the worker's misconduct and the employer's methods for getting to the bottom of things, as well as the effect of any state laws on the topic. If a court rules against your company in an invasion of privacy lawsuit, the company may have to pay financial damages or be subjected to a court order prohibiting it from taking similar action in the future. Because there are no guarantees in this area of the law, most employers should consult with a lawyer before conducting any but the most routine searches.

Here are a few tips that will help you stay on the right side of the law:

- **Make sure policies are in place before you need to search.** If your company warns employees in advance that certain areas (like desks or lockers) may be subject to search, employees will have lower expectations of privacy in those areas—and less reason to complain about a particular search.

- **Search only when necessary.** You need the strongest possible justification for your search—and that means you should have a very compelling reason for digging through employee's belongings.

- **Never search an employee's body.** Some employers become so zealous that they want to physically search workers for stolen items. This is always a bad idea. All of us have a very strong privacy interest in our own bodies and the clothing worn on them. Before you frisk workers, talk to a lawyer—or call in the police.

- **Restrooms and changing areas are off limits.** Most employees legitimately expect that they will not be watched while using the bathroom or changing their clothes—and this expectation is highly reasonable. Some states even have laws prohibiting surveillance of these private areas. If you really think you'll need a bathroom monitor to catch a workplace thief, talk to a lawyer.

Going Undercover

Many private investigators and investigation firms advise placing an operative undercover to unravel complicated employee theft schemes. For example, if you suspect an employee of stealing expensive merchandise for resale, an undercover investigator could pose as a potential purchaser. If you are facing a kickback/bribe scheme, the investigator could pose as a vendor. Or, if you believe several employees are working together in a theft ring, the investigator could come in as a new employee hoping to get in on the deal.

However, using an undercover agent can get fairly complicated. Because the agent must be someone unknown to your employees, you will have to bring in an outsider. And because undercover work is difficult and nuanced, you'll want to bring in a professional—which will quickly run up some significant costs. Only if your company is losing substantial assets will this make financial sense.

There are also legal pitfalls to watch out for. Remember, your company is legally responsible for actions taken on its behalf by an outside agency. This means that if the undercover worker invades an employee's privacy rights by, for example, conducting an illegal search or getting too involved in an employee's life outside the workplace, your company could be on the hook for damages. For all these reasons, if you are seriously considering using an undercover operative, you should hire an experienced and highly recommended investigation firm. For more information on using undercover agents, see *Undercover Investigations in the Workplace*, by Eugene F. Ferraro (Butterworth Heinemann, 2000).

Polygraph Tests

As discussed in Chapter 1, a federal law called the Employee Polygraph Protection Act (EPPA) generally prohibits employers from requiring or even asking employees to take a polygraph test. However, the law carves out several exceptions, and one of them applies to investigations of workplace theft.

Under the EPPA, a private employer may ask an employee to take a polygraph if all of these conditions are met:

- The test is administered in connection with an ongoing investigation of economic loss or injury to the employer's business (see "What the Ongoing Investigation Exception Doesn't Cover," below).

- The employee had access to the property that is the subject of the investigation.

- The employer has a reasonable suspicion that the employee was involved in the incident or activity under investigation.

- The employer gives the employee, at least two working days before the test, a written statement that:

  - describes the specific incident or activity under investigation and the basis for testing the employee

  - identifies the specific loss or economic injury under investigation

  - states that the employee had access to the property in question

  - describes the basis for the employer's reasonable suspicion of the employee

  - is signed by someone who is authorized to legally bind the employer, such as an officer or director of the company, and indicates the time and date when the employee received the statement, and

  - is signed by the employee.

> ## What the Ongoing Investigation Exception Doesn't Cover
>
> The ongoing investigation exception applies to many types of workplace theft, but not all of them. Because the exception applies only to an investigation into a specific incident or activity, an employer cannot rely on the exception to require polygraphs to find out whether theft has occurred or to look into a continuing loss, such as regular inventory shortages that occur all of the time. Testing is allowed only in response to a specific, identifiable incident of loss.
>
> In addition, an employer can test only in response to an economic loss or injury to its own business, not to a customer, client, or coworker. So if a workplace thief is stealing from other employees or from clients, the exception probably doesn't apply.

Even if your situation fits within this exception, you still have to follow a lengthy list of technical requirements, from giving the employee extensive written notices before the test (including an exact list of every question to be asked), to observing a number of rules during the test, to providing the employee with a copy of the test results. You must also use a polygraph examiner who meets specified qualifications. And you can't take any action based on the test results alone, even if you follow all of these rules—you must have additional evidence of the employee's guilt.

Given all of these rules, it probably isn't worth using a polygraph in most theft investigations. If you think that a polygraph is necessary to get to the bottom of things, talk to a lawyer who is familiar with the law—and hire an experienced polygraph examiner.

Gather Documents and Other Evidence

Many theft schemes require—or create—paper trails. Think about what types of documents might be generated by the theft you suspect. An employee engaged in lapping, for example, will probably need a personal set of books to keep track of how much money has been deposited, how much is owed, which checks have been cashed, and so on. A refund or void scheme will yield paperwork in the form of cash register tapes and excessive void or refund slips. A phony vendor scheme generally requires invoices or other requests for payment listing the false vendor name.

Depending on what type of theft you suspect, you may want to look at some of these documents:

- cash register tape and receipts
- void slips
- refund slips
- credits
- purchase orders
- invoices
- deposit slips
- cancelled checks
- bank statements
- vendor records
- financial statements
- tax returns
- expense reimbursement forms
- balance sheets, or
- accounting documents, including ledgers and journals.

You can also collect documents and information outside of the workplace. For example:

- If you suspect an employee of stealing, find out whether the employee is spending lots of money outside the workplace—and where that money came from. Is the employee suddenly buying a vacation home or luxury cars, taking expensive trips, wearing valuable jewelry or clothes? If the employee claims that the money came from a legitimate source, look into it. For example, if an employee claims to have inherited a large amount of money, you could check public probate court records—and obituaries in back issues of the newspaper.

> ⓘ **CAUTION**
>
> **Stick to public records and observable facts.** You might be tempted to start covert surveillance of an employee who seems to be living high on the hog, but that's generally a bad idea. To avoid violating the employee's privacy, limit your investigation to documents that are publicly available—such as records filed with a court or agency—and information that is plainly evident. Noticing that an employee is showing up to work in a brand new Lexus is fair game; calling every real estate agent in town to find out whether an employee is in the market for a new home probably is not.

- If you suspect an employee of a phony vendor scheme, check secretary of state filings. Is the business listed? If so, find out the name(s) of the owners—if it is a phony vendor, the employee or his or her friends or relatives may be listed. Check the business address to see if it matches the employee's address. And if the vendor is supposed to be licensed, check with your state's licensing agency to find out whether this requirement has been met.

Interviews

Once you've gathered and examined relevant documents, you're ready to begin your interviews. In a theft investigation, you'll want to interview your suspect(s) last. Unlike a harassment or discrimination investigation, which begins with the victim, moves to the accused employee, then goes to witnesses and other third parties to confirm or contradict the stories of the main players, a theft investigation moves from the outside in. You'll start your interviews with the most peripheral witnesses, then conclude by interviewing the suspect. That way, you'll have all of the evidence you can possibly gather before confronting the potential thief.

Interviewing Witnesses

The types of witnesses available will depend on the nature of the theft. Once you have a sense of what kind of theft you're dealing with, think about who might have helpful information to offer. In a bribe or kickback scheme, for example, you might want to interview vendors, other employees who are involved in the vendor selection process, the suspect's supervisor, and anyone who might have had an opportunity to witness shady deals (for example, a coworker who accompanies the suspect on sales calls). If you suspect an employee of skimming at a cash register, you might talk to the bookkeeper and to employees who work the same register shifts as the suspect.

Getting Started

As in any investigation, it's best to begin your interviews with an opening statement to put the witness at ease and set the tone for your questions. However, unlike other investigations, you may want to keep your purpose secret at the beginning of the interview, to encourage the witness to reveal as much as possible and to try to prevent the suspect from learning of your interest. Because employees are so reluctant to finger their coworkers for theft, you may want to build up to the topic of your interview slowly, to give yourself time to establish a rapport with the witness.

Experienced investigators advise taking a somewhat vague approach when opening a witness interview. Rather than explaining their purpose in detail, they'll simply say, "The company has asked me to look into something, and I'm hoping you can answer a few questions for me." Or, they might be a bit more specific about the topic: "I've been asked to gather information about our procedures for selecting vendors. Can I ask you some questions about that?"

Of course, if you're dealing with a complaint from a known person, whether employee or outsider, you can be less circumspect in your approach. For example, you might start an interview with a vendor who complained that an employee solicited a bribe by saying, "I understand that you've spoken to _____ about a problem with one of our employees. I've been asked to look into the matter. Can you tell me what happened?"

Questions

The questions you ask the witness will depend on the purpose of the interview. However, your approach should be the same with most witnesses: Move from the general to the specific. If you believe a witness may have seen a coworker stealing from a register, for example, start by finding out what shifts the witness works, when the witness is on the register, and who usually works the nearby registers. You might then ask a general question about theft, such as "Have you ever seen anyone steal from the company?" If the employee responds negatively, get more specific by asking, "Have you ever seen anyone steal from a register?"

> **TIP**
> **Be more direct with a witness who has complained of theft.** If the witness has made a complaint about theft, you can start right in with the facts of the complaint. However, you'll want to make sure to cover basic background questions at some point in the interview, to make sure the witness had the opportunity to see or hear the incidents and to find out about any existing animosity between the witness and the suspected employee.

Closing the Interview

Once you have finished your questions, review your notes with the person you interviewed. Make sure you got everything right and that your notes include all of the important details. Have the employee sign your notes or a written summary of the interview. Ask the employee not to talk about what you've discussed with any coworkers. And ask the employee to come to you immediately with any new information.

> **TIP**
> **Perhaps no theft occurred.** Theft is not the cause of every shortage or loss a business suffers. In some investigations, you will conclude at this point that you are not dealing with employee theft. After examining relevant documents and talking to knowledgeable witnesses, you may decide that accounting mistakes, shoplifting, or faulty inventory procedures

better explain the apparent discrepancies or shortages in question. If this happens, be sure to take steps to shore up any security or procedural problems your investigation uncovered.

Interviewing Suspects

You may find yourself in one of two situations when interviewing a suspect. In some cases, your review of documents and interviews with witnesses will lead you to believe that a particular employee is the culprit. In other cases, you may have narrowed down the range of suspects to two or three employees who had the opportunity to commit the theft. Either way, you'll want to carefully structure your interview to give yourself the best chance of eliciting a confession.

Refusing to Name Names May Be a Sign of Guilt

If you have more than one suspect, ask them who they think is behind the theft. Experts agree that the employee who's guilty very rarely names someone else. Innocent employees often think through the situation, trying to figure out who could have done it. For example, an employee might say, "Well, I put the receipts in the safe every weekday night, and Claire, Frank, and I are the only ones who have a key to the safe. I didn't take the money, so it must have been Claire or Frank." The employee who's guilty, on the other hand, will often go to great lengths to avoid naming names: "Anyone could have taken money from the safe. Someone could have borrowed a manager's key and put it back before it was noticed, or maybe a manager left the safe open by mistake and a customer somehow saw it and took the money."

There are many theories about the reason for this reluctance. Some say the guilty party wants the list of suspects to be as broad as possible and so will pose explanations that suggest anyone could have done it. Others say that guilty employees don't want to name a specific coworker, either because they don't want to get an innocent person in trouble or because they know that it will eventually become clear that the coworker didn't do it, which will cast suspicion back on them.

> (!) **TIP**
>
> **You may have more than one thief.** Many workplace thieves operate alone. Every once in a while, however, more than one employee is in on the scheme. If you have more than one suspect, remember that all of them may be guilty. In this situation, getting one to confess may bring down the whole operation.

Getting Started

As with witnesses, you should begin your interviews with suspects in an innocuous way. This will allow you to develop some rapport with the employee before you start in on the hard questions. Start by saying something like "I've been asked to take a look at our accounting practices" or "I'm gathering some information on sales and inventory procedures," then tell the suspect that you need to ask a few questions.

Preserve the element of surprise. When you're interviewing suspects, time your approach carefully. Make sure that the employee doesn't have something pressing to take care of or a scheduled appointment. Once you tell the employee you want to ask questions, you should conduct the interview immediately. If you delay, the employee may suspect the true reason for your interest—and take steps to foil the investigation (such as destroying documents or getting rid of other evidence of theft) or hide the proceeds of the theft.

Questions

The questions you ask a suspect will, of course, depend on what type of theft you're dealing with and what you already know about it. Because there's such a wide variety of types of theft, it's impossible to provide a list of sample questions, as has been included in other chapters. Instead, let's follow the hypothetical case of Mary, the bookkeeper.

EXAMPLE: Sarah, the HR director of GetGo Enterprises, has been asked to investigate whether Mary, the bookkeeper, is running a lapping scheme. There have been significant lags in posting customer payments; in fact, several customers have complained of receiving a second notice of payment due after they've already paid their bills. To make certain that these discrepancies weren't due to simple errors, Sarah compares the payments the company actually received in the last week (by looking inside the envelopes, already opened in the company mail room, that are being routed to Mary and adding up the checks she found inside) to the amounts Mary has deposited. There is a shortfall of several thousand dollars.

A witness, whose desk is near Mary's, has told Sarah that Mary often writes in a notebook other than the company's ledger and journals, and that she takes this notebook with her everywhere, including to lunch and home at night.

Most interviews will follow the same general pattern:

- **Start with general, open-ended questions.** This will help you get the suspect talking, hopefully before he or she realizes the true purpose of the interview. It will also give you a chance to observe the suspect's body language under fairly normal circumstances. You can compare this to the suspect's demeanor when you start in on the tough topics.

EXAMPLE: Sarah approaches Mary as she's returning from her lunch break. "Hi Mary," she says. "I've been asked to gather some information on our internal accounting procedures. Could you answer a few questions for me?" Mary says that she has to get back to work. "I won't keep you too long," Sarah responds. "Let's go to my office."

Once both are settled, Sarah begins with a few general questions, such as "Please describe your job responsibilities," "Describe a typical day as the company bookkeeper," and "Could you briefly explain what books you keep for the company? What kind of information goes in each of them?"

- **Hone in on the particular procedures or transactions at issue.** Begin with general questions.

EXAMPLE: After Mary has described general bookkeeping procedures, Sarah is ready to ask about customer payments. "You're responsible for processing customer payments, right? Please explain how that works." Sarah's goal is to get Mary to walk her through the process, step by step. Once she's committed herself to a set procedure, she'll have a harder time explaining why she deviated from that procedure for particular customers.

- **Get more specific, and be prepared to lay out documents or other evidence that contradicts the suspect's statements.** If the employee becomes flustered or can't explain the contradictions, raise the possibility of theft in general terms, but don't get angry or speak harshly. If you appear to be sympathetic and nonjudgmental, you'll have better luck getting the employee to admit to something.

EXAMPLE: Mary has explained the procedure for recording and depositing customer payments. Sarah reiterates what Mary has said: "So, you post customer payments on the same day you receive them? And then you deposit the checks immediately?" Mary confirms what she has already said. Sarah then says, "But Mary, you waited several days to deposit this customer's check," and shows her the document. At this point, some employees will realize that the jig is up and will confess. Others will give a justification for the discrepancy. Mary offers an innocent explanation, so Sarah continues presenting evidence: "Last Thursday, the company took in over $6,000 in payments, but you deposited only $3,575. I know that because I added up the checks myself. And here's the deposit slip, filled out in your handwriting." Mary doesn't respond. Sarah says, "Mary, I know you've worked for this company for a long time, and you would only have done something like this if you really needed the money." At this point, Mary—like most suspects in a similar situation—admits to at least some role in the theft.

Convincing a Suspect to Confess

So how do you get from making the suspect uncomfortable to actually eliciting a confession? It varies from person to person, of course, but here are a couple tips from experienced investigators:

- Keep your documents and other evidence hidden, and lay them out one piece at a time. Virtually every workplace theft results in some kind of evidence, and the only person who knows exactly what evidence is available is the thief. If you show your hand only a little at a time, the thief won't know how much evidence you have—and may anticipate evidence you didn't know about.

- Give the suspect an out. Try to think of some way to make confessing to the theft more palatable to the suspect. For example, you could say, "I know you wouldn't do this unless you had a very good reason.

- If the employee confesses, gather as much information as you can about the scope of the theft, whether anyone else was involved, and, perhaps most important, what happened to the proceeds. Get the basics of the confession in writing, if possible. Seek this information right away; once the employee leaves the room, the chances of cooperation voluntarily diminish significantly.

EXAMPLE: Mary has broken down and admitted that she has "borrowed" money from the deposits on occasion, but only because she was financially strapped after her divorce. Now's the time for Sarah to ask questions like these: "When's the first time you borrowed money from a customer payment? This must be hard to keep track of—do you have a written record of which payments you've deposited and which you've withheld? I understand you keep a personal notebook at your desk. Is this why? May I see it now? What have you done with the money? Do you still have any of it?" Mary is reluctant to talk, so Sarah prods her further by adding, "Mary, you can understand that we could run into serious problems with our customers if we don't credit their accounts properly. In fact, several customers have already complained. The first step towards making this right is to undo the damage to our customer relations. For that, we need to know which accounts have been affected."

Getting the Money Back

This interview may be your only chance to convince the suspect to volunteer information that will help you recapture the stolen money or goods. Here are some sample questions that should help you get what you need:

- What happened to the money?
- Is there anything left, or have you spent it? What have you spent it on? Do you still have the items you purchased with the money?
- Have you deposited any of the money in a bank account? Where do you bank? Would you be willing to sign an authorization for us to look at your bank records? [Have such an authorization available, or have one written up while sitting in the interview.]
- You understand that this is the company's money. If you return whatever's left voluntarily, that might help the situation. Will you do that?

Evaluate the Evidence

In theft cases, you will almost always have a strong sense of what happened and who did it by the end of your investigation. If you were successful in getting the suspect to admit to stealing, you will also have a confession. Obviously, in these situations, you won't have to spend much time sifting through the evidence you gathered.

It's relatively rare to close a theft investigation by concluding that you can't decide who, among a group of people, committed the theft. More common is a conclusion that you aren't sure whether you have enough proof that the person you suspect is guilty. For example, if a relatively small amount of money or property is missing, and the loss may be due to shoplifting, accounting errors, or shoddy inventory procedures, it might be tough to pin the blame on an employee you suspect of theft.

If you really can't figure out whether an employee is guilty, your best course of action is to close the investigation without reaching any conclusions (see Chapter 4 for more on how to do this) and take immediate steps to tighten workplace controls.

Take Action

If you find that employee theft occurred, often the only appropriate response is to fire the employee. There may be exceptions to this general rule—for example, if the employee's actions were condoned by management and the employee had reason to believe they were not serious. But these situations will be rare. Remember, two-thirds of employees will steal if they see others stealing and getting away with it. To show employees that your company means business, anyone who steals from the company should probably be fired.

Document the Investigation

Document the investigation, following the guidelines in Chapter 4. Make sure to stick to the facts—theft investigations can lead to defamation lawsuits, in which employees accused of theft claim that you spread false and damaging information about them (in other words, that you called them thieves). Avoid this unhappy result by recounting the facts that your investigation uncovered and detailing the reasons for your conclusions.

Follow Up

When you've finished your investigation, it's time to think about the future: how to get the company's money or property back (if possible) and how to prevent theft going forward.

Recouping Your Company's Losses

Unfortunately, there's no surefire way to get back money or property a workplace thief has stolen. If you're dealing with a thrifty thief who has carefully deposited theft proceeds in a savings account, you might be in luck. In most situations, however, the thief will have spent most of the money already—that's usually why people steal, after all.

There are several avenues of recovery that might be available to your company, depending on the situation. This section will give you some basic information about each. If your company is facing major losses, however, you should talk to a lawyer before deciding how to proceed.

Criminal Prosecution

A criminal prosecution may offer the best opportunity to get money back. Many judges will order a thief who is convicted (or pleads guilty) to make restitution—that is, to pay back what was stolen—to the victim, as part of the sentence. Restitution may also be ordered as a condition of probation. This gives you tremendous leverage to get the company's money back, because the thief risks going to jail for failure to pay. Even if the criminal case never goes to trial, your company can ask the district attorney to require restitution as a condition of any plea bargain or settlement of the charges.

If you want the thief prosecuted, you will need to show the police—and the district attorney—that there is a case to be made against the thief. Among other things, this will require you to be able to present evidence that there was a theft (as opposed to an accounting error, a loss, or a mistake), to show how much was stolen, and to show that the suspect committed the theft. A lawyer can help you figure out how best to convince those in the criminal justice system that your company's case is worth prosecuting.

Civil Lawsuits

Another method for recouping losses is to file a civil lawsuit. The most obvious candidate to sue is the thief, but only if he or she either has the assets to pay a judgment or is likely to land a job in the near future (which would allow your company to garnish his or her wages to guarantee repayment). There's not much point in paying the costs of a lawsuit against an indigent thief whose financial prospects look dim.

If the thief is unlikely to be able to pay a judgment, you might consult with an attorney to figure out whether any third parties could be liable for your company's losses. For example, someone who bought obviously stolen goods from the thief, or a financial institution whose loose controls allowed the thief unauthorized access to your company's accounts, might be legally responsible for at least some of the losses.

Agreement With the Employee

An employee who has confessed to theft may agree to restitution, or to sign a promissory note for the stolen amounts. However, such agreements often aren't worth the paper they're written on. Some employees sign such agreements with no intention of ever making good on their promises. Even if they do intend to pay the company back when they sign the agreement, they might change their mind once the feelings of the moment have passed.

If you try to come up with a restitution agreement, remember these tips:

- **Don't agree to payments over time.** The more time the employee has to pay the money back, the less likely your company is to collect the money. Instead of agreeing to installment payments, require the employee to pay the full amount within a few days or a week of signing the agreement. Let the employee figure out how to come up with the money, through a loan, help from friends and relatives, or some other source.

- **Write a binding contract.** Make sure that your agreement will be enforced as a contract if you ever have to show it to a judge—and explain to the employee that the company will go to court to enforce the agreement if necessary.

- **Negotiate carefully.** Remember the old adage about a bird in the hand? It applies to restitution as well as fowl hunting. If the employee can scrape together a large part of the amount owed, it may make sense to accept that money as payment of the debt. But don't give up too easily—consider the employee's ability to pay and your company's chances of collecting through a lawsuit to decide whether to settle for less than the full amount. Remember, you can always take whatever the employee can give now and retain the right to go after the rest.

Insurance Claims

If your company has a fidelity bond or some other type of employee theft or employee dishonesty insurance, the company may be able to recover at least part of the losses from the insurance company. However, it can be pretty tough to get an insurance company to pay up.

In order to recover, you'll have to follow the company's requirements carefully, and you'll have to be able to prove that the company suffered a covered loss—that is, you'll have to prove the amount of the loss and prove that it was caused by theft. If the company's losses have been substantial and may be covered by insurance, you will probably want to retain a lawyer to represent the company's interests in negotiating with the insurance company.

Deduct Unrecoverable Losses

Your company may be able to take a tax deduction for losses suffered through theft or embezzlement, including stealing by employees. Generally, the IRS will allow businesses to deduct theft-related losses from their income for tax purposes if the business lost more than $100, the loss wasn't repaid from some other source (such as restitution or insurance), and the theft was illegal under the laws of the state where the business is located.

To deduct a business loss due to theft, you'll have to fill out IRS Form 4684, *Casualties and Thefts*, and file it with your tax return. For instructions on filling out the form and more information on qualifying for the deduction, see IRS Publication 547, *Casualties, Disasters, and Thefts* and Publication 584b, *Casualty, Disaster, and Theft Loss Workbook*. You can find these materials on the IRS's website, at www.irs.gov.

Minimize Opportunities for Theft

Now is also a good time to think about how your company can prevent theft in the future. An accountant, auditor, or fraud examiner can review your company's internal systems for weaknesses that give thieves an opportunity to go to work. Here are some basic steps your company can take to reduce the risk of theft:

- **Segregate job duties.** Make sure that no employee is solely responsible for any financial transaction from start to finish. In other words, make sure that every financial transaction requires the involvement of more than one employee. Requiring a second signature on checks, making sure that the employee who counts a deposit is not responsible for taking it to the bank, and requiring a second employee to count out cash register drawers are all examples of segregation of duties.

- **Require authorizations.** Don't let money leave your company through the back door. Adopt rules that require the signature or oversight of a high-ranking official (or the owner) for major transactions.

- **Adopt a proper accounting system.** Loose accounting procedures give employees all kinds of opportunities to steal. An outside accountant or auditor can help you set up a system that leaves less room for money to disappear.

- **Conduct regular audits.** The simple truth is that employees are less likely to steal if they believe they may be caught. Periodic audits of your company's books and inventory will deter theft—or at least, allow theft to be discovered in its earliest stages.

- **Impose paperwork requirements.** Put some extra roadblocks in the way of workplace thieves by requiring documentation for cash outflows. Require receipts for reimbursements for expenses or petty cash. Make employees submit licenses and other paperwork from new vendors, to make sure they're on the up and up. Don't allow refunds unless an employee fills out a form that includes the customer's name, address, and phone number.

- **Get involved.** Remember the old saying, "When the cat's away, the mice will play"? Company officers and high-ranking managers are the cats in this scenario. Don't allow any checks to leave the building without an officer's approval and signature. Have all bank statements sent to the president's home address. The greater (and more public) role company officers play in the company's finances, the fewer problems you will have with theft.

- **Don't bend the rules.** Some companies that follow all of the tips listed above still have significant theft problems. The reason is that they allow employees to ignore or override the rules. It's not hard to avoid this mistake—simply insist that employees toe the line, and discipline any who don't.

- **Make employees happy.** Surveys show that employee satisfaction plays a major role in deterring workplace theft. Employees who feel appreciated are less likely to steal—and more likely to report a coworker for theft.

Investigating Threats and Violence

All of us have heard the horror stories: A disgruntled employee, a worker's former lover, or an enraged client bursts through the door, shooting first and asking questions later. Although workplace violence is not as common as the news might lead us to believe, it is a major problem in the United States. Government studies estimate that there are about two million assaults and threats of violence made against workers each year. According to the Workplace Violence Research Institute (www.workviolence.com), workplace violence costs businesses more than $36 billion each year.

Sometimes, violence comes out of the blue, without warning. Much more often, however, violent workplace incidents are preceded by threats, verbal bullying, and/or physical intimidation. This means that, in most cases of violence by employees and former employees, your company can avert more serious problems by immediately investigating threats and other signs of aggression.

An immediate investigation of every potentially violent situation, no matter how minor it seems, sends the message that violence will not be tolerated. It also gives your company an opportunity to avert more serious problems. Because workplace violence often escalates from threats, outbursts, or an obsession with weapons to physically harming others, you have a chance to stop this cycle if you investigate at the first sign of trouble.

Investigating threats and violence by employees can be distressing. After all, you don't want your investigation to be the very thing that triggers a violent outburst, and you certainly don't want to make yourself a target for a violent employee's rage. You will have to move very quickly, act decisively, and often rely on outside experts to help you assess the situation and figure out how to handle it.

This chapter will help you navigate this rough terrain. It explains the types of workplace violence and when an employer will be held legally responsible for violence in the workplace. It also applies the ten investigation steps to situations involving violence and threatening behavior.

> ! **CAUTION**
> **This book covers workplace violence by current or former employees only.** This book focuses on investigating employee misconduct, not problems caused by people outside the workplace. For this reason, it includes only limited information about third-party assailants—people who come to the workplace solely to commit theft or other crimes, angry customers or clients, or family members or acquaintances of employees. There are certainly steps you can take to prevent third-party violence— "Types of Workplace Violence," below, briefly discusses these other sources of violence and suggests resources that can provide more information.

Threats and Violence in the Workplace

The trick to a successful investigation of workplace violence is to start your inquiry at the very first sign of trouble. This means, in turn, that you have to recognize the early warning signs that often precede violence. If you wait until an employee has seriously injured or killed someone, all you'll have to investigate is what went wrong and what your company should have done differently.

Types of Workplace Violence

Contrary to popular belief, the great majority of violent incidents in the workplace are perpetrated by outsiders—strangers intending to commit a crime—rather than employees. For example, according to the Bureau of Labor Statistics, most workplace homicides are committed by robbers trying to steal from the business, not by current or former workers.

However, employees (particularly former or soon-to-be-former employees), people who know employees (such as romantic partners or family members), and customers or clients also commit workplace violence. This section explains some common types of workplace violence.

Violence by Outsiders

Nonemployee assailants commit most workplace homicides, as well as a substantial proportion of workplace assaults. Motives for this type of violence run the gamut from robbery to revenge to a misguided sense of honor or principle. Consider these examples:

- In 1994, Paul Hill killed a doctor and one of the doctor's escorts as they arrived at the Pensacola Ladies Clinic. Hill claimed that he killed the doctor to prevent him from performing abortions.

- In 1993, Gian Luigi Ferri, a former client of the law firm Pettit & Martin, entered the firm's offices at 101 California Street in San Francisco. Ferri killed eight people and wounded six more before taking his own life.

- In 2003, a doctor was beaten and strangled to death during a physical examination of a patient at a psychiatric hospital in San Leandro, California.

- In 2000, seven workers at a Wendy's restaurant in Flushing, Queens, were shot and five of them killed during a robbery. One of the men convicted in the shooting was a former employee.

High-Risk Occupations

Government statistics certify what most of us already know: Workers who deal with the public are more likely to fall victim to outsider violence. Those at particularly high risk include workers who exchange money with the public, deliver goods or services, work alone or in small numbers during the late evening/early morning hours, or work in jobs that require extensive public contact. Certain industries—including health care, security (including police officers), and retail—are targeted more frequently than others.

It's difficult to predict and prevent violence by outsiders. While some acts of violence (particularly those committed by angry customers or clients, or by those who oppose a company's practices) may be preceded by threats and acts of vandalism, most are committed without warning.

However, there are a few things you can do to reduce the odds that an outsider will target your company. The Occupational Safety and Health Administration (OSHA) offers tips for employers hoping to protect their workers from violence. These include:

- training employees on how to recognize and respond to threatening situations
- securing the workplace by installing surveillance cameras, extra lighting, and alarm systems, and by minimizing workplace access by outsiders through the use of identification badges and guards
- limiting the amount of cash kept on hand, particularly at night
- giving outside workers cell phones and alarms, and requiring them to keep in touch with a contact person throughout their shift, and
- telling employees not to go anywhere where they do not feel safe, and providing an escort in potentially dangerous areas.

RESOURCE

Want more information on preventing violence by third parties? Go to OSHA's website, www.osha.gov, where you'll find fact sheets and tips on how to prevent and minimize violence in various types of businesses, —including retail stores and businesses that specialize in health care. For information on your state's workplace safety rules, contact your state's occupational safety and health agency. You can also find articles and resources on violence and violence prevention at the website of the Workplace Violence Research Institute, at www.workviolence.com.

Domestic Violence

According to the American Institute on Domestic Violence (www.aidv-usa.com), 18,700 acts of violence are committed by intimate partners and spouses (current and former) every year against women in the workplace. And sometimes these incidents go beyond the intended victim to harm other employees as well.

Experts tell us that domestic violence frequently follows a fairly predictable cycle, in which pressure, threats, and coercion precede acts of violence. By the time a batterer shows up at the victim's workplace intending to do harm, chances are good that he has already made threats and committed other acts of violence or property damage. If you encourage employees to come forward and let you know when they fear an abusive partner, you can take steps to prevent that violence from coming to work.

Among the strategies a company can adopt are:

- establishing a confidential way for employees to report domestic violence. Victims of domestic violence are often extremely reluctant to come forward, so you must encourage employees to report abuse—and to report any potential new problems or developments (if the employee's abuser is getting out of jail or has threatened to come to the workplace, for example)

- increasing workplace security by, for example, requiring workplace visitors to sign in and have an escort at all times, installing a locking door between the reception or greeting area and the rest of the workplace, and providing secure, well-lit parking facilities for employees

- getting a restraining order on behalf of the victim and/or your company, requiring the abuser to stay away from the workplace

- if you know that an employee has been threatened, making sure that the security staff in your office or building are aware of any outstanding restraining orders or threats against your employee—and know what the abuser looks like. You may also want to move the victim so she cannot be easily located by her abuser (for example, to a different floor, wing, or worksite), for protection and to buy your company some time to defuse a potentially violent encounter.

If both partners to the relationship work for you, you can investigate using the tips and strategies described below. You also have the option of immediately suspending the abuser. Most often, however, the perpetrator won't be your employee. In this situation, you may need help from the police or a violence consultant.

RESOURCE

Need more information on domestic violence? There are a number of websites that offer information, training, sample policies, and strategies for dealing with domestic violence in the workplace. They include:

- Legal Momentum (formerly the National Organization of Women's Legal Defense and Education Fund), at www.legalmomentum.org
- the Safe at Work Coalition, at www.safeatworkcoalition.org, and
- the American Institute on Domestic Violence, at www.aidv-usa.com.

Violence by Employees and Former Employees

This chapter focuses on investigating incidents in which a current or former employee threatens or assaults others in the workplace. This is the most foreseeable (and therefore, preventable) type of violence. After all, the perpetrators are people you know, sometimes people you see every day. And very few of them simply snap one day and go on a rampage—instead, the problem builds up slowly, and the perpetrator usually sends up a few red flags that violence may in the offing. Here are some examples:

- After the receptionist at the Housing Authority in Richmond, California was fired, he pulled out a gun and opened fire on his coworkers. In the days before he was fired, he told a coworker that he felt like committing a mass murder. The coworker reported his comments, and the receptionist was fired—but was allowed to return to his desk (where he kept his gun) on the way out the door. ("Bulletproof Practices," by Robert J. Grossman (*HR Magazine*, November 2002).)

- Honeywell, Inc., decided to rehire Randy Landing as a custodian—after he was released from prison, having served five years for strangling a Honeywell coworker to death. After he was rehired, Landin sexually harassed female coworkers, challenged a male coworker to a fight, and threatened to kill another coworker—he was transferred twice because of these confrontations. After a female coworker spurned his romantic overtures, he harassed and threatened her, scratched a death threat on her locker door at work, then shot and killed her. *Yunker v. Honeywell, Inc.*, 496 NW2d 419 (Minn. Ct. of Apps., 1993).

- In 1978, former supervisor Dan White shot and killed supervisor Harvey Milk and Mayor George Moscone in San Francisco's City Hall. Although White would later famously claim that he was temporarily insane at the time of the shootings from eating too much junk food (the so-called "Twinkie defense"), he confessed to police that he planned to kill his targets (and others) because they had conspired against his reappointment to the city's board of supervisors.

- In 1999, Byran Uyesugi opened fire on his coworkers at Xerox in Honolulu, killing seven. Uyesugi had been hospitalized six years earlier, after kicking in an elevator door and threatening to kill his supervisor. According to news reports, Uyesugi, a gun collector, was scheduled to attend a meeting to discuss his work performance on the day of the killings.

- In 2000, Michael McDermott, a software developer, killed seven coworkers with an assault rifle at Edgewater Technology. McDermott was having financial problems; the human resources department had just complied with an order to garnish his wages. On the day of the shootings, his car was repossessed from the company parking lot.

Workplace violence runs the gamut from vague threats ("They'll be sorry if they fire me") to pointed threats ("I'm going to bring in a gun tomorrow and take out my supervisor"), bullying, physical and verbal intimidation, stalking, assault, and killing.

Tips for Preventing Violence

Investigating threats and aggressive behavior will help you limit opportunities for violence in the workplace. Other ways to prevent violence include:

- **Screen applicants before hiring.** Check for past criminal convictions (if your state allows it), restraining orders, or a history of difficulties with coworkers.

- **Conduct evaluations—and impose discipline only when it's warranted.** Experts say that employees are more likely to become violent if they believe they have been treated unfairly, taken by surprise, or sandbagged. Prevent these reactions by giving employees fair warning and a chance to improve on minor problems.

- **Treat employees with respect.** Always treat workers decently, especially when you have to discipline or fire them. Don't disparage the employee in front of others or call him or her names.

- **Adopt a workplace violence policy.** Create a policy that states that violence of any kind will not be tolerated.

- **Prohibit weapons in the workplace.** Unless employees have a compelling need to be armed (for example, they work as security guards), don't allow weapons in the workplace. Make sure your state law allows a weapons ban, however: Some states don't allow employers to ban legally owned guns from company property altogether (for example, employees must be allowed to leave their guns in a locked vehicle in the company parking lot). If your state doesn't allow a ban, talk to a lawyer about sensible weapons policies that don't violate the law.

- **Consider an employee assistance program.** Workplace violence often begins offsite—with a failing marriage, a substance abuse problem, or money troubles. Help employees manage these difficulties with an employee assistance program (EAP). An EAP might include counseling, rehabilitation services, or anger management classes.

- **Develop a safety plan.** Instruct employees on what to do if violence starts. Plan escape routes and know where first aid supplies are. And have the telephone numbers of local police or building security handy—preferably on speed dial.

- **Encourage reporting.** Ask employees to come forward and report any incident of violence that they witness.

- **Train managers.** Make sure that managers know the warning signs of violence, the safety plan, and the requirements of company policies.

Warning Signs of Violence

Experts agree that an employee or former employee who commits a violent act often exhibits certain signs of trouble before becoming violent. This is "good" news for employers—it means that your company has a chance to prevent violence if you can read these signals and take action immediately. Of course, no single one of these signs, taken alone, is a sure indicator that an employee may turn violent. And some employees resort to violence without any warning. But managers and human resources professionals should be on the lookout for clues that intervention may be necessary. These include:

- an unexplained rise in absences
- substance abuse
- outbursts at coworkers and customers or poor impulse control generally
- verbal abuse or threats towards coworkers and customers; harassing phone calls or email communications
- strained workplace relationships
- overreaction or resistance to even minor changes in workplace routine; insubordination and belligerence
- lack of attention to personal appearance, including hygiene
- interest in firearms or other weapons; access to weapons
- signs of paranoia ("everyone's out to get me") or withdrawal
- fascination with violent acts or fantasies, or a history of violence
- seeing oneself as a victim and others as persecutors; blaming others for one's problems
- obsessive behavior towards a coworker or customer, up to and including stalking
- comments about suicide
- mood swings, and
- domestic problems, including money troubles or family disputes.

The Workplace Violence Profile

Relying on a profile to determine which employees might act violently is dangerous. Although perpetrators tend to be white men in their 30s or 40s who have few family ties, workplace violence can be committed by anyone, male or female, of any racial and ethnic background, marital status, and age. Using a profile rather than looking at an employee's actual behavior can cause you to miss important clues that violence may be in the offing—or suspect employees who have no violent intentions.

Violence is often a response to stress, whether in the workplace or in other areas of life. In many cases of workplace violence, there is some kind of triggering incident—the last straw for the perpetrator, who then decides to resort to violence. Often, this last straw is a disciplinary action or termination; in some cases, it may be a complaint against the employee for harassment or violation of another work rule. Some violent incidents are triggered by layoffs, economic difficulties outside of work, or an emotional crisis.

Employer Liability for Violence

Generally, employers are legally liable for workplace violence only if they failed to take reasonable steps to prevent or discourage it. Courts have allowed victims of workplace violence (and their survivors) to sue under several different legal theories.

OSH Act Violations

Under the Occupational Safety and Health Act (OSH Act), employers must provide employees with a workplace free of recognized hazards that are causing or are likely to cause serious harm or death. Traditionally, this requirement has applied primarily to hazards created by machinery, poor ventilation, dangerous chemicals, and so on. More recently, however, the Occupational Safety and Health Administration (OSHA), which enforces the OSH Act, has said that workplace violence may also constitute a hazard. This means that employers who don't take reasonable steps to prevent or abate a recognized violence hazard can be punished by OSHA.

OSHA suggests that employers take a number of steps to prevent workplace violence (some are described above). Foremost among these is adopting a zero-tolerance policy toward workplace violence and enforcing that policy through prompt investigation of violence claims and immediate corrective action.

Harassment Laws

In some situations, workplace violence and threats may constitute legally actionable harassment or discrimination. For example, an employee who touches a coworker against her will or threatens to harm her if she dates someone else, may be guilty of both sexual harassment and violence. Or, an employee who gets in a fistfight with another worker after calling him racist names could be committing both racial harassment and violence. For information on harassment, see Chapter 6.

Negligent Hiring, Retention, and Supervision

Someone who is injured by one of your company's employees may be able to sue your company if it failed to take reasonable care in selecting and retaining its workers. Under the legal theories of negligent hiring, retention, and supervision, employers can be sued if they knew or should have known that an applicant or employee was unfit for the job yet did nothing about it. Here are a few situations in which employers have been found liable:

- A pizza company hired a delivery driver without looking into his criminal past, which included a sexual assault conviction and an arrest for stalking a woman he met while delivering pizza for another company. After he raped a customer, he was sent to jail for 25 years, and the company was liable to his victim for negligent hiring.

- A car rental company hired a man who later raped a coworker. Had the company verified his resume claims, it would have discovered that he was in prison for robbery during the years he claimed to be in high school and college. The company was liable to the coworker.

- A furniture company hired a deliveryman without requiring him to fill out an application or performing a background check. The employee assaulted a female customer in her home with a knife. The company was liable to the customer.

- An Amtrak employee who had a history of violent workplace incidents shot his supervisor twice after the supervisor reprimanded him for being absent from work. A jury found that Amtrak's failure to take action after the earlier incidents led to the shooting and ordered it to pay the supervisor $3.5 million in damages.

 TIP

Background checks are a conscientious employer's best friend. To avoid liability for negligent hiring—and make sure that you aren't being fed a line by job applicants—run a background check before you hire anyone. Especially if you are hiring for a position that will have a lot of public contact, a background check can help you make sure that you aren't putting anyone at risk.

Although these lawsuits have not yet appeared in every state, the clear trend is to allow injured parties to sue employers for hiring or keeping on a dangerous worker.

Workers' Compensation Laws May Prevent Employee Lawsuits

In every state, workers' compensation laws require employers to purchase insurance that provides benefits to employees who suffer work-related injuries or illnesses. The system strikes a compromise between employers and employees. Employees are entitled to benefits no matter who caused their injury: themselves, a coworker, or a customer. In return, the employer gets protection from personal injury lawsuits. If a workplace injury or illness is covered by workers' compensation, the worker may not sue the employer over it.

Not all workplace injuries are covered by workers' compensation, however. The injury must be connected to the job—for example, an accident that occurs hours after an employee leaves the workplace probably is not covered. And an employer cannot use the workers' compensation system to escape responsibility for its own intentional or reckless acts.

How does this relate to workplace violence? Some violent incidents are covered by workers' compensation—which means that the employee victims cannot sue their employers for their injuries (although they may be able to sue the person who attacked them). However, if the violence is committed by a supervisor, manager, or officer of the company, or if the company has acted recklessly in allowing violence to occur (for example, by ignoring threats to an employee or retaining an employee who has already engaged in violence), then the incident probably won't be covered by workers' compensation. This means that the victim can sue the employer if one of the legal theories described in this section applies.

The rules on what workers' compensation does and does not cover vary from state to state. To find out about your state's laws, contact your state's workers' compensation office or talk to a lawyer.

Ten Steps to a Successful Investigation of Violence

This section explains how to apply the basic investigation steps covered in Part I of this book to an investigation of workplace threats or violence. If you haven't read Part I, you should do so before getting into this more specific material—the discussion that follows assumes that you are already familiar with basic investigation procedures.

After a Violent Incident

This section assumes that you have learned of threats or relatively minor incidents of violence in time to prevent escalation. However, when serious injuries have already occurred, you are in a different predicament. In this situation, you should immediately contact the police—and emergency medical personnel, if necessary. Make sure that victims receive immediate medical treatment. You will also want to make counseling available to employees and discuss ways to prevent similar incidents in the future.

At some point (and probably with the help of the police), you will have to investigate what happened, to try to figure out what could have been done differently and what should be done to prevent further violence. However, that is a very different investigation from the type covered in this section—and you may well be investigating in the shadow of legal action against the perpetrator and/or your company. In this situation, you will definitely want professional help. See "Take Immediate Action, If Necessary," below, for information on finding a violence consultant.

Decide Whether to Investigate

Whenever you learn of a threat or aggressive behavior by an employee, you need to look into it. Remember, most employees who commit violence give some warning, often in the form of threats, intimidation, and minor acts of physical violence. If you ignore these early warning signs, you are only allowing the problem to escalate towards violence. And if you take a "wait and see" attitude, you might miss your chance to head off a disaster.

> **TIP**
>
> **Employees will appreciate your efforts.** Employees are very concerned about workplace violence—and understandably fearful about working with someone who has made threats or seems to be out of control. If you don't do anything in the face of this kind of misconduct, workplace morale will suffer, absentee rates will rise, and productivity rates will drop. If you take action right away, on the other hand, employees will see and appreciate that the company takes their safety seriously.

So you can't ignore violence—but you also can't take action based solely on a complaint. Not every employee who makes a threat or has an angry outburst moves on to commit violence, and, of course, the truth may be different from what was first reported.

Some employers are so fearful that violence might erupt immediately that they fire first and ask questions later. This is a big mistake. If you are too quick to judge, you might mistakenly assume that an employee who poses no actual threat is violent. This kind of mistake may have disastrous consequences for the employee—and possibly for your company, if the employee decides to sue. You might even provoke the employee into committing a violent act that could have been avoided.

The solution is to investigate every threat and potentially violent act, but to do so very quickly (and often, with professional assistance). The sections that follow explain how.

Learning About Threats

Sometimes, you'll learn about a threat of violence directly from an employee who has been threatened or treated aggressively. That employee might file a formal complaint, talk to a supervisor, or confide in a coworker. Even if no threat has been made, employees might come forward to report that a coworker is acting strangely—talking to him- or herself, mentioning violence, losing control, or looking unusually disheveled and scattered.

You may also hear of anonymous threats: email messages or written notes that threaten harm but don't indicate the author. Some acts of violence—such as defacing an employee's car, vandalizing someone's workspace, or ruining equipment—might also be committed anonymously.

And in some situations, a concerned friend or family member might report the employee. If the employee is ranting to family and friends that he or she wants to kill coworkers or has a plan to harm the boss's children, someone might decide to tip off the company. These reports are sometimes made anonymously—perhaps in a message on the owner's voice mail or an unsigned letter.

Take Immediate Action, If Necessary

Once a threat or violent incident has been reported, your first concern is safety. To keep the workplace safe while you investigate, there are a few things that you'll need to take care of right away. If the threat is serious and immediate, start by contacting a workplace violence consultant to help plan your next moves. Next, you'll have to decide what to do with the suspect while you investigate. And you must figure out whether the company needs to step up security until the matter is resolved.

Lining Up Expert Help

Unless you have an in-house expert on workplace violence (as some larger companies do), your first decision after hearing about a violent or threatening incident should be whether to bring in a consultant. Sometimes called "workplace violence consultants" or "threat assessment specialists," these experts are trained and experienced in figuring out whether or not a particular employee poses a real danger to others.

They can also help you with other aspects of the investigation, including planning, interviewing employees (including the accused employee), giving advice on what disciplinary action to take (and how to deliver the news), following up with police and security personnel, developing antiviolence training and policies, and helping your company avoid violent incidents in the future.

Generally, you should call in a specialist whenever you feel like you are in over your head or don't know what to do. Although hiring a consultant can get pricey, it will be well worth the cost if it helps to head off a violent incident. You should probably talk to an expert if:

- an employee brings a weapon to work, shows a weapon to other employees, talks frequently about owning weapons, or otherwise shows a serious fascination with weaponry

- an employee threatens serious physical violence against another employee or makes repeated references to the possibility of committing violence

- an employee physically harms another employee, in a situation that is neither an accident nor the product of mutual aggression (such as a fist fight or horseplay that gets out of hand)

- an employee stalks or follows another employee, or

- an employee shows a dramatic decline in mood, mental acuity, or awareness, or appears to be losing control.

RESOURCE

Finding a consultant. The best way to find a workplace violence consultant—and any other workplace expert—is to ask those you know and trust for a referral. Of course, not every company will have used a workplace violence expert, but some larger companies may have one on call. Another good source of referrals is your company's business or employment lawyer. Your local or state police may also be able to help you find a workplace violence expert.

Dealing With the Suspect

In every situation involving workplace conflict, you will want to separate the alleged offender and the alleged victim while you sort out what happened. Workplace violence presents a slightly different scenario, however. If a worker has threatened or committed violence against another worker, separating the two won't necessarily solve the problem, even temporarily. For one thing, a worker bent on committing violence can follow through, no matter how far away the victim works. The violent worker can accost the victim in a parking lot, a common space, or the victim's work area. And an employee who has been threatened or treated violently isn't likely to feel much safer if you simply move the offending worker to a different floor or shift.

TIP

Refer an employee accused of violence to your EAP program. If your company has an employee assistance program (EAP), let the accused employee know about it. Many larger companies have these programs, designed to help employees with problems from anger management to relationship difficulties to debt counseling and more. Particularly if the accused employee admits to feeling stress or having difficulties off the job, providing immediate help through the EAP could head off further workplace incidents.

A worker who has resorted to threats or violence could well do so again. Even if separating the workers offers temporary protection to the first victim, it does nothing for the employees who work in the area to which the potentially violent employee is moved, who may quickly become the latest targets of his or her rage and frustration.

All things considered, the best course of action is to immediately suspend an employee accused of violence or threats. When you tell the accused employee about the suspension, emphasize that it's temporary, that no conclusions have been reached about the truth or falsity of the allegations, and that the suspension is not intended to be punitive. Explain that the alleged acts violate company policy and that you must investigate before deciding what to do. Explain that the employee is not to return to the worksite until further notice and that you will be in touch to arrange an interview as part of the investigation. And don't allow the employee to return to the work area after the meeting, except under the escort of a security guard.

 CAUTION

Don't suspend workers without pay. From a legal standpoint, suspending exempt, salaried employees—those who are not entitled to overtime if they work extra hours—without pay while you investigate probably violates wage and hour laws. And even though you can suspend hourly, nonexempt workers without pay, it's not a good idea. A suspension without pay is punitive: It improperly signals that you have made up your mind about the allegations before you've even begun to investigate. A worker who is suspended without pay will probably be angry about it—and you don't want to add fuel to the fire if the worker has a potential for violence. If the allegations turn out to be false, you may be inviting a lawsuit. And unpaid suspensions can be an administrative hassle, as they require you to interrupt your usual payroll system. Avoiding these problems will be worth the wages you pay out to a temporarily suspended employee.

Keeping the Accused Employee in the Loop

In a violence investigation, it's especially important to let the accused employee know exactly what's going on, what you plan to do, and why. As the warning signs of violence indicate, employees who commit violent acts are often suspicious and distrustful of others. They sometimes feel that others are out to get them. They are under stress, and they feel isolated to the point that violence seems like a viable solution to their problems.

One key to preventing a violent reaction to the investigation itself is to keep the accused employee informed. Rather than forcing him or her out of the workplace without an explanation or sending security to march him or her out the door, meet with the accused employee immediately; describe the allegations; tell the employee that the allegations, if true, violate company policy; explain that you will investigate and interview anyone who might have relevant information (including the accused employee), and that the company will make a decision only when all the information has been gathered; and convey that the employee will be immediately suspended, with pay, until the situation is cleared up.

By taking this approach, you accomplish two important objectives: You let the employee know that his or her behavior has been noticed and may result in discipline, and you include the employee in the process, thereby counteracting the employee's feelings of isolation and persecution.

Of course, there may be situations when you have to act more precipitously. For example, if you learn that an employee has gone to the parking lot to retrieve a weapon or has threatened to harm a supervisor when he or she returns from lunch, you won't have a chance to hold this meeting—you'll need to immediately dispatch security to deal with the danger. But, in most cases, you should meet directly with the accused employee to explain where things stand. For information on safety concerns during the meeting, see "Interviews," below.

Restraining Orders

Some states allow employers to get a restraining order against anyone who has threatened or committed violence against their employees. Generally, a restraining order is a court order that prohibits someone from doing something. The prohibited actions depend on the reason for the order—restraining orders are used for a number of purposes, from preventing a neighbor from cutting down a shared tree to prohibiting the government from allowing a new law to go into effect.

In the last few decades, restraining orders have been used as a tool to fight domestic violence. A victim of violence fills out court papers explaining the incidents that have taken place and why she fears further harm. If a judge signs the order, the person accused of violence must stay a specified distance away from the victim (and sometimes also from locations where the victim spends time, like her home or school). If the abuser violates the order (for example, by approaching the victim on the street or coming to her home), the police can arrest the abuser for violating the order before any violence takes place.

In recent years, a number of states have passed laws that allow employers to get restraining orders against anyone who has threatened or committed violence against employees. State laws differ regarding what the employer has to prove to get an order, whom the order can protect (that is, if it applies to all employees or only to those whom the offender has threatened), and other details. (You can find out whether your state has a law—and what the law requires—at http://legalmomentum.org/issues/vio/restraining.pdf.)

EXAMPLE: Lynette, a department manager at USS-Posco Industries, learned that Ezell, one of her employees, violated work rules. Lynette warned Ezell that he would be disciplined for any further violations. Lynette later heard that Ezell had threatened the employees who brought the violations to her attention. Ezell had also made other threats towards his coworkers and bragged that he kept a gun in his car. Ezell was later fired.

The company got a restraining order requiring Ezell to stay away from Lynette and from the workplace. Ezell challenged the order, claiming that he shouldn't be required to stay away from Lynette because he hadn't threatened her directly. The court denied Ezell's challenge, finding that his general threats of violence against employees was enough to allow the company to get the order on behalf of itself and Lynette.

Restraining orders are most effective against terminated employees and other outsiders. It makes sense to apply for an immediate restraining order (if your state allows it) if your company is facing a threat of imminent violence from a former employee or another person who is off-site (such as a customer or the domestic partner of an employee). However, you'll have to weigh the information you have to go on and the severity of the threat. If the threat looks serious and you have credible information to back it up (for example, several employees heard the threat), you may want to get a restraining order even before you investigate. On the other hand, if the threat is unclear and witnesses' stories are conflicting, it may be wiser to wait until you've dug a little deeper. After all, when you seek a restraining order, you are telling a court that you have legitimate reason to fear another person; if you don't have evidence to back that up, you won't get the court order, and you may have some legal trouble with the accused exemployee.

Restraining orders are not as useful for current employees. Because they are required to come to work, a legal order prohibiting them from doing so won't do you much good. In this situation, it's best to complete your investigation before deciding whether a restraining order is necessary (and it may well be, if you decide to terminate the worker for violence). If you suspend the worker while you investigate, you can instruct the worker not to come to the workplace, and enforce that instruction by telling guards and reception personnel that the worker is not to be admitted until you instruct them otherwise.

Security Measures

You will probably want to step up security at your company, at least until you complete the investigation. Depending on the nature of the threat (and how extensive existing security measures are), you may want to adopt some of all of the following precautions:

- Require all workplace visitors to check in, receive a security badge, and be escorted at all times.
- Require all employees to wear a badge or picture ID while at work.
- Install surveillance cameras (check your state's laws first—some prohibit cameras in certain workplace areas), extra lighting, and alarm systems.
- Install a locking door between the entrance or reception area and the rest of the workplace.
- Make sure every employee knows what to do in an emergency.
- Bring in security guards (or additional security guards); if you suspect a particular person, give security a recent photograph and a complete description, with instructions not to allow that person into the workplace.

Choose the Investigator

Chapter 2 explains the qualities that make an investigator particularly effective—such as professionalism, experience, and impartiality. Those considerations always apply, no matter what type of problem you're investigating. However, there are some additional issues to consider in a violence investigation.

Using an Outside Investigator

If you are dealing with a workplace violence or threat assessment consultant, that person may be able to handle the investigation. Of course, the consultant can't make decisions on behalf of the company, especially about what discipline should be imposed following the investigation. However, the consultant should be well equipped to handle the interviews, review documents, and write a report summarizing his or her conclusions. Most experts will also be able to help you decide what to tell other employees, whether you need changes to security plans or personnel policies to deal with violence, and how to train employees and managers to prevent future violence.

Getting the assistance of a consultant is a very good idea in any investigation of serious threats of violence or violent incidents. Experts tell us that much can be learned from reading the nuances of a suspected employee's presentation: key phrases, body language, facial expressions, and gestures. Consultants have years of experience deciphering these signals—and have interviewed many employees who have committed or are suspected of violence. On the other hand, you and your staff may have no training or experience in dealing with violent employees, up until now. Given the high stakes, it's often a good idea to have an expert on hand to help out.

Some consultants will want to handle the whole investigation, while others will be willing to advise you throughout the investigation without taking over entirely. For example, the consultant may give you advice about what steps to take right away to secure the premises, how to get the suspected employee out of the workplace, what documents to gather, and how to handle the interviews (and interpret the responses). Or, the consultant may interview the suspect and victim, while leaving other interviews to you. During your initial contact with a consultant, ask whether the consultant is willing to handle any of the investigative chores—or to be available to advise you throughout the investigation.

Investigator Qualities

In a violence investigation, two of your most important goals are:

- **Laying down the law with the accused employee.** Violence happens, in part, because it is allowed to happen. An employee who has been getting away with intimidating and threatening coworkers may not fully understand that these actions are unacceptable. The longer this situation continues, the more resistant and resentful the employee will be towards any efforts to correct it. The person who interviews the accused employee must be able to clearly explain why the alleged behavior violates company policy and why the company is obligated to take action. This will convey that the employee's actions have consequences—which, in turn, can diminish the chances for further violent incidents.

- **Including the accused employee in the process.** Remember, employees who commit violent acts often feel persecuted and misunderstood. Part of the investigator's job is to convey to the accused employee what is going to happen and why, to make the investigation a transparent process, so the employee doesn't feel that the outcome is inevitable or the company is engaged in a plot against him or her. An accused employee who is included in the process is less likely to see the investigation as a reason to escalate the violence.

The investigator must be able to successfully handle both of these goals. To set limits for the employee, the investigator must have a certain amount of gravitas within the company. This means that a lower-level supervisor or human resources representative might not be the right person for the job; a member of upper management or a company officer might be in a better position to get this message across.

To make sure that the employee sees the investigation as fair and open, you must take special care not to choose an investigator who has had any run-ins or unpleasant dealings with the accused employee. If your investigator has a "past" with the accused employee, the employee may see the investigation as just another workplace conspiracy. Even more distressing, the accused employee may fixate on the investigator as a source of his or her problems in the workplace—which means that the investigator may become a target for violence.

Plan the Investigation

If violence has been threatened or committed, your investigation will have to be especially speedy. With this in mind, you should limit your investigation planning to the bare minimum once you've dealt with any immediate safety concerns.

As always, your first step is to consider what you already know. What happened? If a threat was made, what were the exact words used? If aggressive, intimidating, or violent acts are alleged, what was done? Do you know who made an alleged threat or committed a violent act, or was it done anonymously? Where did it take place? Who was the victim? Who else had the opportunity to witness it?

Your answers to these questions will help you plan your next moves. Specifically, you'll need to figure out:

- **Whom to interview.** The victim or recipient of threats should be first on your list. You'll also want to interview anyone who saw or heard the incidents and, of course, the suspected employee. Other possible candidates include the suspected employee's supervisor or manager and anyone else who may have had an opportunity to witness the work relationship between the victim and the suspect.

- **What documents and evidence to gather.** Start off with the personnel files of the suspected employee and the victim, to see if anything similar has been reported before. If any threats have been put in writing, collect those as well. You'll also want to secure any physical objects that relate to the situation—such as defaced or damaged property (or photographs of the property), weapons, or unsolicited gifts or other objects left for the victim.

- **Whether you will need to review other records.** For example, it may be prudent to run a background check on the accused employee, to find out if he or she has a criminal record, a history of violent behavior, or prior incidents of violence or similar trouble at previous employers. (See "Gather Documents and Other Evidence," below, for more information).

Interviews

Once you've finished your investigation planning, you're ready to start your interviews. Generally, you'll want to interview the victim first, followed by witnesses, and save the accused employee for last. This will give you a chance to gather as much information as possible so you can get the accused employee's response to every allegation.

No matter whom you're interviewing, you should start the interview with some opening remarks to set the employee at ease and explain the process. Next, proceed to your specific questions, remembering to follow up on any new information raised by the witness's responses. Close the interview by letting the witness know what will happen next and inviting him or her to come to you with any concerns or additional information. And conduct follow-up interviews if any new information comes to light.

The Victim

The purpose of your interview with the victim is to find out as much as you can about what happened: what was said or done, when, in what context, how the victim responded, whether similar incidents have happened in the past, and so on. However, most victims will have a different goal during the interview: to find out what is being or can be done to secure their own safety. This is an entirely reasonable concern, and you should address it at the start of the interview.

Getting Started

At the outset, explain that the company is investigating the complaint or incident and that the purpose of the meeting is to gather as much information as possible. Make sure to cover any measures the company has taken to keep the employee safe, such as increasing security, placing the accused employee on leave, consulting with a violence expert, getting a restraining order, and so on. Cover safety measures the employee can take outside the workplace, such as changing established routines, not going out alone, and improving home security—the local police or a violence consultant can help come up with a comprehensive list of security measures for the victim.

Explain how the investigation will proceed and that any employee who has committed misconduct will be disciplined. Ask the victim to come to you immediately if anyone retaliates against him or her for coming forward. Explain that the victim must not talk about the investigation with others in the workplace and that you will protect the victim's confidentiality to the extent possible. Finally, find out if the victim has any questions or concerns about the investigation.

Questions

When you question the victim, you want to find out exactly what happened. Being attacked or threatened is obviously a very upsetting experience; as a result, some victims may be so caught up in how the incident made them feel that they will have trouble relating the facts. For example, a victim might say, "He threatened to kill me!" or "I can't work with someone who attacked me," but this doesn't really tell you very much about what was actually said or done. Although it's important to find out how the victim felt and reacted, remember not to lose sight of the basic facts: who, what, where, when, and how. Here are some sample questions to consider (of course, the actual questions you ask will depend on the facts of your case).

SAMPLE QUESTIONS

- What happened?
- What did [the accused employee] say or do to you?
- How did you respond?
- Did [the accused employee] touch you in any way?
- Did [the accused employee] threaten you? What were his or her exact words?
- What was [the accused employee]'s demeanor? Did he or she make any gestures? What was his or her facial expression? Did he or she yell, speak loudly, use a normal tone of voice?
- Did anyone else see or hear the confrontation?

SAMPLE QUESTIONS (cont'd.)

- What was going on immediately before the incident? Were you interacting with [the accused employee] at all?

- Where and when did the incident take place?

- Has [the accused employee] ever threatened or intimidated you before? Please describe each incident.

- Did anyone witness these prior incidents?

- Have you experienced any unexplained acts of vandalism or property damage? Have you received any unsolicited gifts or other items?

- Do you work with [the accused employee]? What is your working relationship (that is, are you coworkers, does one of you report to the other, do you work together on projects)?

- For how long have you worked together? Describe what your working relationship has been like. Have you worked well together in the past? Have you had difficulty working together in the past?

- Do you know of anyone else who has had similar problems with [the accused employee]? If so, please describe what happened to them.

- Is there anything else you want to tell me about [the accused employee] or about this incident?

- How have the incidents affected you? Did you take any time off as a result of the incidents? Did you seek medical treatment or counseling?

- Are there any documents or other kinds of evidence relating to the incidents? Did you take notes or keep a journal recording these incidents?

- Have you spoken to anyone about this? To whom, and what did you say?

- Is there anything else you'd like to tell me?

Closing the Interview

Once you have finished your questions, review your notes with the person you interviewed. Make sure you got everything right and that your notes include all of the important details. Have the employee sign your notes or a written summary. Ask the employee not to discuss the complaint or the investigation with any coworkers. Remind the employee about retaliation. Ask the employee to come to you immediately with any new information. And let the employee know what will happen next.

Witnesses

Witnesses might be coworkers who heard or saw the incident, others who have had trouble with the accused employee in the past, or the accused employee's supervisor or manager. Like the victim, witnesses may also be concerned about safety—and may be very reluctant to tell you anything that they feel might make them a target.

Getting Started

For witnesses, your opening remarks can be brief. The witness doesn't need to know who complained, who is accused, or what the specific allegations are (although they may already know). Once you have explained that you are investigating a workplace problem and talked about confidentiality and retaliation, you can begin asking your questions.

If the witness raises safety concerns, explain some of the measures you have taken to improve security in the workplace.

Questions

When questioning witnesses, your goal is to gather information without giving too much away. To plan your questions, consider who suggested the witness and why. Did the witness see or hear the incident? Was the witness told about the incident? Is the witness privy to some details of the relationship between the victim and the accused?

Start with general questions about the witness's work; these questions will help you figure out if the witness could have seen or heard the alleged incidents. Next, move on to the specifics of the alleged incidents. Here are some sample questions to consider:

SAMPLE QUESTIONS

- Describe your typical workday or workweek. Who is your supervisor? Where is your workstation? What time do you typically arrive at work each day? What time do you leave?

- Do you work with [the victim] and/or [the accused employee]? How would you describe their work relationship? What is your work relationship like with each of them?

- Has [the victim] ever spoken to you about [the accused employee]? Has [the accused employee] ever spoken to you about [the victim]?

- Have you seen any incidents or heard any communications between [the victim] and [the accused employee] that made you uncomfortable? Describe them to me.

- [If the witness may have seen or heard any incidents, ask questions to figure out whether the witness was there and what happened.]

- Have you heard this or other incidents discussed in the workplace? When, where, and by whom?

- Have you ever had any problems working with [the victim] or [the accused employee]?

- Do you know of anyone else who might have information about the incident? Are there any documents or other evidence that you know of relating to the incident?

- Is there anything else you'd like to tell me?

EXAMPLE: The victim claims that the witness heard the accused employee say, "If you were smart, you'd give me a higher rating. I know you work late sometimes, and it's a long, dark walk to where you park your car. Anything could happen to you." The victim says the accused employee made this statement in the hallway outside her office, late Monday afternoon.

You should start by asking general questions to figure out if the witness was there. For example: "Were you in the office on Monday? What did you do on Monday afternoon? Did you see [the victim] and [the accused employee] in the hallway? What time? What did each of them say?"

If these questions don't get you the information you need, you'll have to ask more specific questions, like: "Did [the accused employee] say anything about his rating? Did he say anything about [the victim's] work hours? Did he say anything that you considered threatening?"

Closing the Interview

Once you have finished your questions, review your notes with the witness. Make sure you got everything right and that your notes include all of the important details. Have the witness sign your notes or a written summary. Ask the employee not to discuss the complaint or the investigation with any coworkers. Remind the employee about retaliation. And ask the employee to come to you immediately with any new information.

The Accused Employee

You have several goals in mind when you interview the accused employee. Of course, you want to hear that person's side of the story, so you can figure out what actually happened. But your primary goal should be threat assessment: determining whether the accused employee really poses a violent threat (and if so, to whom).

> ⚠ **CAUTION**
>
> **Get expert help.** Although this point has already been made in this chapter, it's worth repeating: Assessing whether a particular person will act violently is difficult work, and the consequences of guessing wrong can be disastrous. You should hire an expert for help and advice in any situation that has the potential for violence. The material in this section provides general guidelines, not the comprehensive and individualized assistance that only an expert can provide.

Keep the Interview Safe

Any time you meet with an employee who has the potential for violence, you'll want to take steps to maintain your own safety. First and foremost, you should hold the interview in a room that offers you an escape route—for example, a door that opens directly to the outside of the building. If there is only one door to the room, make sure that the employee doesn't sit between you and that door (rearrange furniture, if necessary).

During the interview itself, be sure to listen to the employee and let the employee know that you are interested in what he or she has to say. Acknowledge the employee's feelings about the allegations, but explain that you need to find out what happened in order for the company to deal with the situation. If the employee becomes agitated or upset, make a special effort to stay calm and focused, to avoid letting the situation escalate. Don't be confrontational in your questioning—maintain the demeanor of an objective fact gatherer. Don't crowd the employee physically or make any agitated movements.

If you have any concerns about safety, bring another person into the interview with you. And make sure that you have security waiting nearby, available to come in if things get out of hand. You should have a telephone in the interview room and a prearranged signal that will let security personnel know that you need some help.

Getting Started

At the outset, explain the purpose of the meeting. Emphasize that the company has not reached any decisions about what happened and that you are interested in hearing what everyone involved has to say before making a decision or taking any action. Because you will probably have to reveal the name of the complaining employee, spend some extra time discussing retaliation—what it is, that the company prohibits it, and that employees who engage in retaliation will be subject to discipline.

Questions

Let the accused employee know that you are investigating alleged threats or violent behavior—and that this behavior, if it happened, violates company policy and will result in discipline. Be very clear that violent behavior has consequences; this will not only set the proper tone for the interview, but will also help dissuade the accused employee from resorting to violence during the interview.

Although the accused employee will probably want to know the specific allegations right away, you are better off postponing this discussion until later in the interview, after you have had a chance to gather some important background information. Assure the accused employee that he or she will have the opportunity to hear and respond to the allegations before the interview is over. Here are some sample questions to consider.

SAMPLE QUESTIONS

- When did you start working for the company? What was the first position you held? Who was your supervisor? What were your job responsibilities? For how long did you hold that position?

- What was the next position you held at the company? [Ask the same questions for each position, up to the current job.]

- What is your current job? Who is your supervisor? What do you think of your coworkers? Do you like your current position? What are some of the things you like about it? Is there anything you dislike about it?

- What is your typical workday or workweek like? What time do you arrive, what time do you leave? What are your job responsibilities?

- Do you supervise any employees? What are their names and positions?

- How would you characterize your working relationship with your direct reports? Your coworkers? Your supervisor?

- [Tell the accused employee what misconduct is alleged or suspected.] What is your response to these allegations?

- Did these things happen? [If the accused employee does not completely deny the allegations:] What did happen? When and where?

SAMPLE QUESTIONS (cont'd.)

- How did [the victim] respond?

- Did anyone witness these incidents?

- Have you told anyone about these incidents?

- Have you kept any notes or a journal about these incidents?

- What is your work relationship like with [the victim]?

- [If the accused employee denies the allegations:] Could another person have misunderstood your actions or statements? Do you think someone made up these incidents? Why?

- Have you ever used foul language in the workplace?

- Have you ever threatened anyone in the workplace? Have you ever had a physical confrontation with another employee? Where and when?

- Do you own any weapons? Do you own any guns? Have you ever used a gun?

- Has anyone ever filed a restraining order against you? Have you ever had any dealings with the police? Please describe the circumstances.

- [For complaints of stalking or romantic obsession:] Have you ever seen [the victim] outside of work? Have you ever had a social relationship with each other? A romantic relationship? Have you ever asked [the victim] out on a date? What was [his or her] response?

- Have you ever been accused of making threats or acting violently, at this job or at previous jobs you've held? Where and when? How were the accusations resolved?

- Do you know of anyone who might have information about these incidents?

- Do you know of any documents or other evidence relating to these allegations?

- How do you think this situation should be resolved?

- Is there anything else you'd like to tell me?

> ⚠️ **CAUTION**
>
> **You must allow the accused employee to respond to the allegations.** Some investigators are so eager to keep the interview civil—or to protect the complaining employee's privacy—that they never confront the accuser with the allegations against him or her. This is a big mistake, one that could undermine the legitimacy of the entire investigation. Courts have held that accused employees who never learn precisely what they are accused of haven't had a fair opportunity to tell their side of the story, to offer the names of relevant witnesses, or to explain why the victim might have made the accusations. You don't necessarily have to say who complained, but you should say whom the employee is accused of threatening or harming. And don't worry about privacy concerns—you have a very compelling business reason for revealing this information.

> 📖 **RESOURCE**
>
> **Need interviewing tips?** For more information on interviewing the accused employee, check out *Dealing With Workplace Violence: A Guide for Agency Planners*, available from the federal Office of Personnel Management, at www.opm.gov (under the heading "HR Practitioners/ Agencies," select "Tools & Resources," then "Guides," then click "To obtain" next to the Guide's title). Written for federal government agencies, this informative resource is now widely used by private companies as well. It offers case examples, planning tips, policy guidance, advice on handling the aftermath of a violent incident, and much more. Although some of the information is relevant only to government workplaces, you'll find most of it to be extremely useful.

Follow-Up Interviews

If any new information comes up during your investigation, you should conduct follow-up interviews with the victim or accused employee. Both employees should have the opportunity to respond to new allegations or defenses, to make sure that you have a complete understanding of the facts when you make your decision and to give you the opportunity to gauge credibility. It is especially important to let the accused employee know of any additional allegations that come up during the investigation. If you don't, you may be accused of unfairness for failing to give him or her an opportunity to respond.

Gather Documents and Other Evidence

Except in very rare circumstances, workplace violence generally escalates from threats, conflicts with coworkers, and intimidation to actual violent acts. This means that, if your company is doing its job right, there may be a paper trail. Check the accused employee's personnel file for any history of problems working with others, abusive behavior, physical altercations, and so on. Find out if anyone has complained about the accused employee before. And review the personnel files of any other employees involved in the incident as well, to see if there's any indication of prior problems with the accused employee.

In addition to official company records, there may be other types of documents and evidence that will help you reach a decision. Here are some examples:

- **Records of threats by the accused employee.** For example, if the threats were made in writing—either on paper or in email—you can get those documents. If threatening messages were left on an answering machine or voice mail service, see if you can get copies. And make sure to ask the victim and witnesses if they've kept any records—for example, a log of threatening phone calls or notes of an intimidating encounter.

- **Medical records or records of treatment sought by the victim.** If a physical assault has occurred, the victim's medical records (if the victim sought treatment) can help you assess what happened. And if the victim has sought counseling or other help to deal with stress created by the accused employee, you might ask for a note from the treatment provider to that effect. (The victim will have to consent to the release of any medical records.)

- **Items collected by the accused employee.** Sometimes, an employee with a propensity for violence collects news articles on other violent incidents, weapons paraphernalia, photographs of or information about the victim, or other items. If the accused employee keeps these things at work, you may be able to collect them. (See Chapter 7 for information on workplace searches.)

- **Nondocumentary evidence.** For example, if the victim's property has been damaged or defaced, you might collect that property (if it's small), or take photographs of the damage. The victim may have received gifts, photographs, or other items from the accused employee, which you can gather and review.

- **Official records.** You may wish to find out whether the accused employee has a criminal record, has been subject to restraining orders, or has been sued for harassment or injuring someone. Many of these records are publicly available; some states restrict an employer's ability to review criminal records (check with your state's department of labor or ask a lawyer about your state's laws).

Evaluate the Evidence

In some violence investigations, the accused employee admits that the incident happened as the victim described. An accused employee who acted under extreme stress and realizes that his or her actions were inappropriate may be willing to own up to the misconduct, while explaining what led to the problem.

EXAMPLE: Marjorie is accused of suddenly turning on a coworker who was walking behind her in a hallway, pushing him away, and screaming, "Just stay away from me! Don't crowd me!" She then ran down the hall to her office and slammed the door. Marjorie's coworkers have noticed that she's been acting strangely for the last month or so—she's been showing up late, falling behind on her assignments, crying, and appearing to be out of it some of the time.

When Marjorie is interviewed, she begins crying. She admits that the hallway incident happened just as her coworker described but explains that her exhusband has been stalking her and threatening to kill her. She is fearful and jumpy, and she thought momentarily that her coworker was her exhusband; when she realized her mistake, she was so embarrassed that she ran away.

An employee who feels justified in resorting to violence or intimidation may also admit to the incident—claiming, in effect, that the victim deserved it. In this situation, the employee feels entitled, inappropriately, to bully others.

EXAMPLE: Marcus is accused of threatening his boss, Sharon, after she promoted one of his coworkers instead of him. Sharon says that Marcus told her, "You'll be sorry for passing me over. You're going to find out what it means to be on my hit list."

When Marcus is interviewed, he readily admits to making the statement but claims that he didn't intend to threaten her with physical violence. "She's been hard on me ever since I started reporting to her, and she never even gave me a chance for that promotion. I wanted her to know that she'd made a mistake and that I wasn't going to forget it."

In many cases, however, the accused employee will deny the allegations, or at least some part of them. For example, the accused employee might claim to have been joking, to have said something slightly different, or to have spoken in a calm tone of voice rather than a shout. To figure out what really happened, consider the factors listed in Chapter 4. In cases of threats and violence, plausibility, demeanor, corroboration, and prior incidents are often especially important.

- **Plausibility.** Whose story makes sense? Does one story defy common sense—or (as may be true in a threat situation) ordinary rules of conversation?

EXAMPLE 1: Charlotte claims that Harry has threatened her and that she has seen him parked outside her house. Harry first denies knowing where Charlotte lives; when confronted with a photograph her husband took of his car, he admits that he may have been in the neighborhood, but it was to visit a friend. He refuses to give his friend's name or address.

EXAMPLE 2: Jamal says that Larry has been angry with him ever since he received a promotion that Larry wanted. Most recently, Jamal claims that Larry told him, "You better hope you don't run into me in a dark alleyway—like the one where you park your car." Larry denies intending to threaten Jamal; he claims that he said, "I worry about you walking to your car at night. You could get hurt." Larry can't explain why he was worried about Jamal, or why he thought Jamal wouldn't be safe walking to his car alone.

- **Corroboration.** Did anyone else hear or see the incident? Should someone else have been able to see or hear it, if it happened the way the victim or accused employee claimed it did?

- **Demeanor.** Victims or recipients of threats or violence are often pretty stressed out and frightened. Does the victim's demeanor make sense, given the allegations? Does the accused employee exhibit the behaviors attributed to him by the victim? Demeanor can't tell you the whole story, but extreme or inappropriate reactions might indicate that things are not what they seem.

EXAMPLE 1: Karen says that Curtis threatened to bring a gun to work and open fire on his coworkers. She says that Curtis said he felt like he was going to explode and couldn't take the pressure of work any more. Karen related these statements in a calm tone of voice, then asked, "Can you really keep someone like Curtis here? I mean, what if he goes through with it?" Curtis appeared to be under no particular stress—until told of Karen's allegations, which he vehemently denied, saying, "Why would she say something like that?" Curtis denies owning a gun and points out the bumper sticker on his car in support of strict gun control. In this case, there may be more to Karen's story than meets the eye.

EXAMPLE 2: John says that Rex has been physically intimidating towards him and other coworkers. John claims that Rex blocks their way in the halls, looms over John when he's sitting at his desk, and gets in John's face whenever he is upset about something. Lately, John says Rex has threatened to harm him. John looks pretty freaked out; he has dark circles under his eyes and expresses concern several times that Rex might hurt him if he finds out that John has complained. During Rex's interview, he crowds the interviewer, raises his voice, and tries to talk over the interviewer. Both John and Rex are acting in ways that support John's story.

- **Prior incidents.** Because violence is usually preceded by warnings, prior incidents of threats or abusive behavior is important evidence. Although it isn't conclusive evidence that the incident in question occurred, a history of violence lends a lot of weight to the victim's version of events.

Take Action

If you conclude that the accused employee is capable of violence, deciding what discipline to impose won't be your only concern. The danger to the victim and other employees doesn't necessarily end once the accused employee is out of the workplace; in fact, firing the accused employee, if handled improperly, could actually increase the risk of a violent incident. In addition to any discipline you will impose, you need to come up a plan to deal with the accused employee and keep the target employee (and workplace) safe.

Disciplinary Action

In some cases, you may conclude that no discipline is warranted for the accused employee. If there appears to have been a genuine verbal misunderstanding, for example, you may reasonably decide to simply end the matter with warnings all around and renewed training about workplace violence.

In some circumstances, you may decide that some form of aggressive behavior occurred but that the accused employee should be excused to some degree. For example, consider the case of Marjorie, discussed above, who pushed a coworker but was under extreme stress because of threats and stalking by her exhusband. Because Marjorie understands that her behavior was inappropriate, it has never happened before, and her current situation is highly unusual, you might choose to give Marjorie a written warning and direct her to some sources of help for her problem with her exhusband (such as the police and an employee assistance program).

However, if you decide that the accused employee made a threat or committed violence absent special circumstances, you will have to decide whether firing is warranted. Generally, you will probably have to fire most employees who actually threaten or physically assault someone. Your company has a legal obligation to keep its employees safe, and retaining an employee who has shown a propensity for violence is not in keeping with that obligation. If the accused employee recognizes that his or her conduct was wrong, is willing to seek help with anger control and appropriate workplace behavior, and can work with you to figure out how to prevent similar problems in the future, it might be worthwhile to keep the employee on board—as long as the behavior was not extreme and you are willing to monitor the situation closely. If you are considering keeping on an employee who has made threats or committed violence, consult with a lawyer and/or workplace violence consultant first.

Coming Up With a Safety Plan

Once you've taken disciplinary measures, you'll have to come up with a plan to keep the workplace safe going forward. This is especially important if you are firing the perpetrator. Remember, termination just gets the employee off your company's payroll; it doesn't solve the underlying problem of the employee's willingness to resort to violence.

How Serious Is the Threat?

Experts say that it is often possible to tell, from the language of a threat or the nature of aggressive behavior, how likely it is that a person will commit violence. Of course, there are no absolutes here—this is all a matter of interpretation and degree, not an exact science. Generally speaking, however, the more detailed and advanced a person's violent thinking has become, the more that person should be considered an immediate danger.

Here are some examples:

- An employee who has focused his or her attention and anger on a particular person is more dangerous than an employee who has vague, general complaints against the company.
- An employee who has threatened someone is more dangerous than an employee who has not.
- An employee who has followed or approached the intended victim, or who has gathered information (such as home address, a favorite route home, or where children go to school), is more dangerous than one who has not.
- An employee who owns or has practiced with weapons is more dangerous that one who has not.
- An employee who conveys a detailed plan for harming the victim (such as how the victim will come to harm, what type of weapon the employee will use, when and where the assault will take place) is more dangerous than one who has not.
- An employee who has rehearsed committing violence is more dangerous than one who has not.
- An employee who feels that he or she must act right away is more dangerous than one who threatens to act at some undefined point in the future.

Consider whether you should pursue any criminal law options— such as informing the police, getting a restraining order, or reporting the accused employee for violating weapons, stalking, or assault and battery laws. Consider taking additional steps to enhance workplace security—talk to your local police for ideas. And make sure to inform your company's workplace security staff that the accused employee is no longer welcome on company property and that police should immediately be called if he or she shows up. A workplace violence expert can help you craft an effective safety plan.

Breaking the News

You will have to inform the accused employee and the victim of the results of the investigation. If you have decided to fire the accused employee, you will want to have security available to assist you, if necessary. Explain what your investigation revealed and why the company decided to fire the employee. Explain exactly what you expect of the employee in the future—that he or she stay away from the workplace, in particular. Give the employee the name of someone in the company to call to wrap up final details, such as continuing health insurance, getting the final paycheck, and so on.

If the employee becomes agitated or threatening, bring in security immediately. Explain that this kind of behavior won't be tolerated and that the employee will be escorted from the workplace immediately. If a termination meeting ends in further threats or aggression, you should probably contact your local police to report the incident.

Always Be Respectful

It is extremely important to treat an employee you are firing with respect and dignity. Hold the termination in private, and don't belabor the employee's failings. Never belittle an employee, and be sure to mention the employee's hard work for the company. Studies show that the way a termination is handled plays a major role in how the fired employee views the company—and if you're dealing with an employee who has the potential to commit violence, you'll want him or her to view the company in the best possible light.

When you meet with the victim, explain the action you have taken and why. Describe the safety plan, including steps you have taken to enhance security, and any criminal proceedings you've set in motion. Make sure the victim knows what to do if he or she sees or hears from the accused employee—for example, if there is a restraining order in effect, the victim should call the police immediately and inform you of the incident.

Find out whether the victim has concerns about his or her own safety—if so, offer to put the victim in touch with someone who can help develop a safety plan for outside the workplace (your local police or a violence consultant can help with this). Ask about the victim's feelings about what happened; in some cases, the victim may be traumatized by the incidents. If the victim needs time off work to recuperate, make that available as an option. You might also offer to have the company pay for a few counseling sessions, if the victim wishes.

Document the Investigation

Document your violence investigation just as you would any other workplace investigation. (See Chapter 4 for details.) Be sure to include any legal actions taken, such as applying for a restraining order or reporting the incident to the police. Also, include your plans for following up with the accused employee or the victim.

Follow Up

Even after you've finished your investigation, there will be quite a few things to do. First of all, you'll want to check in with the victim from time to time, to make sure that he or she feels secure in the workplace and is satisfied with your company's efforts to ensure safety. If you haven't fired the accused employee, you'll also want to meet frequently with him or her, to make sure that any required counseling is completed and to keep track of the accused employee's progress.

In addition to these follow-up meetings, there are several steps you should take to get the workplace back to normal and prevent violence in the future.

Counseling

If actual violence or significant threats have taken place, employees may be traumatized. In addition, after handling the investigation, you may be feeling some stress. If you or others need some help getting back to business as usual, you might consider bringing in some trauma counselors or other workplace advisers, so employees have a chance to express their feelings and have their questions answered.

Policies, Planning, and Training

Most companies learn at least a few things they should be doing different-ly after investigating a violent incident. Try to use this as an opportunity to figure out how better to prevent and address violence in the future. As part of your violence prevention efforts, consider the following strategies:

- **Adopt an antiviolence policy.** Every organization, no matter how small, should have a clear policy prohibiting all kinds of workplace violence, from horseplay and intimidation to threats and assault. You can find a sample policy in Appendix A and on the CD-ROM.

- **Assemble a workplace violence team.** Experts agree that the best way to prevent and address violence is to put together a violence prevention team from different areas of the company—human resources, security, legal, labor, and so on. The team can work together to develop an antiviolence policy, come up with a security plan, decide how to respond to violent incidents, audit potential trouble spots, develop a working relationship with a violence consultant or local police, and figure out how to handle the aftermath of a violent incident.

- **Train your team, managers, and employees.** Once you've got a team in place, consider bringing in a violence consultant to train you in violence prevention and response techniques, including threat assessment. Managers and employees should also be trained on the company's antiviolence policy, how the company handles reports of violence, the warning signs of potential violence, and so on.

- **Do a workplace security audit.** Ask the police or a workplace violence consultant to do a walk-through of your workplace and provide ideas on how your company can improve employee safety.

Workplace Policies

Complaint Policy

Your company's policy should describe the conduct about which employees can complain, how to make a complaint, and what will happen once a complaint is filed.

- **Prohibited conduct.** Spell out, in simple terms, what conduct will be investigated. If your company has a progressive discipline policy, sexual harassment policy, or other written guidelines describing unacceptable workplace behavior, you can use those policies for reference. List the types of misconduct that you would like employees to report (for example, harassment, discriminatory conduct or comments, violent behavior or threats of violence, safety violations, theft, and/or misuse of company property). Include a catchall category at the end of the list, allowing employees to raise concerns about any type of behavior that makes them feel uncomfortable, upset, or unsafe.

For Publicly Traded Companies

Companies that are publicly traded should include an anonymous procedure for making complaints about accounting irregularities. This is required by the Sarbanes-Oxley Act of 2002, as explained in Chapter 7. If your company is publicly traded, add the language set out below. (This should be the third paragraph of your policy.) In the blank space, fill in your company's procedure for making anonymous complaints (for example, by calling a hotline or going to a confidential website for reporting complaints).

> We also encourage employees to come forward with complaints or concerns regarding the company's accounting, auditing, or internal controls procedures, and complaints or concerns regarding possible shareholder fraud. You may raise these issues through the complaint procedures described in this policy, or you may do so anonymously by _____.

- **How to make complaints.** Tell employees how to make a formal complaint if they are victims of, or witnesses to, any of these prohibited behaviors. Make sure that employees can also complain to someone outside of their chain of command: a human resources manager, another supervisor, or even the head of the company. If an employee is being harassed or mistreated by his or her own supervisor, the employee must be able to bypass that person and complain to someone who isn't part of the problem. Even if the employee's direct supervisor is not the source of the complaint, employees may simply feel more comfortable talking to someone who won't be responsible for evaluating their performance and making decisions on promotions, raises, and assignments. However, don't designate too many people. The more people responsible for taking complaints, the greater the likelihood that a complaint could fall through the cracks. Generally, it's sufficient to give employees two or three people to choose from, rather than designating all of your supervisors or managers to hear complaints.

TIP

Make sure that the people you designate to take complaints are accessible to employees. For example, if your human resources department is located in a distant office or your local human resources manager works a part-time schedule, you should choose alternate complaint takers who are local and available.

- **Investigation.** While you need not describe your company's investigative procedures in detail, your policy should assure employees that serious complaints will be investigated quickly, completely, and fairly. It should also explain that employees are expected to cooperate in such investigations.
- **Retaliation.** Assure employees that no action will be taken against them for complaining in good faith. Encourage employees to come forward if they feel retaliated against, and state that the company will act quickly to prevent any further harassment or mistreatment.

- **Managers' responsibilities.** State that managers and supervisors are responsible for reporting violations of company rules and for forwarding any complaints they hear to the appropriate complaint takers.

- **Confidentiality.** Make clear that the company will keep the complaint confidential to the extent possible. You cannot reasonably promise that no one will be told about the complaint; after all, the investigator will have to tell the alleged wrongdoer about the complaining employee's statements and perhaps interview witnesses about the incident.

- **Corrective action.** State that immediate disciplinary will be taken action against employees who violate company policy, following a thorough investigation.

Sample Complaint Policy

Our Company is committed to providing a safe and productive work environment, free of threats to the health, safety, and well-being of our workers. Such threats might include, but are not limited to, harassment, discrimination, violations of health and safety rules, and violence.

Any employee who witnesses or is subject to inappropriate conduct in the workplace may complain to _____ or to any company officer. Any supervisor, manager, or company officer who receives a complaint about, hears of, or witnesses any inappropriate conduct is required to immediately notify _____. Inappropriate conduct includes any conduct prohibited by our company policies about harassment, discrimination, discipline, workplace violence, health and safety, wages and hours, and drug and alcohol use. In addition, we encourage employees to come forward with any workplace complaint, even if the subject of the complaint is not explicitly covered by our written policies.

We encourage you to come forward with complaints immediately, so we can take whatever action is needed to handle the problem. Once a complaint has been made, _____ will determine how to handle it. For serious complaints, we will immediately conduct a complete and impartial investigation.

We expect all employees to cooperate fully in company investigations by, for example, answering questions completely and honestly and giving the investigator all documents and other material that might be relevant. All complaints will be handled as confidentially as possible. When the investigation is complete, the company will take corrective action, if appropriate.

The company will not engage in or allow retaliation against any employee who makes a good-faith complaint or participates in an investigation. If you believe that you are being subjected to any kind of negative treatment because you made or were questioned about a complaint, report the conduct immediately to _____.

Open-Door Policy

An open-door policy can be very informal; indeed, adopting a friendly, informal tone will help encourage employees to come forward with their concerns and ideas. The most important components of an open-door policy are:

- **Purpose.** Describe the reasons for having an open-door policy (for example, to facilitate communication between employees and management, to encourage employees to report work-related concerns, to find out what employees are thinking).

- **Appropriate topics.** Explain what types of issues employees might want to raise—you can also give some examples (such as if an employee is having a problem with a coworker or supervisor, wants to share a good idea, or wants to propose topics for a company meeting or training).

- **Whose door is open.** Tell employees who they should talk to (for example, a supervisor or manager, the company president or CEO, company officers, the human resources department).

- **Encouragement.** Let employees know that the company is eager to hear their concerns. If your employees don't use the policy, it won't do your company any good.

Sample Open-Door Policy

We want to maintain a positive and pleasant environment for all of our employees. To help us meet this goal, our Company has an open-door policy, by which employees are encouraged to report work-related concerns.

If something about your job is bothering you, or if you have a question, concern, idea, or problem related to your work, please discuss it with your immediate supervisor as soon as possible. If for any reason you don't feel comfortable bringing the matter to your supervisor, feel free to raise the issue with any company officer.

We encourage you to come forward and make your concerns known to the company. We can't solve the problem if we don't know about it.

Antidiscrimination Policy

Your company's antidiscrimination policy should explain its commitment to equal opportunity. Here are some issues the policy should cover:

- **Prohibited conduct.** Explain what types of discrimination are prohibited (for example, race, sex, and so on). To find out what antidiscrimination laws your company must follow—and therefore, which types of prohibited discrimination you should list in the policy—see Chapter 5. You'll find a list of state antidiscrimination laws in Appendix D.

- **Complaint procedures.** Explain how employees can complain about discrimination, referring to the complaint policy.

- **Retaliation.** Let employees know that retaliation will not be permitted, and ask employees to report retaliation.

- **Managers' responsibilities.** Require managers to report discriminatory conduct immediately.

- **Corrective action.** State that your company will take immediate and appropriate disciplinary action against any employee who violates the policy.

Antidiscrimination Policy

Our Company is strongly committed to providing equal employment opportunity for all employees and all applicants for employment. For us, this is the only acceptable way to do business.

All employment decisions at our company—including those relating to hiring, promotion, transfers, benefits, compensation, placement, and termination—will be made without regard to [prohibited bases for discrimination].

Any employee or applicant who believes that he or she has been discriminated against in violation of this policy should immediately file a complaint with _____, as explained in our complaint policy. We encourage you to come forward if you have suffered or witnessed what you believe to be discrimination—we cannot solve the problem until you let us know about it. The company will not retaliate, or allow retaliation, against any employee or applicant who complains of discrimination, assists in an investigation of possible discrimination, or files an administrative charge or lawsuit alleging discrimination.

Managers are required to report any discriminatory conduct or incidents, as described in our complaint policy.

Our company will not tolerate discrimination against any employee or applicant. We will take immediate and appropriate disciplinary action against any employee who violates this policy.

Antiharassment Policy

A harassment policy should include the following:

- **Definition of harassment.** Explain what harassment is, and list the prohibited bases for harassment—that is, race, sex, age, and so on. To find out what antidiscrimination laws your company must follow—and therefore, which types of prohibited harassment you should list in the policy—see Chapter 5. You'll find a list of state antidiscrimination laws in Appendix D.

- **Harassment is prohibited.** State clearly that harassment will not be tolerated.

- **Complaint procedure.** Explain how to make complaints of harassment (referring to the complaint policy), and encourage employees to come forward.

- **Retaliation.** Explain that retaliation is prohibited.

- **Managers' responsibilities.** State that managers are required to report harassment immediately.

- **Investigation and corrective action.** State that complaints will be investigated and that anyone who is found to have violated the policy will be disciplined.

Antiharassment Policy

It is our policy and our responsibility to provide our employees with a workplace free from harassment. Harassment on the basis of [prohibited bases for discrimination] undermines our workplace morale and our commitment to treat each other with dignity and respect. Accordingly, harassment will not be tolerated at our company.

Harassment can take many forms, including but not limited to touching or other unwanted physical contact, posting offensive cartoons or pictures, using slurs or other derogatory terms, telling offensive or lewd jokes and stories, and sending email messages with offensive content. Unwanted sexual advances, requests for sexual favors, and sexually suggestive gestures, jokes, propositions, email messages, or other communications all constitute harassment.

If you experience or witness any form of harassment in the workplace, please immediately notify the company by following the steps outlined in our complaint policy. We encourage you to come forward with complaints—the sooner we learn about the problem, the sooner we can take steps to resolve it. The Company will not retaliate, or allow retaliation, against anyone who complains of harassment, assists in a harassment investigation, or files an administrative charge or lawsuit alleging harassment. All managers are required to immediately report any incidents of harassment, as set forth in our complaint policy.

Complaints will be investigated quickly. Those who are found to have violated this policy will be subject to appropriate disciplinary action, up to and including termination.

Antiviolence Policy

Here are some of the issues an antiviolence policy should address:

- **Violence is prohibited.** State that violence will not be tolerated. Explain what violence is and that threats or comments about violence will be taken seriously.

- **Weapons are prohibited.** Indicate that weapons are not allowed in the workplace. If some employees must carry weapons to do their jobs, or if your state does not allow employers to ban weapons from the premises entirely (see Chapter 7), you will have to modify this provision.

- **Procedures.** Explain what employees should do if they witness a threat or violence. Explain how employees can make a complaint about violence.

- **Investigation.** State that all complaints of violence will be investigated and that appropriate corrective action will be taken.

- **Retaliation.** Explain that retaliation is not permitted.

Antiviolence Policy

We will not tolerate violence in the workplace. Violence includes physical altercations, coercion, pushing or shoving, horseplay, intimidation, stalking, and threats of violence. Any comments about violence will be taken seriously—and may result in your termination. Please do not joke or make off-hand remarks about violence.

No Weapons

No weapons are allowed in our workplace. Weapons include firearms, knives, brass knuckles, martial arts equipment, clubs or bats, and explosives. If your work requires you to use an item that might qualify as a weapon, you must receive authorization from your supervisor to bring that item to work or use it in the workplace. Any employee found with an unauthorized weapon in the workplace will be subject to discipline, up to and including termination.

What to Do in Case of Violence

If you observe an incident or threat of violence that is immediate and serious, IMMEDIATELY DIAL 9-1-1 and report it to the police. If the incident or threat does not appear to require immediate police intervention, please contact _____ and report it as soon as possible, using the Company's complaint procedure. All complaints will be investigated and appropriate action will be taken. You will not face retaliation for making a complaint.

Forms and Checklists

CONFIDENTIAL
Complaint Reporting Form

Date of Complaint: _____

Time of Complaint: _____

Name of Complaining Employee: _____

Telephone Number (work): _____

Telephone Number (home): _____

Email address: _____

Complaining Employee's Position: _____

Complaining Employee's Supervisor: _____

Name of Accused Employee: _____

Accused Employee's Position: _____

Accused Employee's Supervisor: _____

Incident(s) at Issue: _____

_____

_____

_____

Potential Witnesses: _____

_____

_____

Has Complaining Employee Told Others of Incident(s)?_____

_____

_____

Documents Relating to Complaint: _____

_____

_____

Other Issues: _____

_____

_____

Complaint Reporting Form (cont'd.)

Name of Intake Person: _____

Signature of Intake Person: _____

The information above is correct and complete, to the best of my knowledge.

Employee Name: _____

Signed: _____

Date: _____

Investigation Notice Form

To: [*Name of Employee*]

From: [*Name of Investigator*]

Date: _____

Re: Investigation of Possible Violation of Company Policy

I am investigating a possible violation of company policy. As part of the investigation, I will be interviewing you today. The purpose of this notice is to provide some important information about what the company expects from you during the investigation.

The company appreciates your participation in this process. We expect you to cooperate fully in the investigation by, for example, answering all questions completely and honestly, providing any documents that are relevant to the investigation, and making yourself available for follow-up interviews, if necessary. You will be excused from your usual work duties for interviews and any other activities necessary to the investigation.

Retaliation against anyone involved in the investigation is strictly prohibited. If you retaliate against anyone involved in this investigation, you will be subject to discipline. If you believe you have been mistreated or otherwise retaliated against because of your participation in this investigation, please tell me immediately.

We expect you to keep the investigation and complaint (if there is one) confidential. This means that you should not talk about the investigation, or the statements you make during the interview, with your coworkers or other company employees. We will maintain the confidentiality of the investigation to the extent possible, revealing information only on a need-to-know basis. If you become aware of any breach of confidentiality—for example, if you hear coworkers discussing the investigation—please tell me immediately.

I encourage you to contact me after our interview today if you remember additional information or if you would like to change or add to your statement for any other reason.

Your signature indicates that you have received and read this notice.

Signed: _____   Date: _____

[Print Employee's Name]

Investigation Report Form
CONFIDENTIAL

To: Investigation File

From: [*Name of Investigator*]

Date:_____

Re: _____

The [Complaint or Allegations]

[*List date of complaint or other information that led to investigation, and the incidents that were investigated. If there are multiple incidents, number each consecutively, starting with oldest incident and moving towards the present.*]

_____

_____

Pre-Investigation Actions

[*List anything you did before the investigation, such as placing an employee on leave, notifying management of the investigation, changing reporting relationships or work locations, etc.*]

_____

_____

The Investigation

I began the investigation [*date and time*].

I interviewed the following witnesses:

[*List each witness, along with date and time of interview.*]

- _____

- _____

- _____

I also had [*number*] follow-up interviews, with:

[*List each witness, along with date and time of interview.*]

- _____

- _____

My notes from these interviews are in the investigation file.

Investigation Report (cont'd.)

I reviewed the following items:

[*List each document or other piece of evidence, including where and when you got it.*]

- _____

- _____

- _____

Copies of these items are in the investigation file.

_____

_____

I also:

[*List any other actions you took, such as visiting the scene of the incidents, taking photographs, etc.*]

_____

_____

I completed my investigation on [*date*].

_____

Conclusions

After reviewing the evidence, I have concluded [*Describe your conclusions and the evidence you considered in reaching them; if you investigated multiple incidents, state your conclusion for each incident.*]

_____

_____

Recommendations

Based on the conclusions listed above, I find that [*List your recommendations as to each person accused of wrongdoing. If you are responsible for taking action, describe what you intend to do or have done—for example, issued a written warning or set up a safety committee.*]

_____

_____

Signed: _____

Date:_____

CONFIDENTIAL
Adverse Action Notice Form

To: [*Employee Name*]
From: [*Manager imposing discipline*]
Re: Adverse action resulting from investigation

On [*date*], an investigation began into allegations of workplace misconduct. The company hired an outside investigator, [*name of investigator or investigative firm*], to perform the investigation. The investigation has now concluded, and the company has determined that you will be subject to the following discipline: [*Indicate discipline imposed, such as written warning or termination of employment.*]

We are providing this adverse action notice as required by the Fair Credit Reporting Act, to inform you of the nature and substance of the investigative report on which this discipline is based.

The report concluded that: [*Summarize the report, without listing the names of the employee who complained or any employees or others who were interviewed.*]

EXAMPLE: (this uses the facts set forth in the hypothetical case in Appendix C; because that case was investigated in-house rather than by an outside investigator, no adverse action notice was required in that case): "Based on interviews with two witnesses and your own statements, it was found that you showed a photograph of two women in a sexual pose to a female coworker, and made a sexual comment about the picture."

Signed: _____
Date:_____

My signature acknowledges that I have received and read a copy of the Adverse Action Notice.

Signed: _____
Date:_____

Checklist: Ten Steps to a Successful Investigation

1. Decide whether to investigate.

2. Take immediate action, if necessary.

3. Choose an investigator.

4. Plan the investigation.

5. Conduct interviews.

6. Gather documents and other evidence.

7. Evaluate the evidence.

8. Take action.

9. Document the investigation.

10. Follow up.

Checklist: Avoiding Common Investigation Mistakes

Avoiding Mistake 1: Failing to Investigate
- ☐ Never ignore complaints.
- ☐ Make sure the problem is minor before you decide not to investigate further.

Avoiding Mistake 2: Delay
- ☐ Get started right away.
- ☐ If you have a good reason for waiting, put it in writing.

Avoiding Mistake 3: Inconsistency
- ☐ Don't punish one employee more severely than another for similar misconduct.
- ☐ Investigate misconduct if your company has investigated similar problems in the past.
- ☐ Make sure your own biases aren't influencing your decisions.

Avoiding Mistake 4: Retaliation
- ☐ Warn employees that retaliation will not be tolerated.
- ☐ Ask the complaining employee to immediately report retaliation.
- ☐ If you must separate workers, move the accused worker, not the worker who complained.

Avoiding Mistake 5: Failing to Be Thorough
- ☐ Investigate every serious complaint or problem thoroughly and carefully.

Avoiding Mistake 6: Compromising Confidentiality
- ☐ Reveal investigation information only on a need-to-know basis.
- ☐ Avoid making negative statements about current or former employees.
- ☐ Don't say anything unless you know it's true.

Avoiding Mistake 7: Losing Objectivity
- ☐ Remember your role: You work for the company.
- ☐ Get help if you need it.

Avoiding Mistake 8: Strong-Arm Investigation Tactics
- ☐ If an employee wants to end an interview, let the employee leave.
- ☐ Don't physically restrain employees by locking doors or blocking the exit.
- ☐ Discipline employees who fail to cooperate with the investigation.

Checklist: Avoiding Common Investigation Mistakes (cont'd.)

Avoiding Mistake 9: Invading Privacy Rights

☐ Ask or search for only what you legitimately need to know.

☐ Make sure your company has policies reserving the right to search.

☐ Make sure there is a sound business reason for searching, questioning, or monitoring any employee.

Avoiding Mistake 10: Using Polygraphs Improperly

☐ Skip the polygraph altogether—the law is too complicated and the results might not be very revealing.

☐ If you use a polygraph, hire a qualified examiner who knows how to comply with the law's technical requirements.

Document Checklist

☐ Company policies

☐ Email messages

☐ Postings to company bulletin boards (electronic or corkboard)

☐ Correspondence

☐ Performance evaluations

☐ Work samples

☐ Written warnings and other disciplinary records

☐ Customer complaints or comments

☐ Commendations

☐ Documents signed by the employees involved
(such as hiring agreements, employment contracts, and other agreements)

☐ Attendance records
(for work generally, required meetings, or training sessions, for example)

☐ Payroll records

☐ Time cards or other records showing hours worked

☐ Work schedules

☐ Inventory records

☐ Expense reports

☐ Computer records (of Internet sites visited, productivity, and so on)

☐ Cash register receipts

☐ Purchase orders

☐ Productivity reports
(such as records of sales completed, deadlines met, or projects finished)

☐ Sales receipts

☐ Equipment logs

☐ Notes taken by an employee involved
(for example, if an employee made a record of threatening or harassing comments by another employee, or kept a diary or journal of workplace incidents)

☐ Files from any previous investigations of the same employees or same types of incidents

Credibility Checklist

☐ **Plausibility:** Whose story makes the most sense? Could the employees involved have heard and seen what they claimed to have witnessed? Should they have heard and seen things that they did not admit?

☐ **Source of Information:** Did the witness see or hear the event directly? Did the witness report firsthand knowledge, or rely on statements from other employees or rumors?

☐ **Detail:** How general or specific was each person's statement? Were details supported by other evidence? Did the accused or suspected employee deny the allegation in detail or only generally?

☐ **Corroboration and Conflicting Testimony:** What witnesses or documents support each side of the story? Does the evidence contradict one person's statements? Do the witnesses support the person who suggested you interview them? If there are conflicts, are they over minor or significant issues?

☐ **Contradictions:** Was each person's story consistent throughout your questioning or on a second telling? Did any of the witnesses contradict themselves? If so, did the change involve a minor issue or a matter of substance?

☐ **Demeanor:** How did the witnesses act during the interview? Did they appear to be telling the truth or lying? Did the accused employee have a strong reaction to the complaint or no reaction at all? Did the complaining employee seem genuinely upset? Were any witnesses' reactions unusual, based on their ordinary demeanor or behavior?

☐ **Omissions:** Did anyone leave out important information during the interview? Is there a reasonable explanation for the omission?

☐ **Prior Incidents:** Does the accused employee have a documented history of this type of misconduct? Has the complaining employee made previous complaints? Have there been other incidents between the complaining and the accused employee?

☐ **Motive:** Does anyone have a motive to lie about, exaggerate, or deny the incident? Is there any history between the employees involved that affects their credibility? Do any of the witnesses have a special loyalty to—or grudge against—anyone involved in the incident?

Discipline Checklist

☐ **Severity:** How serious was the misconduct? If there was a victim, how was the victim affected by the accused employee's actions? What effect did the accused employee's actions have on the workplace?

☐ **Consistency:** Have other employees committed similar misconduct in the past? How were these incidents handled?

☐ **Policy:** Does the company have a progressive discipline policy in which you spell out the types of misconduct that might result in particular disciplinary consequences? Where does this misconduct fall on your company's scale?

☐ **History:** Have there been any similar prior incidents involving this employee? Does the employee have a history of disciplinary problems?

☐ **Knowledge:** Did the employee know that this conduct was prohibited? Did workplace rules and policies clearly spell out the company's expectations? Was the behavior clearly inappropriate, regardless of whether it was explicitly prohibited?

☐ **Evidence:** How strong is the evidence of misconduct? Do you have powerful, firsthand, corroborated evidence of wrongdoing?

Investigation Report Checklist

☐ The name and title of the investigator

☐ The date the report was completed

☐ If there is a complaint, the date of the complaint and name of the employee who complained

☐ If there is no complaint, how and when the company learned of the problem (for example, a fight broke out or an outside audit revealed accounting irregularities)

☐ A summary of the incident(s) under investigation, from the complaint or other information that caused the company to investigate

☐ A summary of any actions taken before the investigation began, such as placing an employee on leave, changing an employee's reporting relationship, or calling in an outside expert

☐ When the investigation began, including the reasons for delaying any part of the investigation (if applicable)

☐ Who was interviewed

☐ The date and time of each interview

☐ The names of any witnesses whom you chose not to interview, and the reasons for your decision

☐ What documents or other evidence were gathered

☐ Where documents or evidence were found (for example, in an employee's personnel file, pinned to the company bulletin board, or in an employee's desk drawer)

☐ When documents or evidence were gathered

☐ Your conclusions and how you came to them, including a summary of the witness's statements and any other facts your considered in relation to the incident(s) under investigation

☐ Any important issues left unresolved

☐ Your recommendations for action or, if you are responsible for taking action, the actions taken as a result of the investigation (for example, discipline against the wrongdoer or workplace training)

Sample Investigation Documents

This appendix provides some sample documents from a fictional sexual harassment case, including an initial complaint, notes from interviews, an investigation report, and a written warning to one of the employees involved. In this case, Jocelyn Evans complained that two of her male coworkers, Bill Martinez and Skip Thompson, acted inappropriately. She brought these concerns to her boss, Brian Haggerty, who didn't take them seriously.

The investigator in this case, Michael Hogan, is the director of human resources for the company. As you'll see, he conducted a thorough and effective investigation, following the guidelines in this book. As soon as he received the complaint, he knew he had to investigate. He took immediate action by suspending one of the men and allowing Jocelyn to take time off, as she requested. He began the investigation right away and concluded it within a week. He interviewed all relevant witnesses, reviewed documents, and visited the scene of an incident alleged in the complaint. He conducted follow-up interviews with Jocelyn and Skip. He reviewed the evidence, made credibility determinations, and concluded that misconduct took place. He wrote a report that addressed each allegation in the complaint. He decided to issue a written warning to one employee; because he doesn't have the authority to terminate employment or to impose discipline on a manager without input from other company officials, he recommended these actions in his report. And he followed up, by actually delivering the written warning and by meeting with Jocelyn.

CONFIDENTIAL
Complaint Reporting Form

Date of Complaint: 8-24-2007

Time of Complaint: 10 a.m.

Name of Complaining Employee: Jocelyn Evans

Telephone Number (work): 555-1212

Telephone Number (home): 555-9898

Email address: jevans@ourcompany.com

Complaining Employee's Position: Sales Representative

Complaining Employee's Supervisor: Brian Haggerty

Name of Accused Employee: Skip Thompson, Bill Martinez, Brian Haggerty

Accused Employee's Position: Brian: Manager of Sales; Bill and Skip: Sales Representatives

Accused Employee's Supervisor: Brian supervises Bill and Skip; Jackson Little, VP of Sales and Marketing, supervises Brian.

Incident(s) at Issue: Jocelyn says Bill showed her a pornographic picture twice; Skip has made sexual comments and touched himself in front of her. Made it difficult to work. Very upset.

(1) On Monday, 8/6, Bill brought in photo from a magazine; two women together, naked, in a sexual pose. Bill said, "I bet you wouldn't mind some of that, would you?" Jocelyn told him that he shouldn't have porn at work, didn't want to be talked to that way. Louise Jay, their administrative assistant, said Bill showed picture to her too.

(2) Next morning, Jocelyn found a copy of the picture taped to her computer screen, with handwritten note on it: "Your girlfriend left this for you." Around 9 a.m. When she saw the picture, Bill and Skip standing in the doorway of her office laughing. Jocelyn mostly out of the office for the rest of that week on calls; tried to avoid Bill and Skip as much as possible.

(3) On Tuesday, 8/14, Jocelyn had to meet with Skip re: upcoming presentation for a client (Clark account). When she went in Skip's office, he said "I was just thinking about you," appeared to be rubbing his genitals. She told him to stop it and to come by her office when he was ready to work. Skip said, "Wow, you really can't take a joke, can you? Are you still mad about that picture?" Jocelyn said that she was angry about the picture and didn't appreciate his comments.

Complaint Reporting Form (cont'd.)

(4) On Friday, 8/17, Sharon Washington and Jocelyn left office together to have a drink after work. Skip made a comment about them going on a "date," said he'd like to "come along for the after party, if you girls ever let a man in on the action." Also made a comment about having a "three-way" with them. Sharon and Jocelyn were shocked, didn't know how to respond. They left immediately; were planning on going to a bar near the office (Midtown Pub), but decided to go to Club V so they didn't run into Skip.

(5) On Wednesday, 8/22, Skip came into Jocelyn's office and shut the door. Jocelyn asked him to open door. Skip: "Don't you want to be alone with me? I think about being alone with you all the time." Jocelyn walked past Skip to open door and ask him to leave; Skip grabbed her arm and said, "You're not being a very nice girl." Jocelyn told Skip to leave immediately; she took the rest of the day off.

(6) On Thursday morning, 8/23, Jocelyn told Brian about all incidents above. He told her to "lighten up"; said Bill and Skip worked hard and had to blow off steam sometimes. Re: touching himself, grabbing her arm: "Skip wouldn't do something like that." Brian said that filing a formal complaint would make things hard for the team; everyone would blame Jocelyn for getting coworkers in trouble.

(7) One hour later, 11 a.m. or so, Jocelyn got email from Skip. Message said "little bird" told him Jocelyn was planning to report him to management. Said none of the men would want to help her with her accounts if she filed complaint against him; they'd be too worried about getting in trouble for saying or doing the wrong thing.

Potential Witnesses:

(1) None to Bill showing Jocelyn the picture.

(2) None. She still has the picture, will bring it in.

(3) Only Skip and Jocelyn were in the office. Sharon saw Jocelyn leaving Skip's office, asked her if anything was the matter. Jocelyn told her, "Skip can be such a jerk." Told her whole story after incident described in (4).

(4) Sharon. Jocelyn thinks that Brian overheard; he was standing nearby and started laughing at Skip's comments.

(5) None. Louise saw Jocelyn crying in the women's room; Jocelyn told her that she wasn't feeling well and was going to take the rest of the day off.

(6) Brian.

(7) None. Jocelyn kept the email message.

Complaint Reporting Form (cont'd.)

Has Complaining Employee Told Others of Incident(s):
See above.

Documents Relating to Complaint:
Jocelyn has the picture that was left on her computer and the email message from Skip. Otherwise, she doesn't know of any other documents.

Other Issues:
Jocelyn is very concerned about having to work with Skip and Brian. Scared to be alone with Skip. Not afraid of Brian that way, but worries he will punish her for complaining somehow. Wants to take the rest of the day off. I told her to take paid leave. Also told her that Skip would be placed on leave immediately pending an investigation. Brian on vacation until next Tuesday.

Name of Intake Person: Michael Hogan, Director of Human Resources

Signature of Intake Person: Michael Hogan

The information above is correct and complete, to the best of my knowledge.

Name: Jocelyn Evans
Signed: *Jocelyn Evans*
Date: August 24, 2007

CONFIDENTIAL
Interview with Bill Martinez

Interview with: Bill Martinez
Date: August 24, 2007
Time: 3 p.m.

Told Bill I was investigating a complaint in his work group. Explained retaliation, confidentiality, and need to cooperate with the investigation. Handed him a written notice form detailing these responsibilities, which he signed. Asked Bill if he was comfortable with me investigating; he said yes.

Work history:

Worked for co. for seven years. Hired as sales rep.

Doesn't supervise anyone. Sometimes works with junior reps on accounts. Junior reps he works with = Skip, Sharon Parker.

Reports to Brian Haggerty.

Usual schedule: Depends. Sometimes lots of meetings, out a lot. Rarely in the office every day of a week. Client calls, etc.

Any way to figure out which days he was in the office, which out? Sign in calendar kept by Louise Jay (admin). If he's in for the day, he writes down when he leaves for a meeting. If he's out whole day, either he or admin make a note. Same for other reps. Calendar is one page per month.

Typical hours: If he comes in, usually here by 8 a.m. Come in early to beat traffic; lives an hour away. Stays only until 4 or so, if working all day. Sometimes different hours, depends on work.

Keep track of hours worked each day? No.

How would you characterize working relationship with Brian? Fine. He mostly leaves me alone. Senior reps work independently, not much supervision.

Meet with Brian regularly? No. If I have a problem, might talk to him.

He meet with you? No. Doesn't really do performance evals, anything like that. If I need feedback on account, might ask him.

Working relationship with Jocelyn? OK, I guess. Senior reps don't work together much. She didn't appreciate joke I made. Probably shouldn't have done it.

What joke? Brought in a picture from a magazine. She talks a lot about differences between women and men, women communicate better, women are more

Interview with Bill Martinez (cont'd.)

sensitive, like that. Showed her a picture of two women naked, joked about how she likes women better than men. Thought she'd find it funny; she didn't.

When was this? Couple weeks ago. Don't remember exact day.

What was picture? Two women naked. Downloaded from the Internet.

At work? No, at home.

Women having sex? Posed to look like. Not really hard-core.

Remember what you said? Something like, "you like women so much, this is probably something you'd like."

Did you say, "bet you wouldn't mind some of that?" Maybe. Don't remember exact words.

She respond? Said she didn't think it was funny. Walked away. Seemed mad.

Why think she'd find it funny? She's talked about her roommate posing for girlie magazines before. Seemed like it didn't offend her.

When did she say this? Maybe a year ago.

Only one time? Yes.

Any other reasons you thought she'd find it funny? Not really. Just a stupid joke. I feel bad about it now.

Ever heard Jocelyn make sexual comments, jokes? Not really. Can't think of anything.

Anyone else there when showed her picture? Don't think so.

Show picture to anyone else? Louise. Asked her if she thought it was offensive after Jocelyn got mad. She said no, but everyone's different.

Anyone else? Skip saw it in my office, asked if he could have it. I said OK. Told him not to let Jocelyn see it, that she was angry I showed it to her.

See picture again? Yes, next a.m. saw it taped to Jocelyn's computer.

Time? Not sure. I'd been at work for a while. Jocelyn just got there.

What happened? Skip came by my office, told me to come with him. Asked why, he said "You'll see." Stopped in coffee room near Jocelyn's office. Said to wait.

Jocelyn came in with her purse, Skip told me to follow him. Went to her office door. She saw picture on her computer, got really mad. Saw us in doorway.

Interview with Bill Martinez (cont'd.)

She say anything? No.

Looked mad? Yes. Turned red. Closed door on us.

You say anything? Might have said "oh shit."

Why? So stupid of Skip. Knew she'd think it was me. Felt bad.

Tell her you didn't do it? Tried to later. She wouldn't stop to talk to me. Asked me to leave her alone.

You say anything? No.

You know Skip doing this? No. Told him not to show it to Jocelyn.

Say anything to Skip? Told him it was stupid. Shouldn't upset Jocelyn; he has to work with her.

Anyone else there? Think Louise was in hallway. Don't know if she saw picture.

Say anything to Louise? No.

Louise say anything? No.

Tell anyone about this? No.

See the picture again after that? No.

Anything else happen between you and Jocelyn since? No. Haven't seen her much. Think she's avoiding me. Been meaning to apologize, but she's been out a lot and seems really upset.

Seen any other incidents between Skip and Jocelyn? No. Just regular work stuff.

Skip talk to you about Jocelyn? Don't think so. Don't remember anything special.

Anything else you want to tell me? Feel really bad about this. Just a stupid joke. Didn't know she'd be so upset. Didn't know Skip would push it further.

Asked Bill to come to me with any additional information, concerns.

My signature below indicates that these notes accurately reflect what was said during the interview.

Signed: Bill Martinez
Name: Bill Martinez
Date: 8-24-07

CONFIDENTIAL
Interview with Louise Jay

Interview with: Louise Jay
Date: August 27, 2007
Time: 9 a.m.

Told Louise I was investigating a complaint in her work group. Explained retaliation, confidentiality, and need to cooperate with the investigation. Handed her a written notice form detailing these responsibilities, which she signed. Asked Louise if she was comfortable with me investigating; she said yes.

Work history:

Worked for co. for six months. Administrative asst. to sales.

Reports to Brian Haggerty.

Usual schedule: Every day, 8:30 to 5.

Calendar by your desk: All reps supposed to sign in and out; either they do it or I do, if they're not in office.

Pretty consistent? Yes. Usually accurate. Have to know where reps are in case client calls. Need to know if other reps have to cover account.

Ever seen sexual photos in the workplace? Yes, few weeks ago. Bill showed me.

Date? Don't remember. Think it was a Monday, not sure.

What was photo? Two naked girls.

Having sex? Maybe. Wasn't super raunchy.

Bill say anything to you when he showed? Asked me if I thought it was offensive. Told me Jocelyn was upset about it.

What did you say? Wasn't a big deal to me. I don't care. Could see why Jocelyn might not like it.

Why? She's very professional.

Heard Jocelyn make sexual comments before? God no. Never.

Heard Bill? Don't think so.

Heard Skip? Don't think so. Doesn't really happen here. Not like my last job.

Bill say anything else? Don't think so. Told him he shouldn't do stuff like that unless he knows the person.

Interview with Louise Jay (cont'd.)

Why? One person might not mind, someone else gets offended. You never know.

He say anything? Think he agreed with me.

Talk to him again about this? No.

Talk to Jocelyn about it? Told her Bill showed it to me, told her he didn't mean any harm.

When? Same day, after Bill showed it to me.

She say anything? Not really. Seemed like she thought it was just a stupid joke.

Tell anyone else about this? My husband. Nobody at work.

Know anything else about picture? Know it was taped to Jocelyn's computer next morning.

How know? Sitting at my desk, saw Bill and Skip outside her door, went and looked, saw her take it off.

She say anything? No. Really angry. Face red. Slammed door.

How Bill and Skip react? Skip laughed. Not sure about Bill.

Bill laughing? Don't think so. Not sure.

You say anything to Bill and Skip? No, I got out of there. Didn't want to deal with it.

Bill say anything to you? No. Saw him talking to Skip, though.

What did Bill say? Not sure; they were in the hallway. Bill looked angry. Skip was laughing.

Skip say anything to you? No.

Jocelyn say anything to you? No.

Tell anyone about this? Husband.

Seen any other incidents between Bill and Jocelyn? Not like this, no.

Skip and Jocelyn? No.

Noticed any change in Jocelyn lately? Seems upset. Saw her crying last week.

When? Don't remember the day. She said she was sick, going home.

Where? The ladies' room.

Interview with Louise Jay (cont'd.)

Any way to figure out day? Would have written that she went home sick on calendar, near my desk. Could check that.

Anything else? Jocelyn working with her door shut more than usual. Taking more time off.

Brian ever say anything to you about this? No.

Brian say anything to you about Jocelyn? No. We don't talk that much, just to say hi in the morning.

Ever meet with Brian to discuss work issues? Never. Think he once told me I was doing fine, something like that. Just in passing.

Anything else? Can't think of anything.

Asked Louise to come to me with any additional information, concerns.

My signature below indicates that these notes accurately reflect what was said during the interview.

Signed: Louise Jay
Name: Louise Jay
Date: 8-27-07

CONFIDENTIAL
Interview with Sharon Washington

Interview with: Sharon Washington
Date: August 27, 2007
Time: Noon

Told Sharon I was investigating a complaint in her work group. Explained retaliation, confidentiality, and need to cooperate with the investigation. Handed her a written notice form detailing these responsibilities, which she signed. Asked Sharon if she was comfortable with me investigating; she said yes.

Go out with Jocelyn Friday night, 8/17? Went out on a Friday, not sure date. That sure was weird.

Why? Skip said this stuff about having a three-way and me and Jocelyn dating each other. It was bizarre.

What did he say? Don't remember exactly. Just made some comment about us having sex together, and all three of us having sex together.

You say anything? I don't remember. Might have told Skip to shut up. We left right after that.

You surprised? You bet.

Why? Never heard anything like that here.

Jocelyn say anything? Don't think so. She was really upset. Said, "let's go."

You say anything to Jocelyn? Something like, "what's that all about?"

She respond? Said Skip had made some sexual comment to her, touched himself in front of her earlier that week.

Touched himself how? Rubbed his crotch over his pants. Said something about being alone with her or fantasizing about her.

Jocelyn say anything else? Said it was freaking her out. Didn't know what to do.

You respond? Told her she should tell Skip to stop. She said already did that. Told her maybe to talk to Brian. Said she might.

Anything else? Yeah, said that's why she was so upset that day. I saw her in the hallway a few days before, she looked really upset. Asked her why, she said something like, "Skip is such an ass." Didn't say any more then. On Friday, told me that was right after Skip did it.

Interview with Sharon Washington (cont'd.)

Jocelyn say anything else? No, don't think so.

Talk to her since about it? No. She's been out of the office a lot, haven't talked to her much. Seems kind of upset.

How? Distracted. Her door is usually open when she's here, but it's been shut for a couple of weeks.

Ever heard Skip make any kind of sexual comment? Just that one.

Bill? No.

Brian? No.

Jocelyn? Not at work. Sometimes we talk about our boyfriends and stuff when we go out, but just between us. She's very professional at work.

Heard Brian talk about any of this? No. Don't see Brian much.

Meet with him? No. If questions about work, I ask Jocelyn or Bill. Brian doesn't have time, works with door closed a lot.

Anything else? Can't think of anything.

Asked Sharon to come to me with any additional information, concerns.

My signature below indicates that these notes accurately reflect what was said during the interview.

Signed: Sharon Washington
Name: Sharon Washington
Date: 8-27-07

CONFIDENTIAL
Interview with Skip Thompson

Interview with: Skip Thompson
Date: August 27, 2007
Time: 3 p.m.

Told Skip I was investigating a complaint in his work group. Explained retaliation, confidentiality, and need to cooperate with the investigation. Handed him a written notice form detailing these responsibilities, which he signed. Asked Skip if he was comfortable with me investigating; he said yes.

Work history:

Worked for co. for two years.

Started as sales asst, made sales rep 4 months ago.

Reports to Brian Haggerty.

Usual schedule: in the office most days. Because he's new rep, doesn't have a large book of clients yet. Helps some senior reps with larger clients. Senior reps = Bill, Jocelyn, Charles Schroeder. Help = preparing paperwork and presentations; goes along on some sales calls and meetings; handles client when senior rep is out for some reason.

Any way to figure out which days he was in the office, which out? Everyone has to sign in and out on the calendar near the admin's desk. Admin writes down if someone is going to be out all day. Not sure how long they keep the calendars; think it's a 12-month calendar.

Typical hours: usually here around 8:30 a.m.; carpools with Tom Barr. Stays until 6; sometimes later.

How keep track of meetings, other work? Write down on day planner in my office. Will give me copy of day planner for last month.

Keep track of hours too? No.

How would you characterize working relationship with Brian? Good, he's been fair to me. Promoted me to sales rep sooner than we originally discussed, because he was happy with my work. Never had any problems.

Meet with Brian regularly? Not really. Talk to him in the hallway.

Meet with Brian in the last week? Don't remember. Would you remember? Not sure.

Interview with Skip Thompson (cont'd.)

Brian come talk to you about anything in the last week? Don't remember. Might have.

Working relationship with Jocelyn? Fine. She's kind of serious, don't think she gets my sense of humor.

What do you mean? She's all about work. Never wants to socialize, doesn't really make small talk. No big deal, she's just serious.

Work with her on any accounts? Help out with Clark account mostly. Sometimes others, but not as much.

Any meetings with her in the last few weeks on Clark account? Don't think so.

On any other accounts? Don't remember any.

Anyone talk to you about Jocelyn in the last week? Brian said something about her not liking my work.

What did he say? Don't really remember. Just that J. wasn't happy with my work on Clark account. Said she'd talk to me about it herself.

Brian say anything else? Don't think so.

Jocelyn talk to you about this? No, don't think so. Not yet.

Where conversation take place? Hallway, I think.

Anyone else there? No.

Ever seen pictures of naked women or men in the office? Might have been a calendar one of the other guys showed him once.

When was that? Don't remember.

Who showed it to you? Don't remember.

What was the picture of? Don't remember.

Is that the only time? I think so.

Someone said that there was a picture of two naked women taped to a computer screen in your work group within the last month. Remember this? I guess I do. Don't know who put it there, though.

You put it there? Not something I would do.

See the picture earlier in Bill's office? Maybe. Yes, I remember now.

Interview with Skip Thompson (cont'd.)

Ask Bill if you could have it? Don't think so.

Remember talking to Bill about the picture at all? Not really. Think he saw it on the computer too. He laughed, thought it was funny.

He say anything? Don't remember.

You think it was funny? I guess.

Where was picture? One of the female rep's offices. Don't remember.

Jocelyn's office? Don't remember.

When? Don't remember – maybe a few weeks ago.

Did you see the picture? Just from a distance.

How did the woman react? Don't know.

In the office on 8/14? Not sure; have to check calendar.

Remember meeting with Jocelyn to talk about the Clark account? No. We were supposed to have a meeting; she was sick and cancelled. Not sure it was that day.

So no meeting? No. She called and cancelled.

Did she come to your office that day at all? Or just call? Just called. Don't think I saw her.

Complaint made that you touched your genitals in front of Jocelyn, said "I was just thinking about you." Did this happen? Can't imagine doing that. Not something I would do.

You didn't touch your genitals in front of Jocelyn? Doesn't sound like me.

Say anything like this to Jocelyn? May have said I was thinking about her, but only re: work. Not personal. Don't know.

Friday, 8/17, in the office when Jocelyn left? Don't remember.

Jocelyn went out for drinks with Sharon? May have. Not unusual.

Recall saying anything to them when they left? Don't know about that day. Once asked if I could come along, wanted to go out with them.

When? Don't remember.

What did you say? Don't remember. Just asking to go along. They said no.

Interview with Skip Thompson (cont'd.)

Ask if they were going on a date? Might have. Didn't mean together, just going out.

Tell them you'd like to get in on the after party? Just said I wanted to go too. Something like that.

Ask if they ever let a man in on the action? Don't remember saying that. Might have said something about "girls' night out," no men allowed, like that.

Say you wanted to have a three-way with them? Doesn't sound like something I would say. Told you, just wanted to join them for drinks.

Did they respond? Said I couldn't come, girls' night out.

Did they seem upset? Don't think so.

Know where they were going? Usually Midtown Pub.

Did you go there that night? Don't remember.

Look for them? Don't remember. Go there sometimes.

Did you see them that night? Don't remember.

Last Wednesday, meet with Jocelyn in her office? Don't remember.

Complaint made that you told Jocelyn "I think about being alone with you all the time." Might have said something about enjoying her company.

Did you make statement? Not like it sounds. I like Jocelyn.

Did you grab her arm? Why would I do that?

Ever touched Jocelyn at all? Don't remember. Might have by accident or something. Don't know. Not on purpose.

Tell her "you're not being a very nice girl"? Don't remember saying that.

Would you remember if you had said it? I think so.

Ever spoken to Brian about Jocelyn? Only remember what I said, she's not happy with something about Clark account.

When was this? Don't remember; last week sometime.

Time? Morning, I think.

Remember anything else about conversation? No.

Where did it happen? Hallway, I think. Very quick.

Interview with Skip Thompson (cont'd.)

Anyone else there? No.

Send Jocelyn an email last Thursday? Send her and other reps email all the time. Can't say for sure.

Message said "little bird" told you she was going to file a complaint? Don't remember.

Showed him copy of message. Did you send? Oh, right. About Clark account. Not happy she complained to Brian.

So you sent? Yes.

Why say "men" wouldn't be happy re: complaint? Not sure. Most reps are men, guess that's why.

What mean by "saying or doing wrong thing?" Just that she's so serious, so critical.

This email about sexual harassment complaint? No, Clark account. Don't know anything about sexual harassment.

Talk to anyone about this email? Don't think so.

Other reps tell you they wouldn't want to work with Jocelyn? Don't think I asked anyone. Just an assumption.

Anything else about this email? No, already explained.

Anything else you want to tell me? Never had a problem with Jocelyn, personally. May not get my sense of humor; maybe she misunderstood something I said. Not happy she criticized me to Brian. Wish she'd come to me first.

Asked Skip to contact me with any additional information, concerns.

My signature below indicates that these notes accurately reflect what was said during the interview.

Signed: Skip Thompson
Name: Skip Thompson
Date: 8-27-07

CONFIDENTIAL
Interview with Brian Haggerty

Interview with: Brian Haggerty
Date: August 28, 2007
Time: 9 a.m.

Told Brian I was investigating a complaint in his work group. Explained retaliation, confidentiality, and need to cooperate with the investigation. Handed him a written notice form detailing these responsibilities, which he signed. Asked Brian if he was comfortable with me investigating; he said yes.

Work history:

Worked for co. for eleven years. Hired as sales rep. Promoted three years ago.

Supervises all sales reps.

Reports to Jackson Little

Usual schedule: Try to get into the office every day. Sometimes go out on calls.

Any way to figure out which days he was in the office, which out? Louise keeps track. Calendar by her desk.

Typical hours: Tries to be here 8:30 til about 6.

Keep track of hours worked each day? No.

Meet with Jocelyn last week? Yes.

Subject of meeting? She was having problems with Skip and Bill.

What problems? Said Bill showed her a picture or something, she didn't like it. Said Skip came on to her.

Came on to her how? Made some comment about having sex, going on a date, something like that.

Remember anything else? Said Skip groped himself. I don't believe that.

Why? Just sounds weird. Who would do that?

Anything else? Don't think so.

Say Skip grabbed her arm? Yeah, think she did.

Anything else about Bill? Don't think so.

How did you respond? Told her I didn't think Skip would do that groping thing. If he grabbed her, probably accidental. Sounded like she overreacted.

Interview with Brian Haggerty (cont'd.)

Why? Skip asks her out, big deal. She can say no.

Did she say Skip asked her out? Something like that. Wanted to go out with her and one of the other girls. They said no, he didn't go.

Say Skip said he wanted to have a three-way? Don't remember that.

Say Skip told her he wanted to be alone with her? Maybe, not sure.

Tell her anything else? No. Told her she should try harder to get along, that I'd talk to Skip if she wanted.

Try harder to get along? Yeah. Most of the sales reps are men. Some of them are going to ask her out. It happens. Don't take it so hard.

How she respond? Said she wasn't overreacting, something like that. Wanted someone to stop it.

What did you say? I'd talk to Skip, but didn't want to stir up a hornet's nest. We all have to work together. Don't want her to be isolated, everyone upset with her.

She say anything else? No, don't think so.

Did you talk to Skip? Yes. Told him something he said upset Jocelyn, to cool it.

Say anything else? Not really. Just don't ask her out any more, she wasn't interested.

Tell him Jocelyn might file a complaint? Maybe, don't remember. Remember telling him to cut it out.

Say anything about the Clark account? No. Why would I?

Say Jocelyn was upset with his work? No, upset about getting asked out.

Skip say anything? Not really. Said OK.

Hear anything else about this? No. Been on vacation; just got back.

Talked to anyone about this? No.

To Jackson? No. Talk to him on the phone maybe once a week. He works out of the Tucson office. Haven't talked to him about this.

Any other employee ever told you about any sexual comments, requests for dates? No.

Working relationship with Jocelyn? Seems fine. Does good work.

Interview with Brian Haggerty (cont'd.)

With Skip? He's going to be a great sales rep, once he learns ropes.

Bill? Also does good work. Been here a long time, probably knows job better than me.

Ever heard anyone make sexual comments in the workplace? No. Heard this stuff from Jocelyn, but didn't sound that bad.

Ever made sexual comments yourself? No. Wouldn't do that.

Asked Brian to come to me with any additional information, concerns.

My signature below indicates that these notes accurately reflect what was said during the interview.

Signed: Brian Haggerty
Name: Brian Haggerty
Date: 8-28-07

CONFIDENTIAL
Interview with Jocelyn Evans (Follow-up)

Interview with: Jocelyn Evans (Follow-up)
Date: August 28, 2007
Time: Noon

Told Jocelyn meeting to follow up on some things that came up in investigation.

Ever told Bill about roommate posing for nude magazines? Yes, think I did.

How come up? Were at auto parts company, sales call. Had a calendar or something with naked women. Bill mentioned it later; told him my roommate did that stuff.

Anything else? Don't think so.

Talked to Bill about difference between men and women? Don't think so.

About women being more sensitive? Oh, yeah. We have.

What? His wife complains how he forgets her birthday, never talks to her about his feelings, stuff like that. I tell him "women like that stuff, Bill." Talked about how women use more of their brain for language, more important to them.

Anything else? No. Just chatting; no big deal. Didn't mean to say women are better or anything.

Bill ever try to talk to you about the picture? Don't think so. Might have. I didn't want to talk to him.

Try to approach you? Might have. Really didn't want to hear anything more from him.

Louise tell you Bill didn't mean any harm? Might have. Honestly, I felt different after it was taped to my computer. If he just showed me picture & made stupid joke, wouldn't have been such a big deal. But I told him it upset me and he kept at it.

You know Bill put it on your computer? Guess I assumed. He had the picture.

Were you in office Tuesday, 8/14? Yes, told you, that was day Skip touched himself.

Why were you in his office? Supposed to meet re: Clark account.

Interview with Jocelyn Evans (Follow-up) (cont'd.)

What time? Afternoon sometime, not sure. Could check calendar.

Did you cancel meeting? No. Went to his office, he touched himself, told him to come to my office when ready to work. He never did.

Tell Brian you weren't happy with Skip's work on Clark account? No. Told him about touching himself, not happy with that. And other stuff I told you. Nothing about his work.

Brian tell you he'd talk to Skip? Sort of. Made it sound like it would cause all these problems.

Brian say you were overreacting? Something like that. Don't know if he used those words, but that's what he meant. Said I would cause problems, make it hard for people to work with me. Said I should be used to guys asking me out.

Anything else you want to tell me? No.

Asked Jocelyn to come to me with any additional information, concerns.

My signature below indicates that these notes accurately reflect what was said during the interview.

Signed: Jocelyn Evans
Name: Jocelyn Evans
Date: 8-28-07

CONFIDENTIAL
Interview with Skip Thompson (Follow-up)

Interview with: Skip Thompson
Date: August 28, 2007
Time: 2 p.m.

Told Skip I had few more questions after interviewing others. Asked who I interviewed; told him it was confidential.

What did Brian say to you about Jocelyn? Upset about something on Clark account, I told you.

Tell you that you upset her? Yes, about work.

Did he say that? Upset about work? Think so.

Tell you not to ask her out any more? Don't remember that.

Tell you she wasn't interested in going out with you? Don't remember that.

Asked Skip to contact me with any additional information, concerns. Told him he was still on paid administrative leave pending outcome of investigation.

My signature below indicates that these notes accurately reflect what was said during the interview.

Signed: Skip Thompson
Name: Skip Thompson
Date: 8-28-07

CONFIDENTIAL
Investigation Report

To: Investigation File
From: Michael Hogan
Date: August 30, 2007
Re: Complaint by Jocelyn Evans

The Complaint
On August 24, 2007, I took a complaint from Jocelyn Evans regarding inappropriate sexual behavior. (See Complaint Form in file.)

Jocelyn complained of seven incidents:

(1) On Monday, 8/6/07, Bill Martinez showed her a photo from a magazine; two women together, naked, in a sexual pose. Bill said, "I bet you wouldn't mind some of that, would you?" Jocelyn told him that he shouldn't have porn at work, didn't want to be talked to that way.

(2) Tuesday morning, 8/7/07, around 9 a.m., Jocelyn found a copy of the picture taped to her computer screen, with handwritten note on it: "your girlfriend left this for you." When she saw the picture, Bill and Skip Thompson standing in the doorway of her office laughing.

(3) On Tuesday, 8/14/07, Jocelyn had to meet with Skip about an upcoming presentation for a client (Clark account). When she went in Skip's office, he said "I was just thinking about you" and appeared to be rubbing his genitals. She told him to stop it and to come by her office when he was ready to work. Skip said, "wow, you really can't take a joke, can you? Are you still mad about that picture?" Jocelyn said that she was angry about the picture and didn't appreciate his comments.

(4) On Friday, 8/17/07, Sharon Washington and Jocelyn left office together to have a drink after work. Skip made a comment about them going on a "date," said he'd like to "come along for the after party, if you girls ever let a man in on the action." Also made a comment about having a "three-way" with them. Sharon and Jocelyn were shocked, didn't know how to respond. They left immediately; were planning on going to a bar near the office (Midtown Pub), but decided to go to Club V so they didn't run into Skip.

(5) On Wednesday, 8/22, Skip came into Jocelyn's office and shut the door. Jocelyn asked him to open door. Skip: "Don't you want to be alone with me? I think about being alone with you all the time." Jocelyn walked past Skip to open door and ask him to leave; Skip grabbed her arm and said, "you're not being a very nice girl." Jocelyn told Skip to leave immediately; she took the rest of the day off.

Investigation Report (cont'd.)

(6) On Thursday morning, 8/23, Jocelyn told Brian about all incidents above. He told her to "Lighten up"; said Bill and Skip worked hard and had to blow off steam sometimes. Re: touching himself, grabbing her arm: "Skip wouldn't do something like that." Brian said that filing a formal complaint would make things hard for the team; everyone would blame Jocelyn for getting coworkers in trouble.

(7) One hour later, 11 a.m. or so, Jocelyn got email from Skip. Message said "little bird" told him Jocelyn was planning to report him to management. Said none of the men would want to help her with her accounts if she filed complaint against him; they'd be too worried about getting in trouble for saying or doing the wrong thing.

Pre-Investigation Actions

When I took her complaint, Jocelyn told me that she was afraid of Skip. She also told me that she was concerned that Brian might retaliate against her for complaining. She asked for time off. I told her that retaliation was prohibited, and that the company would take action against anyone who retaliated against her. She reiterated that she wanted time off, that she didn't want to have to deal with everyone right now. I agreed that she could take several days off, with pay, while I investigated. I told her that I would check in with her on Tuesday of the following week.

After I finished taking Jocelyn's complaint, I immediately called Jackson Little, the vice president of Marketing and Sales and Brian Haggerty's immediate supervisor, and informed him of the allegations. I placed this call at about noon, to Jackson's cell phone. I told Jackson of the allegations because Brian was accused of wrongdoing. I told Jackson that I had given Jocelyn permission to take a few days off, and that I intended to place Skip on leave right away. Jackson agreed with these actions and asked me to inform him when the investigation was complete.

I went immediately to the sales office at about 12:30 p.m. I told Skip that he was being placed on immediate administrative leave, with pay, pending a misconduct investigation. I told Skip that I would be conducting an investigation into what happened, and was eager to hear his side of the story. I told him I would conclude the investigation as soon as possible. We scheduled an interview for the following Monday afternoon at 3 p.m. at a coffee shop near the office. I escorted Skip from the building and asked him not to come back until he heard further from me.

Brian was on vacation until the following Tuesday morning. I left a message on his voice mail asking that he come directly to my office when he arrived at work.

Investigation Report (cont'd.)

The Investigation

I began the investigation immediately, on the afternoon of August 24, 2007.

I interviewed the following witnesses:

- Bill Martinez, on August 24 at 3 p.m.
- Skip Thompson, on August 27 at 3 p.m.
- Louise Jay, on August 27 at 9 a.m.
- Sharon Washington, on August 27 at noon
- Brian Haggerty, on August 28 at 9 a.m.

I also had two follow-up interviews, with:

- Jocelyn Evans, on August 28 at noon
- Skip Thompson, on August 28 at 2 p.m.

My notes from these interviews are in the investigation file.

I reviewed the following items:

- A photograph provided by Jocelyn when she filed her complaint, on August 24
- An email message provided by Jocelyn when she filed her complaint, on August 24
- A copy of the office calendar kept by Louise, the administrative assistant for sales; I made copies of this calendar at about 5 p.m. on August 24, after learning about it during my interview with Bill.

Copies of these documents are in the investigation file.

I also visited the sales department and looked at the hallway and office layout. My diagram of the office is in the investigation file.

I completed my investigation on August 29, 2007.

Conclusions

After reviewing the evidence, I have concluded that the incidents Jocelyn complained of occurred much as she described.

(1) Bill showing Jocelyn the photo: Bill admitted that he showed the photo to Jocelyn, that he said something like, "You like women so much, this is something you'd probably like," and that Jocelyn was upset. The photo is of two naked women, posed in a sexual position.

(2) The photo taped to the computer: Bill and Louise confirm that they saw the photo taped to Jocelyn's computer, and that Jocelyn was very angry. Bill says that Skip saw the photo in his office the previous day and asked if he could have it; Bill then gave it to him. The next morning, Skip told Bill to come with him and led him down

Investigation Report (cont'd.)

the hallway to a coffee room near Jocelyn's office. When Jocelyn arrived at work, Skip led Bill to her doorway, where they saw her notice the picture and get angry. Bill said Skip was laughing; Bill was upset about the incident and later told Skip it was stupid. Louise said that she was sitting at her desk and saw Bill and Skip outside Jocelyn's door, and that she saw Jocelyn tear the picture from her computer. I confirmed, by visiting the office, that there is a coffee room diagonally across from the doorway to Jocelyn's office, and that Louise's desk is right down the hallway. Skip talked about the incident only when asked a very direct question, then claimed not to know whose office it was in or when it happened. Because the incident happened just a few weeks ago and was reported in essentially the same way by Jocelyn, Bill, and Louise, I find Skip's statement not credible.

(3) The Clark account meeting: Skip stated that Jocelyn cancelled this meeting by phone because she was out sick. In response to the specific claims of touching himself, he said, "That doesn't sound like me" and "That's not something I would do." Sharon stated that she ran into Jocelyn in the hallway outside of Skip's office that afternoon, and Jocelyn looked upset. Sharon asked what was wrong, and Jocelyn said, "Skip is such a jerk." Sharon also said that Jocelyn later told her that Skip touched himself and made a sexual comment that day. The calendar for the sales department indicated that Jocelyn was at work all day. Jocelyn's statement is corroborated by the calendar and by Sharon's statements. Skip's denials were indirect; also, his demeanor during this portion of the interview was very calm—he didn't appear to be angry about the accusation. For these reasons, I conclude that Skip's statement is not credible.

(4) The Friday night drinks incident: Jocelyn and Sharon described this incident consistently. Sharon confirmed that Jocelyn was very upset, and later told her about incident (3), above. She also confirmed that they decided to go to Club V to avoid Skip. Skip said he didn't remember the incident, then said he may have made a "joke" about going out with them, but didn't remember exactly what he said. I find Skip's statement is not credible.

(5) Grabbing her arm: Skip again said he didn't remember this, that he might have said he enjoyed her company, and might have touched her by accident. Brian said that he thought he remembered Jocelyn saying that Skip grabbed her arm, although he didn't think it would have happened on purpose. Louise stated that she saw Jocelyn in the bathroom crying afterwards, and that Jocelyn said she was going home sick. The calendar confirms that Jocelyn went home sick that afternoon. On balance, I find Jocelyn's statements to be more credible than Skip's.

Investigation Report (cont'd.)

(6) Meeting with Brian: Brian confirmed that Jocelyn met with him and complained about Bill and Skip. He said she complained about Bill showing her a picture, about Skip touching himself, grabbing her arm, and making sexual comments. He stated that he told Jocelyn she was overreacting, and told her to try harder to get along with the other reps. He also told her that he didn't want to see her isolated and have everyone upset with her for making a big deal of it. I find that Brian's statement corroborates Jocelyn's allegation.

(7) The email message: Skip denied any recollection of the message, sent just a few days earlier, until I showed it to him. He then claimed that it was about a complaint Jocelyn made to Brian about his work on the Clark account. He could not explain why he referred to the other "men" in the message, other than to say that no one would want to work with Jocelyn if she was overly critical. Brian stated that he talked to Skip about his meeting with Jocelyn, that he told Skip to "cool it" and to stop asking her out. Brian stated that he did not say anything to Skip about problems on the Clark account. Brian also stated that he might have told Skip that Jocelyn was thinking about filing a complaint. I find that Skip's explanation for the email is not credible, and that he sent the email after learning that she had discussed the above allegations with Brian.

Recommendations and Actions

Based on the conclusions listed above, I find that Skip violated company policy and committed serious misconduct. He posted a sexual picture in Jocelyn's office after being told that it would upset her. He touched himself in front of her, made sexual comments, and grabbed her arm. He also attempted to discourage her from filing a complaint. Because his conduct was repeated, serious, and apparently intended to intimidate Jocelyn, I recommend that Skip's employment be terminated immediately.

I also find that Bill violated company policy. Showing Jocelyn the picture and making a sexual remark was inappropriate and warrants discipline. Because Bill admitted his misconduct and has expressed remorse for it, I determined that he should be retained, given a written warning, and required to attend sexual harassment training. These actions are within my authority as human resources director, and I have taken them. I met with Bill earlier today to issue the written warning. (See written warning form in file.)

Brian's conduct was also serious and inappropriate. As a manager, Brian is required by company policy to report misconduct to my office immediately. Instead, Brian apparently made light of Jocelyn's complaints and attempted to discourage her from filing a complaint. He told her that he didn't believe some of her allegations. He also informed Skip of Jocelyn's complaint, which resulted in Skip's email message.

Investigation Report (cont'd.)

This conduct is more damaging because Brian is the only manager in his office. I recommend that Brian receive a written warning, be required to attend sexual harassment training for managers, and be transferred to the Tucson office, where he will be one of several managers. I also recommend that Jackson, Brian's supervisor, meet with Brian to discuss his managerial skills and style, and perhaps arrange for regular coaching. All of the witnesses I interviewed said that they rarely met with or spoke to Brian for any reason, which may indicate a need for management training.

Signed: *Michael Hogan*

Date: August 30, 2007

Written Warning

Date: August 30, 2007
Employee Name: Bill Martinez
Manager Name: Issued by Michael Hogan, HR director

Incident Description
On August 24, 2007, I received a complaint of misconduct. The complaint alleged that you had shown a photograph of two naked women in a sexual pose to Jocelyn Evans, and said, "I bet you wouldn't mind some of that, would you?"

I interviewed you later that day regarding the complaint. You confirmed that you had shown the photo to Jocelyn. You didn't remember the exact words you said to her, but thought you said something like, "You like women so much, this is probably something you'd like." You stated that Jocelyn told you she didn't think this was funny and appeared to be angry. You also stated that you felt bad about the incident and tried to apologize, but Jocelyn did not want to speak to you.

Prior Incidents
No prior reported incidents of similar behavior.

Improvement Plan:
Bill, your conduct violates company policies on appropriate workplace behavior. Specifically, your conduct violates our policy on Professional Behavior (p. 23 of the Employee Handbook) and Harassment (p. 12). You showed poor judgment in bringing a sexual photograph into the workplace, showing it to Jocelyn, and making a sexual comment. Although you said that you thought Jocelyn would find this funny, you were incorrect. Jocelyn was angry and offended by this inappropriate attempt at humor.

You are not to make sexual comments or jokes in the workplace, bring sexual photos to work, or otherwise participate in behavior that constitutes harassment under company guidelines. To make sure you understand the difference between appropriate and inappropriate behavior, I have scheduled you to attend a sexual harassment training workshop on September 12. If you have any questions about whether particular conduct is appropriate following this training, please talk to me.

In addition, you are not to retaliate or take any action against Jocelyn or anyone else involved in this investigation. Any retaliation on your part will be subject to discipline.

Written Warning (cont'd.)

Employee Comments:

I'm very sorry for showing the photo to Jocelyn. It was a stupid joke, and I did think she'd find it funny, but I can see now that she didn't.

Signed: Michael Hogan
Date: 8-30-07
Employee: Bill Martinez
Date: 8-30-07

CONFIDENTIAL

To: Investigation File
From: Michael Hogan
Date: August 31, 2007
Re: Meeting with Jocelyn Evans

I met with Jocelyn Evans this afternoon. I told her that the investigation was completed and that Bill had been disciplined. I told her that Skip was no longer with the company and that Brian would not be working in this office any more. Jocelyn asked me some questions about what discipline Bill had received and whether Brian would be demoted; I told her this information was confidential.

I asked Jocelyn whether she was comfortable continuing to work with Bill. She said that Bill had apologized very sincerely to her the day before, and told her that he didn't tape the picture to her computer screen. Because of this, and because their working relationship was fine until this incident, Jocelyn said that she thought it would be fine to keep working with Bill.

Jocelyn expressed some concern about going back to work and being blamed for Skip and Brian having to leave. I assured her that the company would not allow any retaliation against her for making a complaint and set up a meeting in a few weeks to see how things were going. I asked Jocelyn to come to me right away if she had any concerns or felt that she was being retaliated against.

Signed: Michael Hogan

Resources

State	Law applies to employers with	Private employers may not make employment decisions based on			
		Age (protected ages, if specified)	Ancestry or national origin	Disability	AIDS/ HIV
Alabama *Ala. Code §§ 25-1-20, 25-1-21*	20 or more employees	✓ (40 and older)			
Alaska *Alaska Stat. §§ 18.80.220, 47.30.865*	One or more employees	✓ (40 and older)	✓	Physical and mental	✓
Arizona *Ariz. Rev. Stat. §§ 41-1461, 41-1463*	15 or more employees	✓ (40 and older)	✓	Physical and mental	✓
Arkansas *Ark. Code Ann. §§ 16-123-102, 16-123-107, 11-4-601, 11-5-403*	9 or more employees		✓	Physical and mental	
California *Cal. Gov't. Code §§ 12920, 12940, 12941, 12945, 12926.1; Cal. Lab. Code § 1101*	5 or more employees	✓ (40 and older)	✓	Physical and mental	✓
Colorado *Colo. Rev. Stat. §§ 24-34-301, 24-34-401, 24-34-402, 27-10-115*	One or more employees	✓ (40 to 70)	✓	Physical, mental, and learning	✓
Connecticut *Conn. Gen. Stat. Ann. §§ 46a-51, 46a-60, 46a-81*	3 or more employees	✓ (40 and older)	✓	Present or past physical, mental, or learning	✓
Delaware *Del. Code Ann. tit. 19, §§ 710, 711*	4 or more employees	✓ (40 and older)	✓	Physical or mental	✓

State Laws Prohibiting Discrimination in Employment

[1] Employees covered by FLSA.

Gender	Marital status	Pregnancy, childbirth, and related medical conditions	Race or color	Religion or creed	Sexual orientation	Genetic testing information	Additional protected categories
✓	✓ (Includes changes in status)	✓ Parenthood	✓	✓			Mental illness
✓			✓	✓		✓	
✓		✓	✓	✓		✓ [1]	
✓	✓	✓	✓	✓	✓	✓	• Gender identity • Medical condition • Political activities or affiliations
✓		✓	✓	✓			• Lawful conduct outside of work • Mental illness
✓	✓	✓	✓	✓	✓	✓	Mental retardation
✓	✓	✓	✓	✓		✓	

State Laws Prohibiting Discrimination in Employment (cont'd.)

State	Law applies to employers with	Age (protected ages, if specified)	Ancestry or national origin	Disability	AIDS/ HIV	
		Private employers may not make employment decisions based on				
District of Columbia *D.C. Code Ann. §§ 2-1401.01, 2-1401.02, 7-1703.03*	One or more employees	✓ (18 and older)	✓	Physical or mental	✓	
Florida *Fla. Stat. Ann. §§ 760.01, 760.02, 760.10, 760.50, 448.075*	15 or more employees	✓	✓	"Handicap"	✓	
Georgia *Ga. Code Ann. §§ 34-6A-1 and following, 34-5-1, 34-5-2*	15 or more employees (disability) 10 or more employees (gender)			Physical or mental		
Hawaii *HI Const. Art. 1, § 3* *Haw. Rev. Stat. §§ 378-1 and 2*	One or more employees	✓	✓	Physical or mental	✓	
Idaho *Idaho Code §§ 39-8303, 67-5902, 67-5909*	5 or more employees	✓ (40 and older)	✓	Physical or mental		
Illinois *775 Ill. Comp. Stat. §§ 5/1-102, 5/1-103, 5/2-101 to 5/2-103, Ill. Admin. Code tit. 56, § 5210.110* *775 ILCS 5/1-103*	15 or more employees One or more employees (disability)	✓ (40 and older)	✓	Physical or mental	✓	

2 wage discrimination only

Gender	Marital status	Pregnancy, childbirth, and related medical conditions	Race or color	Religion or creed	Sexual orientation	Genetic testing information	Additional protected categories
✓	✓ (includes domestic partnership)	✓ Parenthood	✓	✓	✓	✓	• Enrollment in vocational, professional, or college education • Family duties • Source of income • Place of residence or business • Personal appearance • Political affiliation • Smoker • Gender identity or expression • Any reason other than individual merit
✓	✓		✓	✓			Sickle cell trait
✓[2]							
✓	✓	✓	✓	✓	✓	✓	Arrest and court record (unless there is a conviction directly related to job)
✓		✓	✓	✓		✓	
✓	✓	✓	✓	✓	✓	✓	• Citizen status • Military status • Unfavorable military discharge • Gender identity • Arrest record

State Laws Prohibiting Discrimination in Employment (cont'd.)

State	Law applies to employers with	Private employers may not make employment decisions based on				
		Age (protected ages, if specified)	Ancestry or national origin	Disability	AIDS/ HIV	
Indiana *Ind. Code Ann. §§ 22-9-1-2, 22-9-3, 22-9-2-1, 22-9-2-2*	6 or more employees	✓ (40 to 70) (One or more employees)	✓	Physical or mental (15 or more employees)		
Iowa *Iowa Code §§ 216.2, 216.6, 729.6*	4 or more employees	✓ (18 or older)	✓	Physical or mental	✓	
Kansas *Kan. Stat. Ann. §§ 44-1002, 44-1009, 44-1112, 44-1113, 44-1125, 44-1126, 65-6002(e)*	4 or more employees	✓ (18 or older)	✓	Physical or mental	✓	
Kentucky *Ky. Rev. Stat. Ann. §§ 344.010, 344.030, 344.040, 207.130, 207.150, 342.197*	8 or more employees	✓ (40 or older)	✓	Physical or mental	✓	
Louisiana *La. Rev. Stat. Ann. §§ 23:301 to 23:352, 23:368*	20 or more employees	✓ (40 or older)	✓	Physical or mental		
Maine *Me. Rev. Stat. Ann. tit. 5, §§ 19302, 4552, 4553, 4571- 4576*	One or more employees	✓	✓	Physical or mental		
Maryland *Md. Code 1957 Art. 49B, §§ 15, 16, 17*	15 or more employees	✓	✓	Physical or mental		
Massachusetts *Mass. Gen. Laws ch. 149 § 24A, ch. 151B, §§ 1, 3A, 4*	6 or more employees	✓ (40 or older)	✓	Physical or mental	✓	

	Gender	Marital status	Pregnancy, childbirth, and related medical conditions	Race or color	Religion or creed	Sexual orientation	Genetic testing information	Additional protected categories
	✓			✓	✓			
	✓		✓	✓	✓		✓	
	✓			✓	✓		✓	Military status
	✓			✓	✓			• Smoker or nonsmoker • Occupational pneumoconiosis with no respiratory impairment resulting from exposure to coal dust
	✓		✓ (Applies to employers with 25 or more employees)	✓	✓		✓	Sickle cell trait
	✓		✓	✓	✓	✓	✓	• Gender identity or expression • Past workers' compensation claim • Past whistleblowing
	✓	✓	✓	✓	✓	✓	✓	
	✓	✓		✓	✓	✓	✓	• Military service • Arrests

State Laws Prohibiting Discrimination in Employment (cont'd.)

State	Law applies to employers with	Private employers may not make employment decisions based on				
		Age (protected ages, if specified)	Ancestry or national origin	Disability	AIDS/ HIV	
Michigan *Mich. Comp. Laws §§ 37.1201, 37.1202, 37.2201, 37.2202, 37.1103, 750.556*	One or more employees	✓	✓	Physical or mental	✓	
Minnesota *Minn. Stat. Ann. §§ 363A.03, 363A.08, 181.81, 181.974*	One or more employees	✓(18 to 70)	✓	Physical or mental	✓	
Mississippi *Miss. Code Ann. § 33-1-15*						
Missouri *Mo. Rev. Stat. §§ 213.010, 213.055, 191.665, 375.1306*	6 or more employees	✓ (40 to 70)	✓	Physical or mental	✓	
Montana *Mont. Code Ann. §§ 49-2-101, 49-2-303, 49-2-310*	One or more employees	✓	✓	Physical or mental		
Nebraska *Neb. Rev. Stat. §§ 48-1101, 48-1102, 48-1001 to 48-1003, 20-168, 48-1111, 48-1104*	15 or more employees	✓ (40 to 70) (Applies to employers with 25 or more employees)	✓	Physical or mental	✓	
Nevada *Nev. Rev. Stat. Ann. §§ 613.310 and following*	15 or more employees	✓ (40 or older)	✓	Physical or mental		

Gender	Marital status	Pregnancy, childbirth, and related medical conditions	Race or color	Religion or creed	Sexual orientation	Genetic testing information	Additional protected categories
✓	✓	✓	✓	✓		✓	• Height or weight • Arrest record
✓	✓	✓	✓	✓	✓	✓	• Gender identity • Member of local commission • Perceived sexual orientation • Receiving public assistance
							• Military status (all employers) • No other protected categories unless employer receives public funding
✓		✓	✓	✓		✓	
✓	✓	✓	✓	✓			
✓	✓	✓	✓	✓		✓ All employers	
✓		✓	✓	✓	✓	✓	• Lawful use of any product when not at work • Use of service animal

State Laws Prohibiting Discrimination in Employment (cont'd.)

State	Law applies to employers with	Private employers may not make employment decisions based on			
		Age (protected ages, if specified)	Ancestry or national origin	Disability	AIDS/HIV
New Hampshire *N.H. Rev. Stat. Ann. §§ 354-A:2, 354-A:6, 354-A:7, 141-H:3*	6 or more employees	✓	✓	Physical or mental	
New Jersey *N.J. Stat. Ann. §§ 10:5-5 to 10:5-12, 10:5-29.1, 34:6B-1, 43:21-49*	One or more employees	✓ (18 to 70)	✓	Past or present physical or mental	✓
New Mexico *N.M. Stat. Ann. §§ § 24-21-4, 28-1-2, 28-1-7*	4 or more employees	✓ (40 or older) (Applies to employers with 20 or more employees)	✓	Physical or mental	
New York *N.Y. Exec. Law §§ 292, 296; N.Y. Lab. Law § 201-d*	4 or more employees	✓ (18 and over)	✓	Physical or mental	✓
North Carolina *N.C. Gen. Stat. §§ 143-422.2, 95-28.1, 127B-11, 130A-148, 168A-3, 168A-5*	15 or more employees	✓	✓	Physical or mental	✓
North Dakota *N.D. Cent. Code §§ 14-02.4-02, 14-02.4-03, 34-01-17*	One or more employees	✓ (40 or older)	✓	Physical or mental	

[3] Employers with 15 or more than employees.

Gender	Marital status	Pregnancy, childbirth, and related medical conditions	Race or color	Religion or creed	Sexual orientation	Genetic testing information	Additional protected categories
✓	✓	✓	✓	✓	✓	✓	
✓	✓ (Includes domestic partner)	✓	✓	✓	✓	✓	• Predisposing genetic characteristics • Military service or status • Smoker or nonsmoker • Accompanied by service or guide dog • Gender identity (effective June 17, 2007)
✓	✓ (Applies to employers with 50 or more employees)	✓	✓	✓	✓[3]	✓	• Gender identity (employers with 15 or more employees) • Serious medical condition
✓	✓	✓	✓	✓	✓	✓	• Lawful use of any product when not at work • Military status • Observance of Sabbath • Political activities • Accompanied by service dog
✓			✓	✓		✓	• Lawful use of any product when not at work • Military service • Sickle cell trait
✓	✓	✓	✓	✓			• Lawful conduct outside of work • Receiving public assistance

State Laws Prohibiting Discrimination in Employment (cont'd.)

State	Law applies to employers with	Private employers may not make employment decisions based on			
		Age (protected ages, if specified)	Ancestry or national origin	Disability	AIDS/HIV
Ohio *Ohio Rev. Code Ann. §§ 4111.17, 4112.01, 4112.02*	4 or more employees	✓ (40 or older)	✓	Physical, mental, or learning	
Oklahoma *Okla. Stat. Ann. tit. 25, §§ 1301, 1302; tit. 36, § 3614.2; tit. 40, § 500; tit. 44, § 208*	15 or more employees	✓ (40 or older)	✓	Physical or mental	
Oregon *Or. Rev. Stat. §§ 659A.001 and following, 659A.303*	One or more employees	✓ (18 or older)	✓	Physical or mental (Applies to employers with 6 or more employees)	
Pennsylvania *43 Pa. Cons. Stat. Ann. §§ 954-955*	4 or more employees	✓ (40 to 70)	✓	Physical or mental	
Rhode Island *R.I. Gen. Laws §§ 28-6-18, 28-5-6, 28-5-7, 23-6-22, 12-28-10, 28-6.7-1*	4 or more employees One or more employees (gender-based wage discrimination)	✓ (40 or older)	✓	Physical or mental	✓
South Carolina *S.C. Code §§ 1-13-30, 1-13-80*	15 or more employees	✓ (40 or older)	✓	Physical or mental	
South Dakota *S.D. Codified Laws Ann. §§ 20-13-1, 20-13-10, 60-12-15, 60-2-20, 62-1-17*	One or more employees		✓	Physical, mental, and learning	
Tennessee *Tenn. Code Ann. §§ 4-21-102, 4-21-401 and following, 8-50-103, 50-2-201, 50-2-202*	8 or more employees One or more employees (gender-based wage discrimination)	✓ (40 or older)	✓	Physical or mental	

Gender	Marital status	Pregnancy, childbirth, and related medical conditions	Race or color	Religion or creed	Sexual orientation	Genetic testing information	Additional protected categories
✓		✓	✓	✓			
✓			✓	✓		✓	• Military service • Smoker or nonsmoker
✓	✓	✓	✓	✓		✓	
✓		✓	✓	✓			• Familial status • GED rather than high school diploma • Use of guide or service animal
✓		✓	✓	✓	✓	✓	• Domestic abuse victim • Gender identity or expression
✓		✓	✓	✓			
✓			✓	✓		✓	Preexisting injury
✓			✓	✓			

State Laws Prohibiting Discrimination in Employment (cont'd.)

State	Law applies to employers with	Private employers may not make employment decisions based on			
		Age (protected ages, if specified)	Ancestry or national origin	Disability	AIDS/HIV
Texas *Tex. Lab. Code Ann. §§ 21.002, 21.052, 21.101, 21.402*	15 or more employees	✓ (40 or older)	✓	Physical or mental	
Utah *Utah Code Ann. §§ 26-45-103, 34A-5-102, 34A-5-106*	15 or more employees	✓ (40 or older)	✓	Follows federal law	✓
Vermont *Vt. Stat. Ann. tit. 21, § 495, 495d; tit. 18, § 9333*	One or more employees	✓ (18 or older)	✓	Physical or mental	✓
Virginia *Va. Code Ann. §§ 2.2-3900, 2.2-3901, 40.1-28.6, 40.1-28.7:1, 51.5-41*	Law applies to all employees	✓	✓	Physical or mental	
Washington *Wash. Rev. Code Ann. §§ 38.40.110, 49.60.040, 49.60.172, 49.60.180 to 210, 49.12.175, 49.44.090; Wash. Admin. Code § 162-30-020*	8 or more employees One or more employees (gender-based wage discrimination)	✓ (40 or older)	✓	Physical, mental, or sensory	✓
West Virginia *W.Va. Code §§ 5-11-3, 5-11-9, 21-5B-1, 21-5B-3, 21-3-19*	12 or more employees	✓ (40 or older)	✓	Physical or mental	✓
Wisconsin *Wis. Stat. Ann. §§ 111.32 and following*	One or more employees	✓ (40 or older)	✓	Physical or mental	✓
Wyoming *Wyo. Stat. §§ 27-9-102, 27-9-105, 19-11-104*	2 or more employees	✓ (40 or older)	✓	Not specified	

[4] Equal pay laws apply to employers with one or more employers.

Gender	Marital status	Pregnancy, childbirth, and related medical conditions	Race or color	Religion or creed	Sexual orientation	Genetic testing information	Additional protected categories
✓		✓	✓	✓		✓	
✓		✓	✓	✓		✓	
✓			✓	✓	✓	✓	Place of birth
✓	✓	✓	✓	✓		✓	Use of a service animal
✓	✓	✓	✓	✓	✓	✓	• Hepatitis C infection • Member of state militia • Use of a trained guide dog • Gender identity
✓[4]			✓	✓			• Smoking away from work
✓	✓	✓	✓	✓	✓	✓	• Arrest or conviction • Lawful use of any product when not at work • Military service or status
✓			✓	✓			• Military service or status • Smoking off duty

Current as of February 2007

State Agencies That Enforce Laws Prohibiting Discrimination in Employment

Alabama
EEOC District Office
Birmingham, AL
205-212-2100
800-669-4000
www.eeoc.gov/birmingham/index
.html

Alaska
Commission for Human Rights
Anchorage, AK
907-274-4692
800-478-4692
http://gov.state.ak.us/aschr

Arizona
Civil Rights Division
Phoenix, AZ
602-542-5263
877-491-5742
www.azag.gov/civil_rights/index
.html

Arkansas
Equal Employment Opportunity
Commission
Little Rock, AR
501-324-5060
www.eeoc.gov/littlerock/index
.html

California
Department of Fair Employment
and Housing
Sacramento District Office
Sacramento, CA
916-445-5523
800-884-1684
www.dfeh.ca.gov

Colorado
Civil Rights Division
Denver, CO
303-894-2997
800-262-4845
www.dora.state.co.us/Civil-Rights

Connecticut
Commission on Human Rights and
Opportunities
Hartford, CT
860-541-3400
800-477-5737
www.state.ct.us/chro

Delaware
Office of Labor Law Enforcement
Division of Industrial Affairs
Wilmington, DE
302-761-8200
www.delawareworks.com/
industrialaffairs/welcome.shtml

District of Columbia
Office of Human Rights
Washington, DC
202-727-4559
http://ohr.dc.gov/ohr/site/default
.asp

Florida
Commission on Human Relations
Tallahassee, FL
850-488-7082
http://fchr.state.fl.us

Georgia
Atlanta District Office
U.S. Equal Employment
Opportunity Commission
Atlanta, GA
404-562-6800
800-669-4000
www.eeoc.gov/atlanta/index.html

Hawaii
Hawai'i Civil Rights Commission
Honolulu, HI
808-586-8636
www.hawaii.gov/labor/hcrc/

Idaho
Idaho Commission on Human
Rights
Boise, ID
208-334-2873
www2.state.id.us/ihrc

Illinois
Department of Human Rights
Chicago, IL
312-814-6200
www.state.il.us/dhr

Indiana
Civil Rights Commission
Indianapolis, IN
317-232-2600
800-628-2909
www.in.gov/icrc

Iowa
Iowa Civil Rights Commission
Des Moines, IA
515-281-4121
800-457-4416
www.state.ia.us/government/crc

State Agencies That Enforce Laws Prohibiting Discrimination in Employment (cont'd.)

Kansas
Human Rights Commission
Topeka, KS
785-296-3206
www.khrc.net

Kentucky
Human Rights Commission
Louisville, KY
502-595-4024
800-292-5566
www.kchr.ky.gov

Louisiana
Commission on Human Rights
Baton Rouge, LA
225-342-6969
www.gov.state.la.us/HumanRights/
humanrightshome.htm

Maine
Human Rights Commission
Augusta, ME
207-624-6050
www.maine.gov/mhrc

Maryland
Commission on Human Relations
Baltimore, MD
410-767-8600
www.mchr.state.md.us

Massachusetts
Commission Against
Discrimination
Boston, MA
617-994-6000
www.state.ma.us/mcad

Michigan
Department of Civil Rights
Detroit, MI
313-456-3700
www.michigan.gov/mdcr

Minnesota
Department of Human Rights
St. Paul, MN
651-296-5663
www.humanrights.state.mn.us

Mississippi
Department of Employment
Security
Jackson, MS
601-321-6000
www.mdes.ms.gov

Missouri
Commission on Human Rights
Jefferson City, MO
573-751-3325
www.dolir.state.mo.us/hr

Montana
Human Rights Bureau
Employment Relations Division
Department of Labor and
Industry
Helena, MT
406-444-2884
800-542-0807
http://erd.dli.state.mt.us/
HumanRight/HRhome.asp

Nebraska
Equal Opportunity Commission
Lincoln, NE
402-471-2024
800-642-6112
www.neoc.ne.gov

Nevada
Equal Rights Commission
Reno, NV
775-688-1288
http://detr.state.nv.us/nerc/NERC_
index.htm

New Hampshire
Commission for Human Rights
Concord, NH
603-271-2767
www.nh.gov/hrc

New Jersey
Division on Civil Rights
Newark, NJ
973-648-2700
www.state.nj.us/lps/dcr

New Mexico
Human Rights Division
Santa Fe, NM
505-827-6838
800-566-9471
www.dol.state.nm.us/dol_hrd
.html

New York
Division of Human Rights
Bronx, NY
718-741-8400
www.dhr.state.ny.us

North Carolina
Employment Discrimination
Bureau
Department of Labor
Raleigh, NC
919-807-2796
800-NC-LABOR
www.nclabor.com/edb/edb.htm

State Agencies That Enforce Laws Prohibiting Discrimination in Employment (cont'd.)

North Dakota
Human Rights Division
Department of Labor
Bismarck, ND
701-328-2660
800-582-8032
www.nd.gov/labor

Ohio
Civil Rights Commission
Columbus, OH
614-466-5928
888-278-7101
www.crc.ohio.gov

Oklahoma
Human Rights Commission
Oklahoma City, OK
405-521-2360
www.hrc.state.ok.us

Oregon
Civil Rights Division
Bureau of Labor and Industries
Portland, OR
971-673-0761
www.oregon.gov/BOLI/CRD

Pennsylvania
Human Relations Commission
Harrisburg, PA
717-787-4410
www.phrc.state.pa.us

Rhode Island
Commission for Human Rights
Providence, RI
401-222-2661
www.richr.state.ri.us/frames.html

South Carolina
Human Affairs Commission
Columbia, SC
803-737-7800
800-521-0725
www.state.sc.us/schac

South Dakota
Division of Human Rights
Pierre, SD
605-773-4493
www.state.sd.us/dol/boards/hr

Tennessee
Human Rights Commission
Knoxville, TN
865-594-6500
www.tennessee.gov/humanrights

Texas
Commission on Human Rights
Austin, TX
512-463-2642
www.twc.state.tx.us

Utah
Anti-Discrimination and Labor
Division
Labor Commission
Salt Lake City, UT
801-530-6801
800-222-1238
http://laborcommission.utah.gov/
Utah_Antidiscrimination_Labo/
utah_antidiscrimination_labo.htm

Vermont
Attorney General's Office
Civil Rights Division
Montpelier, VT
802-828-3657
www.atg.state.vt.us

Virginia
Council on Human Rights
Richmond, VA
804-225-2292
http://chr.vipnet.org

Washington
Human Rights Commission
Seattle, WA
206-464-6500
800-233-3247
www.hum.wa.gov

West Virginia
Human Rights Commission
Charleston, WV
304-558-2616
888-676-5546
www.wvf.state.wv.us/wvhrc

Wisconsin
Equal Rights Division
Madison, WI
608-266-6860
www.dwd.state.wi.us/er

Wyoming
Department of Employment
Cheyenne, WY
307-777-7261
http://wydoe.state.wy.us

Current as of February 2007

Resources on HR and Employment Available from Nolo

Nolo offers a variety of resources on HR compliance and employment law.

Books

Nolo publishes many titles for employers, managers, and human resources professionals, including:

- *The Essential Guide to Federal Employment Laws*, copublished by Nolo and SHRM, which explains the requirements, record-keeping obligations, coverage, and deadlines imposed by 20 important laws, including the Americans With Disabilities Act, Fair Labor Standards Act, and Title VII

- *Dealing With Problem Employees*, a comprehensive resource for handling tough employee issues, including detailed information on minimizing legal exposure if you have to fire an employee

- *Create Your Own Employee Handbook,* which provides the information and policies you need to draft or update your company handbook, and includes a CD-ROM that allows you to cut and paste policies into a handbook

- *The Performance Appraisal Handbook*, which explains how to effectively track and evaluate employee performance without getting into legal trouble

- *The Progressive Discipline Handbook: Smart Strategies for Coaching Employees*, a step-by-step guide to handling employee discipline, including information on how to communicate effectively with employees and how to identify, correct, and document problems

- *The Job Description Handbook*, which explains how to create, use, and update job descriptions effectively, and includes a PowerPoint training presentation on CD-ROM

- *The Essential Guide to Family and Medical Leave*, a comprehensive resource that explains every aspect of the Family and Medical Leave Act, from figuring out company coverage to reinstating employees when leave is over, including how to handle the overlap between the FMLA and state leave laws, workers' compensation statutes, the Americans With Disabilities Act, and more

- *The Manager's Legal Handbook*, an introduction to many of the legal issues managers face every day, including discrimination, wage and hour issues, firing and layoffs, employer privacy concerns, protecting trade secrets, and much more

- *The Employer's Legal Handbook*, a comprehensive guide to employment law, written with the small business owner in mind, and

- *Consultant and Independent Contractor Agreements*, which provides all of the information and sample contracts you need to work well with independent contractors—and avoid having them reclassified as employees.

Nolo's Website

You can find free articles on a wide variety of employment and HR topics on Nolo's award-winning website, www.nolo.com. From the home page, click "Business & Human Resources" to view articles on:

- hiring employees
- hiring independent contractors
- wage and hour laws
- personnel policies and procedures
- family, medical, and other types of leave
- discrimination
- workplace privacy
- firing workers, and
- obligations to workers who are leaving the company.

If you select "Rights and Disputes" from the home page, you'll find articles on dispute resolution, mediation, arbitration, and working with lawyers.

From the home page, you can also find podcasts on a variety of topics (including employment and HR issues), Nolo's lawyer directory, and much more.

Resources on HR and Employment Available from SHRM

Some of SHRM's resources are available to nonmembers; access to much of our comprehensive HR information is a benefit of membership. For additional information, go to the SHRM home page, www.shrm.org, or to the membership benefits page at www.shrm.org/memberkit. Below are some of the SHRM resources most directly related to legal compliance.

SHRM Books and Electronic Supplements

SHRM's professional books give practical help to HR professionals and contribute to the stature of the profession. SHRM members receive discounts if they buy from the Society. Go to www.shrm.org/books or www.shrm.org/shrmstore. Among SHRM's titles are:

- *Understanding the Federal Wage & Hour Laws: What Employers Must Know about the FLSA and its Overtime Regulations* succinctly but thoroughly covers all aspects of the Fair Labor Standards Act for HR professionals.

- *Managing to Stay Out of Court: How to Avoid the 8 Deadly Sins of Mismanagement* shows how to improve employee relations, provide workplace leadership, and help keep your company out of court.

- *Legal, Effective References: How to Give and Get Them* provides practical much-needed guidance about the realities, legalities, and practicalities of reference checking.

- *Investigating Workplace Harassment: How to Be Fair, Thorough, and Legal* details specific, experience-tested techniques for investigating allegations of all types of harassment, with how-to's for planning, documenting, interviewing, weighing evidence, and making a decision.

- *Outsourcing Human Resources Functions: How, Why, When, and When Not to Contract for HR Services* (with CD-ROM) provides a roadmap to success for the challenging task of selecting, contracting, and managing providers and services. The CD-ROM includes a sample RFP, RFI, and contract.

- *HIPAA Privacy Source Book* (with CD-ROM) is an all-in-one resource with everything you need to understand the HIPAA Privacy Rule and comply with it.
- *Human Resources Essentials: Your Guide to Starting and Running the HR Function* provides a thorough, practical overview of human resource knowledge—and of how HR activities can be linked to a company's overall strategies and goals.
- *Performance Appraisal Source Book: A Collection of Practical Samples* (with CD-ROM) covers the basics of performance review systems and plans and puts the best practical examples of good performance-appraisal materials at your fingertips.
- *Hiring Source Book: A Collection of Practical Samples* (with CD-ROM) reviews hiring principles and puts samples of good materials and best practices at your fingertips.
- *The Comprehensive, All-in-One HR Operating Guide: 539 ready-to-adapt human resources letters, memos, procedures, practices, forms…and more* provides sample materials covering the complete spectrum of HR communications in ten sections: Strategic Planning, Employment, Compensation and Benefits, Employee and Community Services, Employee Relations, Labor Relations, Organizational Development and Planning, Safety and Security, General Administration, and International and Immigration Programs.

Periodicals

Members receive SHRM's periodicals as part of their benefits; some publications are available to nonmembers by subscription or request.

- *HR Magazine* (monthly) features in-depth analysis of trends and events affecting human resource management. Key articles also appear on SHRM's website. Go to www.shrm.org and highlight "Knowledge Center" to see a list of SHRM's periodicals.
- *SHRM Legal Report* (members, quarterly) provides in-depth analysis of current legal issues affecting human resource management. Go to www.shrm.org/law/report.

Governmental Affairs—Website

The Governmental Affairs section (www.shrm.org/government/) reflects the activities of the Governmental Affairs Department, which anticipates and addresses regulations and legislation that could change the way HR professionals perform their jobs. Particularly useful sections include:

- the Federal Affairs section (www.shrm.org/government/federal/), which includes resources related to federal legislative, regulatory, and judicial public policy that impacts HR professionals, and

- the State Affairs section (www.shrm.org/government/states/), which offers information about proposed and enacted legislation in all 50 states that may impact the HR profession. This section also provides tools to help SHRM members become involved in the state legislative process.

HR Focus Areas (Members)—Website

The HR Focus Areas (www.shrm.org/focusareas/) include news, features, research materials, webcasts, discussion areas, and more on a wide spectrum of HR disciplines. Most directly relevant are:

- the Workplace Law Focus Area (www.shrm.org/law), which aggregates SHRM's employment law content in one convenient location. Included are weekly Court Report articles on selected decisions by federal appeals and other courts, monthly Legal Trends columns from HR Magazine, in-depth analysis of compliance issues from the quarterly Legal Report, and State Workplace Law Resources. The Workplace Law Bulletin (members, periodic) reports on new legal decisions, legislative and regulatory news and provides analysis of what they mean, and

- the Compensation and Benefits Focus Area (www.shrm.org/rewards), which includes frequent updates on legal compliance-oriented topics involving employee and executive compensation, health care benefits, and retirement benefits.

HR News Online—Website

HR News is a twice-daily online news service that reports on breaking news and events. Some articles are available to nonmembers. Highlights are sent to members on Mondays in the HR Week email, and shorter versions of some articles are published in *HR Magazine*. Go to www.shrm.org/hrnews_ published.

HR Knowledge Center (Members)—Website

The HR Knowledge Center (www.shrm.org/kc/) is home to a wide variety of resources running the whole gamut of human resource practices. Resources include:

- *HR Toolkits* (www.shrm.org/hrtools/toolkits_published/), collections of resources on a long list of topics. The toolkits contain articles, links, and other practical information related to the topics, which include:

ADA	Interviewing
ADEA	Investigations
Affirmative Action	Layoffs
Bankruptcy	Payroll
Benefits	Pension/Retirement
COBRA	Performance Management
Compensation	Personnel Records
Drug Testing	Recruiting
Employee Handbooks	Social Security Mismatch
FLSA	Termination
FMLA/Leave	Unemployment
HIPAA Privacy Act	Visas
HR Liability	Workers' Compensation
Independent Contractors	Workplace Safety
International Antidiscrimination	Workplace Security
Laws	

- *The Glossary of Human Resources Terms* (www.shrm.org/hrresources/ hrglossary_published/), commonly used terms and definitions that are significant to the HR profession. Many compliance-oriented terms are included in this continuously updated feature.

- *SHRM White Papers* (www.shrm.org/hrresources/whitepapers_ published/), offer focused analyses on a wide variety of HR topics, including many that are compliance oriented.
- *HR Solutions* (www.shrm.org/kc/solutions/articles/Solutions%20TOC. asp), presents weekly questions and answers on an assortment of HR issues, including many workplace law issues.

Webcasts (Members)—Website

Free webcasts include presentations by noted experts on a broad range of HR topics, including employment law. Presentations are followed by Q&A sessions. Webcasts are archived for viewing at any time. Go to www.shrm. org/webcast.

Information Center (Members)—Online and by Phone

Information Specialists who are all HR professionals assist with HR-related questions via email, instant messaging, or phone and conduct research on members' behalf in the SHRM Information Center Library. (SHRM assistance is provided as general information and is not a substitute for legal or other professional advice.) Members can reach the Information Center at 1-800-283-SHRM (select Option 5), or at www.shrm.org/hrinfo.

How to Use the CD-ROM

The tear-out forms in Appendixes A, B, and C, as well as some helpful audio files, are included on a CD-ROM in the back of the book. This Windows CD-ROM contains files that you use with software programs that are already installed on your computer. The CD-ROM is not a standalone software program. Please read this appendix and the README. TXT file included on the CD-ROM for instructions on installing the files from the CD.

To access these form files, you have two options:

(1) open them from the CD-ROM or

(2) install them onto your computer.

Note to Mac users: This CD-ROM and its files should also work on Macintosh computers. Please note, however, that Nolo cannot provide technical support for non-Windows users.

Two different kinds of resources are included on the CD-ROM:

• Electronic versions of the forms from Appendix A, B, and C. Each form file is included in two formats:

(1) Rich Text Format (RTF), which can be opened, completed, printed, and saved by most current word processing programs, and

(2) Portable Document Format (PDF), which can be viewed with Adobe Reader and are designed to be printed out and filled in by hand or with a typewriter.

• MP3 audio files that you can listen to using your computer's media or MP3 player.

See the end of this appendix for a list of CD-ROM resources, their file names, and their file formats.

In accordance with U.S. copyright laws, remember that copies of the CD-ROM and its files are for your personal use only.

Please do not call Nolo's technical support if you have questions on how to use Adobe Reader, your word processor, your media player, or your computer.

Option 1:
Accessing Investigation Resources from the CD

All forms and audio can be directly accessed from the Main Menu file (MainMenu.pdf). You must have the Adobe Reader installed on your computer to use the Main Menu file. Adobe Reader is available for all types of Windows and Macintosh systems. If you don't already have this software, you can download it for free at www.adobe.com.

To open the Main Menu file, insert the CD-ROM and do the following:

Windows 2000, XP, and Vista Users

Follow the instructions that appear on the screen. If nothing happens when you insert the Forms CD-ROM, then:

1. Double click the My Computer icon.
2. Double click the icon for the CD-ROM drive into which the Forms CD-ROM was inserted.
3. Double click the file WELCOME.EXE.
4. Click "View Investigation Resources."

Macintosh Users

1. If the "Investigation Resources CD" window is not open, open it by double clicking the "Investigation Resources CD" icon on your desktop.
2. Select and open the "Investigations Resources" folder.
3. Open the Main Menu file (MainMenu.pdf).

Option 2:
Installing and Accessing Investigation Resources on Your Computer

To install the Investigation Resources to your computer, insert the CD-ROM and do the following:

Windows 2000, XP, and Vista Users

Follow the instructions that appear on the screen. If nothing happens when you insert the Forms CD-ROM, then:

1. Double click the My Computer icon.
2. Double click the icon for the CD-ROM drive into which the Forms CD-ROM was inserted.
3. Double click the file WELCOME.EXE.
4. Click "Install Investigation Resources."

To access the installed resources, do the following:

1. Click the Windows "Start" button.
2. Open the "Programs" folder.
3. Open the "Investigations Resources" subfolder.
4. Click "Main Menu."

Macintosh Users

1. Use the Finder to go to the folder to which you copied the CD-ROM's files.
2. Open the "Investigations Resources" folder.
3. Double click MainMenu.pdf.

To access the installed resources, do the following:

1. If the "Investigation Resources CD" window is not open, open it by double clicking the "Investigation Resources CD" icon.

2. Select the "Investigations Resources" folder icon.

3. Drag and drop the folder icon onto the icon of your hard disk.

All installed forms and audio resources can be directly accessed from the Main Menu file (MainMenu.pdf) in the Start menu. You must have the Adobe Reader installed on your computer to use the Main Menu file. Adobe Reader is available for all types of Windows and Macintosh systems. If you don't already have this software, you can download it for free at www.adobe.com.

Files Included on This CD-ROM

The following files are in Adobe Acrobat PDF Format:

FILE NAME	FORM TITLE
Complaint.pdf	Complaint Policy
OpenDoor.pdf	Open-Door Policy
Antidiscrimination.pdf	Antidiscrimination Policy
Antiharass.pdf	Antiharassment Policy
Antiviolence.pdf	Antiviolence Policy
ComplaintReport.pdf	Complaint Reporting Form
InvestigationNotice.pdf	Investigation Notice Form
InvestigationReport.pdf	Investigation Report Form
AdverseAction.pdf	Adverse Action Form
InvestigationSteps.pdf	Checklist: Ten Steps to a Successful Investigation
InvestigationMistakes.pdf	Checklist: Avoiding Common Investigation Mistakes
Document.pdf	Document Checklist
Credibility.pdf	Credibility Checklist
Discipline.pdf	Discipline Checklist
InvestigationChecklist.pdf	Investigation Report Checklist

The following files are in rich text format (RTF):

FILE NAME	FORM TITLE
Complaint.rtf	Complaint Policy
OpenDoor.rtf	Open-Door Policy
Antidiscrimination.rtf	Antidiscrimination Policy
Antiharass.rtf	Antiharassment Policy
Antiviolence.rtf	Antiviolence Policy
ComplaintReport.rtf	Complaint Reporting Form
InvestigationNotice.rtf	Investigation Notice Form
InvestigationReport.rtf	Investigation Report Form
AdverseAction.rtf	Adverse Action Form
InvestigationSteps.rtf	Checklist: Ten Steps to a Successful Investigation
InvestigationMistakes.rtf	Checklist: Avoiding Common Investigation Mistakes
Document.rtf	Document Checklist
Credibility.rtf	Credibility Checklist
Discipline.rtf	Discipline Checklist
InvestigationChecklist.rtf	Investigation Report Checklist

The following files are in MP3 format:

FILE NAME	FORM TITLE
Complaint.mp3	Scenario 1: Taking a Complaint
ComplaintInterview.mp3	Scenario 2: Interviewing the Complaining Employee
InterviewAccused.mp3	Scenario 3: Interviewing the Accused Employee

Index

SELECTED ADDITIONAL TITLES FROM
THE SOCIETY FOR HUMAN RESOURCE MANAGEMENT (SHRM®)

Building Profit through Building People: Making Your Workforce the Strongest Link in the Value-Profit Chain
> By Ken Carrig and Patrick M. Wright

Diverse Teams at Work: Capitalizing on the Power of Diversity
> By Lee Gardenswartz and Anita Rowe

The Comprehensive, All-in-One HR Operating Guide: 539 ready-to-adapt human resource letters, memos, procedures, practices, forms...and more
> By R.J. Landry

Human Resource Essentials: Your Guide to Starting and Running the HR Function
> By Lin Grensing-Pophal, SPHR

Outsourcing Human Resources Functions: How, Why, When, and When Not to Contract for HR Services
> By Mary F. Cook and Scott R. Gildner

Understanding the Federal Wage & Hour Laws: What Employers Must Know about FLSA and its Overtime Regulations
> By Seyfarth Shaw LLP

HR SOURCE BOOKS

Employment Termination Source Book: A Collection of Practical Samples
> By Wendy Bliss, J.D., SPHR and Gene R. Thornton, Esq., PHR

Hiring Source Book: A Collection of Practical Samples
> By Cathy Fyock, CAP, SPHR

Performance Appraisal Source Book: A Collection of Practical Samples
> By Mike Deblieux

Trainer's Diversity Source Book: 50 Ready-to-Use Activities from Icebreakers through Wrap Ups
> By Jonamay Lambert, M.A. and Selma Myers, M.A.

PRACTICAL HR

Legal, Effective References: How to Give and Get Them
> By Wendy Bliss, J.D., SPHR

Investigating Workplace Harassment: How to Be Fair, Thorough, and Legal
> By Amy Oppenheimer, J.D., and Craig Pratt, MSW, SPHR

Proving the Value of HR: How and Why to Measure ROI
> By Jack J. Phillips, Ph.D. and Patricia Pulliam Phillips, Ph.D.

TO ORDER SHRM BOOKS
SHRM offers a member discount on all books that it publishes or sells.
To order this or any other book published by the Society, contact the SHRMStore®.

ONLINE: www.shrm.org/shrmstore
BY PHONE: 800-444-5006 (option #1); or 770-442-8633 (ext. 362); or TDD 703-548-6999
BY MAIL: SHRM Distribution Center, P.O. Box 930132, Atlanta, GA 31193-0132, USA

Get the Latest in the Law

(1) **Nolo's Legal Updater**
We'll send you an email whenever a new edition of your book is published!
Sign up at **www.nolo.com/legalupdater**.

(2) **Updates at Nolo.com**
Check **www.nolo.com/update** to find recent changes in the law that
affect the current edition of your book.

(3) **Nolo Customer Service**
To make sure that this edition of the book is the most recent one, call us at
800-728-3555 and ask one of our friendly customer service representatives
(7:00 am to 6:00 pm PST, weekdays only). Or find out at **www.nolo.com**.

(4) **Complete the Registration & Comment Card ...**
... and we'll do the work for you! Just indicate your preferences below:

- -

Registration & Comment Card

NAME _____ DATE _____

ADDRESS _____

CITY _____ STATE _____ ZIP _____

PHONE _____ EMAIL _____

COMMENTS _____

WAS THIS BOOK EASY TO USE?   (VERY EASY)   5   4   3   2   1   (VERY DIFFICULT)

☐ Yes, you can quote me in future Nolo promotional materials. *Please include phone number above.*

☐ Yes, send me **Nolo's Legal Updater** via email when a new edition of this book is available.

Yes, I want to sign up for the following email newsletters:

    ☐ **NoloBriefs** (monthly)
    ☐ **Nolo's Special Offer** (monthly)
    ☐ **Nolo's BizBriefs** (monthly)
    ☐ **Every Landlord's Quarterly** (four times a year)

☐ Yes, you can give my contact info to carefully selected
partners whose products may be of interest to me.

NOLO

NVST 1.0

Nolo
950 Parker Street
Berkeley, CA 94710-9867
www.nolo.com

YOUR LEGAL COMPANION